Democracy and Development

Democracy and Development
Allies or Adversaries?

R.C. BHARDWAJ
K. VIJAYAKRISHNAN

Ashgate
Aldershot • Brookfield USA • Singapore • Sydney

© R.C. Bhardwaj and K. Vijayakrishnan 1998

All rights reserved. No part of this publication may be reproduced, stored in a retrieval system, or transmitted in any form or by any means electronic, mechanical, photocopying, recording or otherwise without the prior permission of the publisher.

Published by
Ashgate Publishing Limited
Gower House
Croft Road
Aldershot
Hants GU11 3HR
England

Ashgate Publishing Company
Old Post Road
Brookfield
Vermont 05036
USA

British Library Cataloguing in Publication Data
Bhardwaj, R. C.
 Democracy and development : allies or adversaries. –
(Commonwealth parliamentary association)
 1.Democracy 2.Economic development 3.Human rights
 4.Political development
 I.Title II.Vijayakrishnan, K.
 321.8

Library of Congress Cataloging-in-Publication Data
Bhardwaj, Romesh Chander, 1961–
 Democracy and development : allies or adversaries / R.C. Bhardwaj,
 K. Vijayakrishnan.
  p. cm.
  This publication presents highlights of a conference titled:
 Parliamentary democracy and development—allies or adversaries?,
 held in 1996, in Wiston House, West Sussex, England.
  Includes bibliographical references and index.
  ISBN 1-84014-033-X (hc.)
  1. Economic development—Political aspects—Congresses.
 2. Economic development—Social aspects—Congresses. 3. Democracy—
 Economic aspects—Congresses. I. Vijayakrishnan, K.
 II. Parliamentary democracy and development—allies or adversaries?
 (1996 : Wilton Park (Conference Center), West Sussex, England)
 III. Title.
 HD82.B469 1998
 338.9—dc21   98-18564
                                                                                              CIP

ISBN 1 84014 033 X

Typeset by Manton Typesetters, 5–7 Eastfield Road, Louth, Lincolnshire, LN11 7AJ, UK.
Printed and bound in Great Britain by MPG Books Ltd, Bodmin, Cornwall

Contents

Foreword vii
by the Hon. Billie Miller MP, Deputy Prime Minister,
Minister of Foreign Affairs, Tourism and International
Transport, Barbados
Preface ix

1	The Contribution of Democracy to Economic Development	1
2	Creating an Enabling Economic Environment for Development	21
3	Human Rights, Good Governance and Development	31
4	Gender and Development	45
5	Freedom of the Press	59
6	Promoting an Efficient and Independent Public Administration	69
7	The Relationship between Government and the Military	77
8	The Singapore Model	89
9	Development and Democracy in the Island States of the Caribbean	99
10	Indirect Democracy in Uganda	107
11	The Role of Parliamentary Associations in Facilitating the Proper Functioning of Parliaments	119

Appendices

1	List of Conference Participants	137
2	Conference Programme and Presenters	145
3	Discussion Group A: Indirect Democracy in Uganda	149
4	Discussion Group B: The Singapore Model	153
5	Discussion Group C: Aid and Good Governance	157

Bibliographies

1	Development and Human Rights	161
2	Parliamentary Democracy and Development	164
3	Facilitating the Proper Functioning of Parliament	178

4	Freedom of the Press	179
5	The Relationship between Government and the Military	179
6	The Singapore Model	180
7	Development and Democracy in the Island States of the Caribbean	183
8	Indirect Democracy in Uganda	184
9	Gender and Development	186
10	Creating an Enabling Economic Environment for Development	191
11	Aid and Good Governance	210
12	Promoting an Efficient and Independent Public Administration	213

Index 217

Foreword

The promotion of good governance as a prerequisite for development has been the popular focus of an array of international organizations throughout the last decade of the twentieth century. Existing governmental and non-governmental organizations have redirected their efforts into programmes to foster the democratic ethos in various societies, and a host of new groups have sprung up to advocate particular aspects or forms of democratic government. This work has generated tensions in many societies which have attempted to reconcile demands for improvements to both their standards of living and their standards of democracy.

The Commonwealth Parliamentary Association (CPA) has eight decades of experience in this field, working behind the scenes to enable Parliamentarians and officials to enhance the effectiveness of their own democracies by exchanging ideas within the Commonwealth parliamentary community. By comparing practices elsewhere and adapting promising ideas to their own political cultures, Parliamentarians have worked together to reduce their own deficits, both democratic and economic. This is the Commonwealth way.

Since 1994, the Association has broadened this approach with a series of joint conferences with Wilton Park, a policy analysis agency of the United Kingdom government's Foreign and Commonwealth Office. One of these conferences forms the basis of this insightful book.

The CPA-Wilton Park conferences have exposed Commonwealth Parliamentarians to the diverse perspectives of a largely European network of diplomats, senior civil servants and academics, and exposed the Europeans to Commonwealth ways. I participated in the first conference, an examination of the development of ever more responsible Parliaments, and found it a most enlightening experience. This was not just because of what I gleaned from the discussions; it was also because I witnessed at first hand the Commonwealth connection being made time and again, and saw the Europeans marvelling at the ease with which representatives from different Commonwealth backgrounds could so easily communicate with each other.

This book, stemming from the second conference in this series, focuses on the struggle of all nations to achieve higher standards of economic and democratic development. But it looks particularly at the argument so often, and erroneously, made that developing countries cannot afford both development and democracy at the same time, that somehow putting a durable roof over our heads and nutritious food in our stomachs cannot be accomplished while we are nurturing great ideas in our minds. The authors of this text, an eminent former Secretary-General of the Lok Sabha of India, and his colleague on the current Lok Sabha Secretariat staff come from a country which offers ample evidence that this is not the case. India, still a rapidly developing country in many economic respects, is an extremely advanced parliamentary democracy.

The issues aired here touch on the fundamental challenge facing all peoples: How can we best frame a global society which respects our right to a decent, stable and sustainable way of life, and which respects our right to a voice in determining what that way of life should be.

Hon. Billie Miller, MP
Deputy Prime Minister and Minister of Foreign Affairs, Barbados
Chairman, Commonwealth Parliamentary Association Executive Committee

Preface

The last decade of this millennium has been witness to the reassertion of democracy yet again, this time transcending all geographical barriers. The collapse of the Soviet Union and its Eastern bloc allies has advanced the onward march of democracy as never before. The 'democratization' and 'parliamentarization' of political order globally has resulted in a revival of the debate on the correlation between political democracy and economic development. Even as many transitional economies are grappling with the new ground realities, societies which had been suppressed for too long are demanding instant positive results, very often threatening the survival and sustenance of democracies there. Elsewhere, several newly industrialized countries have been consolidating their economic progress, though their polities may not conform to the basic tenets of classical democracy. Some of the enduring democracies in the developing world, in the meanwhile, have embarked on economic reforms and structural adjustment programmes, discarding their earlier approaches to economic administration. What is manifest is the resurgence of a democratic spirit worldwide, as also is a new thrust to the imperative of sound economic management. The unfolding situation offers both challenges and opportunities. The need of the hour is statesmanship which can convert these challenges into opportunities and make this world a better place to live in.

In mid-February 1996, the Commonwealth Parliamentary Association (CPA), which is a repository of the best traditions of parliamentary democracy, jointly organized a conference, *Parliamentary Democracy and Development: Allies or Adversaries?*, with Wilton Park, an international agency of the British Foreign and Commonwealth Office, at Wiston House, West Sussex, United Kingdom. The week-long conference was attended by parliamentarians, diplomats, administrators, political scientists, economists and specialists in diverse fields from Commonwealth countries as well as from outside the Commonwealth, and also from the European Union and several international organizations. The distinguished participants, with long-standing experience in their areas of specialization, discussed at length the varied subjects on the conference agenda. The thought-provoking presentations were followed by lively and informed discussions. Away from the hubbub of politics and the rough and tumble of decision-making, the conference participants shared their views and experiences, not in the least constrained by their nationalities or political ideologies, and in the process making the sessions even more meaningful. The tranquil environs of the stately Wiston House provided the ideal setting for such purposeful interaction.

Bearing in mind the topical relevance of the subject-matter, the CPA felt that it would be useful to produce a publication highlighting the many ideas and views that were aired at the discussion sessions at the conference. The CPA also suggested that such a volume should try to put together related streams of thought on the subjects discussed at Wiston House which would be of help to interested readers. This work attempts such an effort to present essentially a parliamentary perspective on the relationship between two critical concepts in the present-day world, democracy and development. Within this broad framework, several aspects of the main theme are discussed. The discussions on the sub-themes have helped in arriving at a better understanding of the differing perceptions on the larger concepts of democracy and development.

The authors would like to make clear that this volume does not claim to be an authentic verbatim report of the Wilton Park Conference; rather, it is a modest endeavour to present the high points of the conference in the light of current thinking on the subject-matter. For those interested in academic discourses on the themes, there are any number of good studies by eminent scholars. The bibliographical references in this book give useful indicators to further reading on the different topics.

It was an honour to be invited by the CPA to be the rapporteurs for the 461st Wilton Park Conference. We are greatly beholden to the Secretary-General of the CPA, Arthur Donahoe, for this privilege. We should like to express our profound gratitude to the Hon. Billie Miller MP who gladly agreed to write the Foreword for this publication. We are also grateful to all those who gave us permission to make use of the papers they presented to the conference in finalizing this work. Several friends at the CPA Headquarters Secretariat were of the utmost help to us in more ways than one – the Director of Administration, Raja Gomez, the Editor, Andrew Imlach, the Assistant Editor and Information Officer, Diana Reynolds and the Assistant Director of Finance, Mahbub Alam. The Wilton Park academic staff, particularly Senior Assistant Director Dr. Nicholas Hopkinson, were also immensely helpful. Some of our colleagues in the Parliament Library and Research and Information Service also assisted us in giving shape to this volume. The authors would like to make it clear that the views presented in this publication have no connection with the Lok Sabha Secretariat, with which we are both associated. We hope that this book will be found useful and informative by parliamentarians, policy-makers and students of parliamentary political science.

R.C. Bhardwaj
K. Vijayakrishnan

1 The Contribution of Democracy to Economic Development

Introduction

The journey of democracy as a system of governance from the city states of Greece of the sixth and fifth century BC to the nation states of Eastern Europe at the end of the twentieth century has been a long and uneasy one. It has been proved to be a saga of the assertion of the will of the people, notwithstanding many trials and tribulations. Over the millennia, the nature and content of democracy underwent recurrent transformations in tune with changing times and varying climes. Yet the underlying core of democracy survived the cataclysmic changes all around. Over two thousand years later, one finds that the sovereign will of the people on which the edifice of parliamentary democracy rests has come to occupy centrestage of political systems across the globe.

The fact, however, remains that the world is still beset with myriad problems of various kinds. A few stark global statistics may help us to underscore the scale of the challenge which confronts us:

- Somewhere, still, every 2.4 seconds of every day, a small child dies from poverty.
- 1.3 billion people (a fifth of the world's population) live in absolute poverty, a figure expected to rise to over 2 billion by the end of the decade.
- 1.75 billion people have no access to safe water and 3 billion are without basic sanitation.
- The number of refugees has risen from 2.5 million in 1970 to a desperate 18.5 million or more today, and there are between 24 and 30 million internally displaced people without even the theoretical

protection of the United Nations High Commissioner for Refugees (UNHCR) because they have not crossed a frontier.[1]

These figures speak for themselves, and make a mockery of the inflated claims of national development proffered by world leaders. It is true that several countries have been able to achieve rapid strides in socio-economic development, yet poverty still haunts most of the population, even as we are nearing the next millennium. It is in this context that the debate on the correlation between democracy and development gains added significance.

Democracy and Capitalism

At the outset, it may be helpful to define the concepts of democracy and development. There is very often a tendency to confuse democracy with capitalism, and in many cases capitalism is equated with economic development. Democracy is widely accepted to be a method of political organization for the purpose of arriving at decisions, and capitalism has been identified as a system for the economic organization of society. Further, while democracy requires periodic free and fair elections with political pluralism, capitalism does not. Development encompasses economic reform and adjustment; sustenance of macroeconomic stability; predictability of the policy environment; institutional structures conducive to sustainable growth with equity; and achievement and maintenance of competitiveness in a global setting.[2]

Is parliamentary democracy an ally of economic development or is it a hindrance?[3] The best way to approach the subject is to look to historical experience,[4] which shows that the emergence of capitalism and accelerated economic and industrial development preceded truly democratic institutions in Western Europe. John Healey observes that, from the sixteenth century onwards, societies emerged which were more dynamic in technological and economic terms than their predecessors. This was largely made possible by the emergence of a commercial class operating in markets where clear rules gave certainty for doing business and owning private property, and where people were relatively free from excessive and arbitrary intervention by the state. In view of this, many scholars argue that full democracy must wait for the development of an independent and robust capitalist class to challenge the power of political leadership and to ensure an environment or set of rules which permit accelerated economic activity. It is seen that the sustained democratic systems of the twentieth century, mainly in northern Europe and North America, have mostly been in countries which have had capitalist economic development and high standards of living. On the other hand, it is also seen that less economically developed countries (LEDCs) such as India and Jamaica have been genuinely democratic for nearly half a century.

Does this mean that the introduction of the full democratic process should or can be delayed until considerable economic development has taken place? Does it also mean that it is necessary for a society with more limited political and civil freedoms, with a single-party system and a powerful central state, first to achieve economic development? These questions bring to the fore examples of Singapore and the 'miracle economies' of East Asia which have achieved spectacular economic development with a less than full democratic system. There are many who cite the success of the newly industrialized countries (NICs) of South-East and East Asia to argue that some form of centralized authoritarian rule is required to provide the 'firm hand' in guaranteeing high rates of saving and investment, ensuring economic growth. Overall, the statistical evidence on the association between a country's civil and political rights record and its economic growth is inconclusive. Intuitively, one can name as many single-party countries which have achieved a good economic performance as those which have not.

Economic Growth and Political Stability

The best correlations are probably between the economic performance of countries and the extent of their democratic stability. Frequent political changes have an adverse impact on the predictability of the business environment, which in turn has a cumulative unfavourable effect on economic performance. There is also evidence to suggest that countries with genuine electoral participation have been generally less unstable and politically violent though there may be exceptions, as in the case of Sri Lanka, a consolidated democratic culture, which has been trying to tackle protracted ethnic strife. Sri Lanka has often been cited as a vibrant democracy which has achieved considerable success in providing appreciable socio-economic progress for its people. However, the Sri Lankan developmental process has suffered in the wake of its ethnic crisis. If societies are fundamentally very polarized, not only is a democratic process more difficult to operate but so also is a sound economic policy.

Democracy and Competitive Market Environment

Is democracy consistent with a liberal, competitive market environment? A certain critical degree of free and competitive economic activity, especially competition with the rest of the world, has been a major factor in economic performance, as is evidenced in the East Asian countries. By and large, in Latin America and sub-Saharan Africa, economic performance has suffered because of excessive and arbitrary interventions by officials and politicians in prices and allocation decision in all areas of life – trade, foreign exchange, borrowing, production, investment, movement of goods, and so on. In addition, excessive arbitrary protection and subsidy has interfered with enterprise and initiative. In principle, democratic systems are consistent with market economies as both involve freedom of activity – one in the political arena and the other in the economic arena. Both also help in achieving decentralization and wider participation in the decision-making process. A genuinely liberal democracy allows the free formation and operation of civic interest groups which help in lobbying for specific interests. The state is then under pressure from these economic interests which can ossify the economic system by preventing the functioning of competitive, innovative action. Patronage politics and privileges for élite interests have been the bane of many authoritarian single-party regimes, as in the case of the Africa of the 1970s and the 1980s. In the recent past, there is no correlation between the type of political system and the degree of free market orientation of the policies pursued. In the period between the 1960s and the 1980s, there was a build-up of excessive market interference in Latin America, sub-Saharan Africa and South Asia without much regard to democratic rights.

The question then arises as to whether a democratic system or democratization is likely to aid a shift towards a more liberal competitive environment. Essentially, periodic elections permit democracy to replace the political leadership whose economic policies have not delivered the goods, opening up the way for alternative models or policies. Democracy also provides for the ventilation of grievances, and the leadership is bound to listen to the people's voices. In addition, in a democratic set-up, independent interest groups have the chance to express their viewpoints favouring change or liberalization when the economy is cracking. Furthermore, there is every possibility of making change by compromise and negotiation, probably by incremental steps.

Electoralism and Economic Reforms

Electoral multi-party systems have successfully changed the economic agenda in certain aspects, as in the case of Sri Lanka in the 1960s and the 1970s and Jamaica over a longer period. In Botswana, the frequency and fairness of elections and the culture of the 'appeal' to the ordinary people have helped to sustain economic success. More important has been its basically democratic culture of consultation, compromise and slow, cautious change. In Senegal, however, the key to improvement in its performance was the need for economic reform. Elections took place and mandates for economic reforms were given, though the reforms faltered in the 1980s. President Abdou Diouf, himself a technocrat, who obtained a mandate for reform through elections, did not create a coalition of interests which favoured reforms, from Parliament, farmers and businessmen. From the late 1980s, the new electoralism in Africa has resulted in few changes of government or fresh coalitions committed to economic reforms. In some countries, such as Benin, electoral change in government has had perverse effects on economic reforms. In Kenya, Cameroon and Côte d'Ivoire, the somewhat 'massaged' elections have not resulted in any significant change in either government or policy. Economic reform, however, has been sustained in Ghana and Uganda where there have been no multi-party elections or change of government.

The Indian Experience

According to Healey, India, the world's largest democracy, has long had modest economic growth, partly due to the existence of a substantial entrepreneurial capitalist class and considerable potential dynamism. The Indian economy has suffered from its dirigiste and protectionist policies and practices with overvalued exchange rates, controlled prices, excessive discretionary state licensing, control over movement of goods and widespread subsidies. However, in the last few years, India has embarked on an economic reform programme which has been sustained. The political system and culture has had the following features which has made this possible despite the odds:

- a range of freely functioning groups to protect and lobby for the interests of many different people means that the system is both broad based but also fluid and flexible when new opportunities or challenges appear;
- the use of formal political bargaining processes and mediation through parties, provincial and national legislatures, business groups, trade unions, industry groups;
- the use of informal mechanisms to achieve compromise deals for economic change, though usually with the need to appeal to the electorate for validation;
- a capacity to find compromises which allow the losers from economic change to have some compensation for the changes that benefit others;

- a 'gradualist' approach or the willingness to make the changes incremental and slow so that they are politically sustainable;
- the use of a federal democratic structure which allows resistance to economic change to be diffused away from an excessive focus on the centre and to decentralize the resolution of conflicts to the level of the provincial governments.

Interestingly, economic reforms have been a crucial aspect of the electoral planks of all political parties, though the nature, content and approach towards the reform process have varied from party to party. The Indian National Congress which was instrumental in launching the reforms was replaced by the Bharatiya Janata Party (BJP) in the 1996 elections. The BJP too, in spite of their very brief stay in power, emphasized the need for reforms. The present United Front government, supported by an alliance of political parties, including the left of centre parties, have also stressed the importance of reforms. In India, the need today is for more transparency in the reform process.

Democratization and Economic Growth

It is now evident that the control of public-sector deficits and inflation are prerequisites for sustained recovery and faster economic growth. How does democratization impact on the will and capacity of the government to stabilize an economy? During the transitional period from authoritarian rule to a multi-party electoral democracy, popular expectations are particularly high and hitherto repressed social demands and grievances are released. The new democratic politician in the arena may be inexperienced. In such a situation, there is likely to be much less restraint in public expenditure and budget deficits than if there are rulers who come to power and remain in power by non-constitutional means.

The democratization experience shows that 'strong' democracies like Costa Rica facilitate macro-economic reform process because of a tradition of consultation with business and labour. It is more possible if the democratic government has solid support in society or some consensus on the need for action. 'Weak' democracies are those in which the ruling regime cannot command support from divided parties, coalitions, legislatures or key support groups. In greatly divided societies, whether by ethnicity or economic differences, a democratic solution to economic problems is more difficult. None the less, single-party authoritarian regimes have not always been better than democracies at bringing inflation and imbalances under control. Overall, research indicates that there is no major electoral cycle in public spending, nor is there any systematic evidence that democratic regimes have greater difficulty in controlling public expenditure and inflation.

Ensuring Accountability

In principle at least, democracy ensures governmental accountability to the people. But are governments really accountable? Experiences vary from country to country. In several countries, elected parliaments have played a weak 'rubber-stamping' role on public expenditure, while civic groups and independent media do not seem to have much role or impact on economic policy formulations or public expenditure priorities. Even on the question of how public funds were spent in relation to intentions, countries have different stories to tell. As regards public spending, it is seen in the case of Zambia, Sri Lanka, Botswana and Jamaica that the distribution of public social expenditure has been fairly widespread, though not normally targeted on the poorer sections. On another front, studies show that regularly elected assemblies and competitive party politics have not ensured an effective 'watch-dog' role for the control and use of public funds.

Parliamentary or other varieties of democratic systems do not guarantee better economic performance. However, they do offer mechanisms which are better adapted to peacefully overcoming obstacles to economic change and accountable use of public resources. Such systems imply – or should imply – a democratic culture which involves consultation and compromise which take account of a wide range of interests in society. Economic change which always create some 'losers', even if the society on the whole benefits, is best negotiated under such a democratic culture. In this process, changes in economic policies and practices and hence economic programmes are likely to be rather slow but, much more importantly, these should be more sustainable.

Democracy and Development: Differing Perceptions

The discourses on the relationship between democracy and development have been going on for a long time. There are different dimensions to this relationship, as is evident from studies. Says Erik Paul:

> It is widely assumed that the process of industrialization creates conditions which are necessary for the emergence of a democracy.... . Another prerequisite for democratization is the existence of a civil society.... . A third condition is a political culture which supports the desirability for a more open society.... .

Another important factor is the influence of the external environment on domestic political change.[5]

Carlos Waisman argues that 'all liberal democracies in the contemporary world have existed in capitalist societies, and all non-capitalist economies have had non-democratic polities, but not all capitalist societies have had liberal democratic polities'.[6] Mahmood Monshipouri propounds three propositions: democratization is logically preceded by economic liberalization and by the building of a civil society; the pace and scope of liberalization are shaped by *de facto* socio-economic and political conditions; and cultures historically are dynamic and adjustable to changing conditions.[7] According to Larry Diamond, socio-economic development promotes democracy in two senses: where democracy already exists, sustained development contributes significantly to its legitimacy and stability, especially in the early life of the regime. 'Where democracy does not exist, it leads (sooner or later) to the eventually (if not initially) successful establishment of democracy.'[8]

Writing on the relationship between economic development and good governance, which is an important factor in societal progress, Joan Nelson observes:

> In the 1970s and 1980s, the view was widely held that authoritarian governments were more capable than democracies of taking difficult economic management decisions and promoting growth more generally.... . By the late 1980s, there was a growing consensus on two points: over-extended, inefficient and often corrupt governments were perhaps the key obstacle to economic growth in many developing countries. But good government (rather than minimal government) is crucial to development. The best way to ensure better government, many concluded, is to broaden participation and accountability.[9]

Stephen Haggard and Robert Kaufman argue that the consolidation of democracy and the consolidation of economic reforms are closely related, but have different political foundations:

> Democracy is a decision-making system in which there is a degree of uncertainty concerning substantive outcomes. Democracy provides opportunities for competing interests to contest and change policies, including economic ones. But democracies are unlikely to become institutionalized if broad assumptions underlying the management of the economy lack widespread support or are subject to continuous challenge.[10]

On the prospects of economic development in democracies, Georg Sorensen is of the view that:

the prospects of economic development ... depend on the nature of the ruling coalitions behind the democracies. Highly restricted, élite-dominated democracies may be virtually 'frozen' in that their room for manoeuvre in addressing welfare issues, and also in promoting resources for economic growth, is set within very narrow limits of continued support for the *status quo*... . Mass-dominated democracies, on the other hand, contain the potential for substantial reform which can restrain vested interests. But the process risks leading to confrontation with élite forces and the subsequent undermining of democracy itself. Yet there is a space in between these extremes, where relatively stable democracy and economic progress can work in conjunction.[11]

How does one link growth with democracy? A study conducted by three Swiss economists attempted such a link between democracy and growth. Out of the sixteen empirical studies they made, three found a negative correlation (the more democratic a country, the lower is the growth rate); three found a positive one, and ten found no conclusive results either way.[12] Eleven other studies have attempted 'instability indices', all of them showing that the more unstable a political regime was, the lower its economic growth was likely to be (exceptions are to be found, such as Thailand).[13]

Building appropriate institutional mechanisms for creating an enabling environment is an important factor in developing countries. More than that, to some observers, there is the need for a full and unequivocal endorsement of the democratic spirit. As Alhaji Sir Dawda Kairaba Jawara says, referring to developments in some African countries, 'In this atmosphere of debate and dissent, breakdowns in the body politic will become fewer, course correction faster, and discontinuities will be avoided, rather than when there is unquestioning conformity.'[14]

Adrian Leftwich, making use of a simple two-by-two table of democracy and non-democracy, development and non-development, has worked out four ways in which these variables may be combined (based on the available data about their economic and political characteristics). These are:[15]

- democratic development (Botswana, Malaysia);
- non-democratic development (Korea, Taiwan, China and Indonesia);
- democratic non-development (Jamaica, the Gambia, Costa Rica);
- non-democratic non-development (Haiti, Zaire).

It is generally accepted that, even though there is no firm evidence to link democracy with successful economic reforms or fast economic growth, democracy does not harm growth. There does, however, seem to be a strong connection between freedom and other components that are known to boost growth.[16] Leftwich identifies certain factors that have been characteristic of successful developmental experience. Says Leftwich:

Successful developmental outcomes, both historically and in the modern era, seem to have depended less on whether regimes have been democratic or not and more on such factors as internal stability...; on acceptability in international economic and political markets; on positive relations with dominant economies; on the relative autonomy of the state in both democratic and non-democratic polities; on sound infrastructure and competent administration; on low levels of corruption; on a critical minimum degree of consensus between groups and regions about the objectives of growth and the rules of the game for achieving it; and on an increasing degree of both regional and social equality in the distribution of the costs and benefits of that growth.[17]

Human Development

In recent years, much stress has been laid on the human aspect of development. According to Mahbub ul Haq, the chief architect and principal author of the *Human Development Report*, the four essential components in the human development paradigm are equity, sustainability, productivity and empowerment.[18] The first *Human Development Report* worked out the concept of human development and its measurement. It explored the relationship between economic growth and human development, showing that economic growth is necessary but not essential for human development. The right kind of economic environment and policies are required to translate the benefits of growth into the lives of the people. It also showed that commitment and political will, not always resources, are often the main constraints to taking care of economic growth and human development simultaneously. Furthermore, it explained that sustainable development strategies should meet the needs of the present generations, without compromising the ability of future generations to meet their needs.[19] The *Human Development Report 1995* took the concept forward and argued that:

- development must put people at the centre of its concerns;
- the purpose of development is to encourage all human choices, not just income, so that the human development concept focuses on the entire society, not just the economy;
- human development is concerned with both expanding human capabilities (through investment in people) and ensuring the full use of these capabilities (through an enabling framework);
- human development is created on four essential pillars: productivity, equity, sustainability and empowerment;
- the human development approach defines the ends of development and analyses the options for achieving them.[20]

According to Paul Streeten, human development is six-times blessed, as it is an end in itself that needs no further justification. It is a means to higher productivity. It slows human reproduction by lowering the desired family size. It is also good for the physical environment. Reduced poverty contributes to a healthy civil society, increased democracy and greater social stability. The political appeal will reduce civil disturbances and increase political stability, though this will depend on the relation between aspirations and material improvements.[21]

Mahbub ul Haq is of the view that the development plans should start with a human balance sheet: targets must first be expressed in basic human needs and only later translated into physical targets for production and consumption; both production and distribution objectives should be integrated and given equal status; and strategies must be decentralized to involve community participation and self-reliance. In addition, such plans must contain a human framework for analysing their performance.[22] It is interesting to note that, increasingly, the political leadership the world over is stressing the importance of development with a 'human face'.

As regards problems faced by developing countries, the modernization theorists assign the obstacles to development internally in the countries concerned.[23] Proponents of the dependency theory attribute the problems of developing countries chiefly to their external economic relations. André Gunder Frank is credited with the view that the developing countries occupy positions as satellites which are economically and therefore also politically inferior to the capitalistic metropoles of the Western world.[24] The fact remains, however, that many developing countries have not been able to devise appropriate strategies which could promote economic development. For example, the developmental experience in the LEDCs has been characterized by bureaucratic and political corruption. According to a study by the Transparency International,[25] a Berlin-based multinational organization dedicated to curbing corruption in international business, the developing countries emerge as the most corrupt. New Zealand ranks first as the least corrupt country, followed by Denmark, Sweden, Finland and Canada. Scandinavia emerges as the region with the cleanest administration and the least corruption.

Yet another area where developing countries are found lagging is in competitiveness. The Geneva-based World Economic Forum[26] published its *Global Competitiveness Report 1996* covering 49 nations to assess which country showed the best prospects for economic growth in the next five to ten years. The report rated Singapore as the most competitive, followed by Hong Kong and New Zealand.

The East Asian Miracle

Singapore is often cited as a remarkable example of economic achievement, though not exactly within the classical democratic framework. Singapore, along with its East Asian counterparts, has been promoted as a model of development by many. According to a World Bank study, the defining characteristics of the East Asian economies in comparison with the other LDCs are:

- high average rate of economic growth;
- reduced inequality;
- more rapid output and productivity growth in agriculture;
- higher rates of growth of manufactured exports;
- earlier and steeper declines in fertility;
- higher growth rates of physical capital, supported by higher rates of domestic savings;
- higher initial levels and growth rates of human capital;
- generally higher rates of productivity and growth.[27]

According to the World Bank study, the rapid economic growth in the East Asian economies was primarily due to the application of a set of common, market-friendly economic policies, leading to both higher accumulation and better allocation of resources. It is essential for developing countries to get the policy fundamentals right. It is also desirable that a two-track approach to development process emphasizing macro-economic stability on the one hand and investments in people on the other be pursued.[28] In some economies, mainly in north-east Asia, some selective interventions contributed to growth. This succeeded because of three essential prerequisites: they addressed the problems in the functioning of markets; they took place within the context of good, fundamental policies; and their successes depended on the ability of governments to establish and monitor appropriate economic performance criteria related to the interventions.[29] Lewis Preston argues that the

> economies studied used very different combinations of policies, from hand-offs to highly interventionist. Thus, there is no single 'East Asian model' of development. This diversity of experience reinforces the view that economic policies and policy advice must be country-specific if they are to be effective.[30]

What are the lessons from the Singapore model? According to an observer, Singapore has had a vital ingredient of effective plan implementation. There has also been a clever blend and combination of what appears to be top-down planning and market forces.[31] The net result of these two factors of a strong, development-oriented government and the harnessing of market forces to such development planning efforts is a coherent and consistent model of economic development.[32] To Preston, the study of the East Asian miracle shows that extraordinary growth has been due to superior accumulation of physical and human capital. They have also been better able than most to allocate physical and human resources to highly productive instruments and to acquire and master technology.[33] He adds: 'in this sense, there is nothing "miraculous" about the East Asian economies' success; each has performed these essential functions of growth better than most other economies'.[34]

The Lessons from Kerala

There are several developing countries definitely more democratic than Singapore, or any of its East Asian neighbours, which have achieved considerable human development, though not approximating their economic development. Sri Lanka, for example, has been successful in raising its literacy level, reducing its infant mortality rate and lowering the birth rate, which are considered to be key indicators of development. Very often, proponents of the 'Singapore model' overlook the fact that it is the case of a city state which has a small population. In this context, the case of the southern Indian province of Kerala has been much more interesting and is attracting the attention of the world.[35]

Kerala had a history of benevolent rulers in the pre-independence days who laid emphasis on the education and health of their subjects. In the years after independence, Kerala has been a laboratory of experiments which the rest of India has tried to emulate. In 1957, the province created history when, for the first time anywhere in the world, the Communists were voted to power. Ever since, the people of Kerala have exercised their franchise to change governments in successive elections. Kerala's voting percentage has always been in the range of 70 per cent of the eligible voters, much higher than the rest of India. Politics in Kerala has been characterized by coalitions of various parties and groups, and the province has an almost continuous history of coalition governments.

The province of Kerala is small, with an area of 38,863 sq.km. The population, according to the 1991 census, is about 29 million. People belonging to various religious faiths, including Hindus, Christians and Muslims, live in relative harmony. Successive governments have built upon the early start given by the kings of the past and taken initiatives to provide a better life for the people. Among the Indian provinces, Kerala has been prominent in land reform legislation. Today, however, Kerala is being discussed in many quarters for its achievements in the social sector. Kerala has achieved human development indicators which are comparable to several East Asian and European countries. As Tables 1.1 and 1.2 show, Kerala has a very high literacy rate at 89.8 per cent. In fact, Kerala has now been declared a 100 per cent literate province. The life expectancy at birth in Kerala is 71.3 while in Singapore it is 74.8 and in China 68.5. The infant mortality rate for Kerala is 16 per thousand live births whereas the figures for Singapore and China are 6 and 44 respectively. The corresponding figures for the whole of India bring into sharper focus the achievements of Kerala. The province has also been able to bring down its birth rate to 17.3 (as per 1994 provisional statistics) whereas the figure for India is 28.6. While the growth rate of population is 2.13 for India, the figure for the province is 1.35. Similarly, the sex ratio for Kerala is 1036 females for 1000 males whereas the all-India figure is 927 females for 1000 males. Kerala's health care system is also taken as a model by many, and the province is considered to be very neat and clean. Yet Kerala's economic performance has been gloomy, with a per capita income lower than that of India as a whole. This does not, however, mean that there is rampant poverty in the province, though the unemployment rate in Kerala is very high. What has to be appreciated is that whatever achievements Kerala has made are within a highly democratic, pluralistic set-up. According to Jean Drèze and Amartya Sen, Kerala's experience has not received the international attention that is given to achievements of countries such as Sri Lanka, South Korea, Costa Rica and Hong Kong, especially considering the fact that, with a population of over 29 million, Kerala is more populous than countries like Sri Lanka (18 million), Costa Rica (3.2 million), Hong Kong (5.8 million) and Singapore (2.8 million):[36] 'To achieve as much as Kerala has done for a population of its size is no mean record in world history.'[37] The *Human Development Report 1996* has lauded the human development gains made by Kerala which have far exceeded other provinces in India and many developing countries. The report says:

> The critical conditions for Kerala's progress are replicable: mass literacy, agrarian reform, improvement in the status of the oppressed castes and enlightened attitudes towards girls' and women's education and status. All these have been supported by public policy at the state level.[38]

Mahbub ul Haq has underlined the point that there is no automatic translation of the income of a society into the lives of its people.[39] For example, Saudi Arabia has a per capita income which is 16 times that of Sri Lanka, but a much lower literacy rate. The infant mortality rate in Brazil is four

Table 1.1 Select Indicators (all India and Kerala)

	Life expectancy at birth (years) (1988–92)	Literacy rate (1991) Total male/female (%)			Sex ratio (Females/1000 males) (1991)	IMR (1994)*	Death rate (1994)*	Birth rate (1994)*	Growth in population (1981–91)
All India	58.7	52.21	64.13	39.29	927	73	9.2	28.6	2.13
Kerala	71.3	89.81	93.62	86.17	1036	16	6.0	17.3	1.35

Notes: *as per Sample Registration System (per thousand)

Sources: Economic Survey 1995–96 (Ministry of Finance, Economic Division, Government of India); *India's Social Sectors, February 1996* (Centre for Monitoring Indian Economy (CMIE))

Table 1.2 Select Indicators (Kerala and some other countries)

Country/state	Area ('000 sq.km.)	Population (million) mid-1993	Adult literacy (%) 1992	Life expectancy at birth (years) (1992)	IMR per 1000 live births (1993)	Annual growth of adult population 1980–93
China	9,561	1,178.4	79.3	68.5	44	1.4
Republic of Korea	99	44.1	*	71.1	11	1.1
Singapore	1	2.8	*	74.8	6	1.1
Sri Lanka	66	18	89.3	71.9	17	1.5
Thailand	513	58.1	93.5	69.0	36	1.7
Kerala	38.8	29.6 (1991)	89.8 (1991)	71.3 (1988–92)	16 (1993)	1.35 (1981–91)

Notes: * according to UNESCO, illiteracy is less than 5 per cent

Sources: *Census of India 1991*; *Economic Survey 1995–6*; *India's Social Sectors, February 1996*; *Human Development Report 1995*; *World Development Report 1995*

times higher than that in Jamaica, even though the former enjoys twice the per capita income. Oman has three times the per capita income of Costa Rica but about one-third its literacy rate and seven fewer years of life expectancy. Similarly, the life expectancy of Black males in Harlem in New York city is lower than that in Bangladesh or Sudan.[40] In the light of the above, the Kerala experience is fascinating – relatively high levels of human development, though not the desired levels of economic development.

Thus, the debate on the correlation between democracy and development continues to create divergent viewpoints. It is seen that confusion between the concepts of democracy and capitalism still exists. While many capitalist countries are democracies, capitalism can exist without democracy. Studies and evidence prove that democracy is largely a prerequisite for economic development. Conversely, it is essential to have a certain level of economic development for democracy to be sustainable and meaningful.

The question of whether democracy is an ally or adversary of economic development is important, since the introduction of multi-party democracy in many developing countries has been linked to declining living standards and increasing political instability. There is empirical evidence to prove both sides of the question as to whether or not democracy is a facilitator of development. Democracy is more a facilitator of development than a controller of the developmental process. There cannot, of course, be any universal prescription because there cannot be any universal economic truths. The absence of any clear, universally accepted definitions of democracy and development, especially economic development, makes it difficult to arrive at any specific conclusions. In any case, democracy and development do not interact in isolation – there are very many factors that influence this tenuous relationship. There is, indeed, a need for a better and improved understanding of the relationship between these two key concepts which have the maximum bearing on the future of peoples and nations.

References

1 Lord Judd, in his keynote address at the conference, *Parliamentary Democracy and Development: Allies or Adversaries?*, Wiston House, UK, 12 February 1996.

2 Percy Mistry, in his presentation at the conference, *Parliamentary Democracy and Development: Allies or Adversaries?*, Wiston House, UK, 15 February 1996.

3 This discussion has benefited from the presentation by John Healey at the conference, *Parliamentary Democracy and Development: Allies or Adversaries?*, Wiston House, UK, 12 February 1996.

4 For detailed studies on the relationship between democracy and development, *see* Axel Hadenius, *Democracy and Development* (Cambridge, 1992), Amiya Kumar Bagchi (ed.), *Democracy and Development* (Proceedings of the IEA Conference held in

Barcelona, Spain) (Basingstoke, 1995); and Adrian Leftwich (ed.), *Democracy and Development: Theory and Practice* (Cambridge, 1996).
5   Erik C. Paul, 'Prospects for Liberalization in Singapore', *Journal of Contemporary Asia*, vol.23, no.3, 1993, p.292.
6   Carlos H. Waisman, 'Capitalism, the Market and Democracy', in Gary Marks and Larry Diamond (eds), *Re-examining Democracy: Essays in Honour of Seymour Martin Lipset* (Newbury Park, 1992), p.140.
7   Mahmood Monshipouri, *Democratization, Liberalization and Human Rights and the Third World* (Boulder, Col., 1995), pp.5–6
8   Larry Diamond, 'Economic Development and Democracy Reconsidered', in Marks and Diamond, *op. cit.*, p.125.
9   Joan M. Nelson, 'Good Governance: Democracy and Conditional Economic Aid', in Paul Mosley (ed.), *Development Finance and Policy Reform: Essays in Theory and Practice of Conditionality in Less-Developed Countries* (Basingstoke, 1992), p.310.
10 Stephen Haggard and Robert R. Kaufman, *The Political Economy of Democratic Transitions* (Princeton, New Jersey, 1995), p.16.
11 Georg Sorensen, 'Conditionality, Democracy and Development' in Olav Stokke (ed.), *Aid and Political Conditionality* (London, 1995), p.407.
12 *The Economist*, cited in *The Times of India* (New Delhi), 2 February 1996.
13 *Ibid.*
14 Alhaji Sir Dawda Kairaba Jawara, 'The Commonwealth and Human Rights', *The Round Table*, no.321, January 1992, p.40.
15 Adrian Leftwich, 'Two Cheers for Democracy? Democracy and the Developmental State', in Adrian Leftwich (ed.), *Democracy and Development: Theory and Practice* (Cambridge, 1996), p.282.
16 *The Economist*, vol.318, no.7713, 29 June 1991, p.15.
17 Adrian Leftwich, 'On the Primacy of Politics in Development', in Leftwich, *op. cit.*, pp.19–20.
18 Mahbub ul Haq, *Reflections on Human Development* (Delhi, 1996), p.16.
19 *Human Development Report 1995*, p.124.
20 *Ibid.*, p.122.
21 Paul Streeten, Foreword to Mahbub ul Haq, *op. cit.*, pp.ix–x.
22 Mahbub ul Haq, *op. cit.*, pp.4–5.
23 See Axel Hadenius, *Democracy and Development* (Cambridge, 1992), p.91.
24 *Ibid.*
25 Batuk Ghatani, in *The Hindu* (Delhi), 6 June 1996.
26 Jaishree Balasubramanian, in *The Times of India* (New Delhi), 31 May 1996.
27 The World Bank, *The East Asian Miracle* (Oxford, 1993), p.27.
28 Lewis Preston, Foreword to *ibid.*, p.(vi).
29 *Ibid.*
30 *Ibid.*
31 Somsak Tambunlertchai and S.P. Gupta (ed.), *Development Planning in Asia* (Kuala Lumpur, 1993), pp.248–49.
32 *Ibid.*
33 Preston, *op. cit.*, pp.v–vi.
34 *Ibid.*, p.vi.
35 For a study of Kerala and its achievements, *see* Richard W. Franke and Barbara H. Chasin, *Kerala: Development through Radical Reforms* (New Delhi: Promilla and Co., in collaboration with the Institute for Food and Development Policy, San Francisco, 1994); Robin Jeffrey, *Politics, Women and Well-being: How Kerala became a Model*

(Basingstoke, 1992); Jean Drèze and Amartya Sen, *India: Economic Development and Social Opportunity* (Delhi: Oxford University Press), 1995; and Jean Drèze and Amartya Sen (eds), *Indian Development: Selected Regional Perspectives* (Delhi: Oxford University Press), 1996.

36 Jean Drèze and Amartya Sen, *India: Economic Development and Social Opportunity* (Delhi, 1995), p.199.
37 *Ibid.*
38 *Human Development Report 1996*, p.81.
39 Mahbub ul Haq, *op. cit.*, p.51.
40 *Ibid.*

2 Creating an Enabling Economic Environment for Development*

The need for creating an enabling environment for economic development is a subject which has long been on national and international agendas. There are, of course, different viewpoints and differing perceptions of even the definition of the term 'development'. Decision-makers in various countries, particularly in the developing world, have presented their own 'models' of development in the name of appropriate paradigms which take account of the ground realities in their societies. In most of these cases, the models have not been able to deliver the goods. The collapse of the Soviet bloc and the rejection of its economic system have added to the intensity of the debate on development and the need for a facilitating environment for economic growth and all-round progress. Many democratic societies, especially in the developing world, have not been able to provide respectable standards of living for their citizens, thereby posing the serious question of whether democracy is an ally of development or a hindrance. The fantastic rate at which economic development has taken place in the NICs of East Asia has brought to the fore the argument that discipline in society as also in financial management is required even more than democracy. All countries insist that they have mechanisms and institutions which would foster economic development, but development experience in recent times exposes these claims. At the very end of the twentieth century, poverty and privation are the lot of a substantial section of the world population.

---

* This discussion is largely based on the presentation by Percy Mistry at the conference, *Parliamentary Democracy and Development: Allies or Adversaries?*, Wiston House, UK, 15 February 1996.

What is Development?

More than ever before, nations are today fully conscious of the imperative to create an enabling environment for development, though the concept of development is both multi-dimensional and complex. In this study, a narrow economic concept of development is adhered to. In this sense, it means economic reform and adjustment; sustenance of macro-economic stability; predictability of the policy environment; institutional structures conducive to sustainable growth and equity; and achievement and maintenance of competitiveness in a global setting which is increasingly dynamic and interwoven. Development is associated with economic growth and stability, and the enabling environment is one which facilities these two objectives.

Lessons from the Development Experience

In early development theory, the LDCs were perceived as disadvantaged owing to shortage of capital and foreign exchange. It was argued that if these *two gaps* could be covered, development could occur with a proactive role by the state. Forty-five years later, development is seen as a much more complex process and its absence is identified with *one gap*, a shortage of human capital and its concomitant derivative, the inadequacy of the institutional infrastructure.

Other lessons have also been learnt during these four and a half decades. Market systems are more development-friendly than variants of non-market systems. There should be properly regulated markets with the fewest possible imperfections and with explicit mechanisms to substitute or compensate for markets in conditions of market failure. The role of markets and prices needs to be understood in the context of market-supporting institutions without which markets do not work at all except in 'informal economies'.

Excessively pervasive and intrusive states are distinctly developmentally unfriendly, especially when the state or state-owned enterprises and institutions attempt to replace or substitute for the market in producing or pricing goods and services and mobilize or allocate resources by fiat rather than through competition. Sound markets need strong regulation by strong and credible states whose capacity and enforcement resolve are not continually put to test by market forces and market agents in their ceaseless attempts to establish where the frontiers of compromise or co-optation lie. Weak states and weak governments are not conducive to the functioning of strong markets, although there are exceptions like Thailand.

Attempts to achieve high rates of untrammelled economic growth – at least in the early stages of development – have proven to be superior in delivering the goods than have attempts to achieve equality first, or even the more usual growth-with-equity. However, growth for its own sake, without appropriately balanced concerns about the distribution of the benefits of such growth, is simply not sustainable in the long run. The East Asian experience has demonstrated clearly that growth with reasonable distribution is indeed sustainable for very long periods, especially when success in competition becomes an entrenched national habit. But distribution is best achieved through market-based incentives which make it immediately clear to wealth-creators that the distribution of gains is in their own interest, rather than through government intervention in wage policies or in 'soak the rich, help the poor' tax policies. Such interventions usually result in unnecessarily high rates of unemployment and levels of capital intensity which are misaligned with fundamental factor endowments and in a loss of revenue. Governments often forget that the rich and their assets are mobile while the poor are not. As a result, populist tax policies invariably backfire, usually resulting in the poor being soaked to help the rich!

Progressive taxation is neither progressive nor efficient. Attempts to achieve social justice through tax policies invariably fail. They do not achieve social justice but, even worse, they even compromise the raising of sufficient revenue for the functions of basic governance to be performed. Taxation policies should focus only on revenue raising and not on social engineering.

A high level of direct taxes on personal and corporate incomes and on trade transactions usually results in dependency on a very narrow taxable base in developing countries, with revenues becoming vulnerable to various and frequent shocks. A low level of indirect taxation spread across a very broad tax base is usually more efficient, more buoyant and more robust. In developing countries, taxation of income and savings is entirely counterproductive and is far less efficient than taxation on expenditure or on domestic value-added at each stage of a transaction's cycle.

States which attempt to produce goods and services as well as govern usually end up neither producing anything efficiently nor governing particularly well, especially if they happen to be democratic socialist states in the developing world.

Enabling Conditions for Sustained Economic Development

These are some of the significant lessons which have been learnt from the development experience of the post-war world. In the light of these, what then are the enabling conditions which democratic or even undemocratic states must provide for sustained economic development? These fall into the following broad areas: governance; infrastructure (physical and social); relations within civil society domestically; relations with the international business community; international relations with states and civil society interest groups; and competitiveness issues.

Basic Governance

Good governance has been stressed as one of the crucial factors in economic management. There are a host of components needed in laws of good governance. An efficient, capable and competent public administration is a prime requisite. While it is not possible to weed out corruption completely, every effort should be made to ensure that corruption does not work against development. While East Asia can hardly be termed as uncorrupt, it has managed to make corruption and development compatible, rather than antithetical. The bane of many countries in Asia, Africa and Latin America has been corruption in the polity and the civil service which has worked to the detriment of these societies. It is essential that civil services should perform minimum functions well rather than multiple functions badly. The civil services should be lean and small and not bloated and all-pervasive. More importantly, civil services should not be confused with social security systems or employment programmes for the extended families of politicians. Politicians and civil servants are certainly not above law just because they make, interpret or apply the law.

Another prerequisite for basic governance is transparency, predictability and stability in relations and transactions between government and business. Policies inevitably need to be stable over the long term. Policy changes, except in the case of a complete change in the economic paradigm, need to be evolutionary rather than revolutionary. If they do involve paradigm shift, then they need to be brutal and swift. Governments should be clear in their minds that the private sector does not exist or function to suit their interests and purposes. On the contrary, politicians and governments exist to serve the interests of the private sector (broadly defined) and not the interests of just that part of it which accommodates the private agenda of public officials.

Another component of good governance is a fair, transparent and decisive mechanism for arbitrating or overruling conflicts of interest between opposing vested interest groups (like management–labour or producers–consumers). There has to be adherence to rule-based decision where the rules are clear and applicable to all players. The application of the rule of law in settling criminal suits and civil contractual disputes must be swift. Governments should not be cavalier in their treatment of private property rights; instead, they should have respect for such rights.

Good governance warrants clearly articulated objectives and approaches to management of macro-economic policy and a firm commitment to the relentless pursuit of macro-economic stability, with adjustment being made to preserve stability rather than stability being compromised to accommodate domestic political exigencies. This is particularly necessary for fiscal management, monetary management, a low inflation rate and nominal exchange rate stability within margins that can reasonably be covered by affordable forward premiums.

It is essential to pursue sensible foreign policies which define national interests clearly and rationally in the contexts of internal and external security; regional considerations and good neighbourly behaviour; expanding cross-border trade and investment; avoiding the usual political temptation to indulge in chauvinism and xenophobia; avoiding aid dependence; and avoiding the surrender of economic sovereignty to the international financial institutions.

The provision of genuinely public goods as efficiently as possible at as low a cost as possible with full cost recovery pricing is another aspect of basic governance. The distribution between public and private goods in the context of particular countries remains a grey area which needs to be dealt with pragmatically, rather than theoretically, ideologically or theologically. Infrastructure and primary education are still generally regarded as public goods, although many areas of infrastructure can be more efficiently provided by the private sector.

Emphasis should be laid on the rapid development of indigenous human capital within the capacity of public budgets and private affordability. Similarly, domestic savings and investment, avoiding over-reliance on foreign savings and investment but not shutting the door to these, should be stressed.

Governments should have a liberal approach to foreign investment and foreign technology without being overly prescriptive about defining areas in which they are welcome and the areas in which they are not. Exclusions should be limited and economically justifiable, not just a matter of political preference.

Unless countries have the political culture and public management capacity of countries such as Singapore or Switzerland, governments should have a major commitment to privatizing virtually all state-owned enterprises (SOEs) that can reasonably be privatized to avoid political agendas colliding with commercial common sense at the expense of the taxpayer. Moreover, SOEs have proven to be extraordinarily wasteful of capital with low incremental capital output ratios (ICORs) and much higher capital intensity than private firms.

Governments need to have a proclivity toward under-prescription and over-enforcement of simple and clear rules in every area where government and the private sector interact. However, there is today hopeless over-prescription of petty rules accompanied by even more hopeless enforcement which has inevitably resulted in the credibility of ostensibly rules-based systems being completely eroded.

Infrastructure

Good governance should also pay attention to the provision of proper market-supporting infrastructure and services by both public and private sectors, especially with regard to legal systems and standards; accounting systems and standards; business information support; capable tax advisory and management consulting industries; access to efficient communications and office/information technology; access to efficient, capable, trained manpower at a competitive cost; safety and security of physical being, plant and property, and of transactional rights; satisfactory regulation and competition (enforcing laws and enforcement capacities); and swift recourse to legal redress and the enforcement of property rights.

In competing for private capital to drive investment and be the engine of growth, governments which do not pay sufficient attention to the importance of infrastructure usually lose out to those which do. Private firms are perfectly willing to take normal commercial risks. They are usually unwilling to include in their cost structure those items which they properly believe is the business of government to provide (roads, railways, well-developed transport arteries), or arrange for the provision of power, water, telecommunications, airlines, airports, shipping connections, etc., through private investment.

Private investors are also unwilling to include in their cost base expenditure for social infrastructure – especially health, education, recreation and culture – which they also believe to be the preserve and responsibility of governments. On another front, it is a mistake for governments in developing countries to believe that low labour costs and cheap land are sufficient to attract investment. These advantages are only attractive when all other things are equal. When they are not, the attractions to private investment are quite different from what governments believe them to be.

Relations with Civil Society

Development and growth are powerfully affected by the way in which governments deal with other powerful elements in civil society, such as labour and trade unions, non-governmental organizations (NGOs), and single-issue special interest groups whose particular interests no longer respect national borders (e.g. environmentalists, gender militants, civil liberties groups, etc.). Those who generate growth usually do not care for governments which deal with civil society in either too clumsy a fashion or with those which pander excessively to special interests. A reasonably happy balance between the two, i.e. firm handling of situations where conflicts of interest between different elements of civil society arise, is usually seen as the most desirable.

Relations with the International Business Community

The attitude of governments to foreign investors – direct and portfolio investors – has become a critical indicator of enabling conditions, especially as global private capital flows have, since 1990, dwarfed flows from official sources.

Governments which play to the domestic voting gallery, of playing the xenophobia card at times of electoral convenience, could invite trouble. The same is true of governments which do double somersaults to attract foreign investors at the expense of domestic investors. The best approach is a relatively open and neutral regime (for all private investments) without special favours, tax breaks or other incentives to attract one type of investment but not another. Level playing fields are not easy to maintain by governments in which the private agenda of public officials intrudes too obviously.

Governments which say one thing and do another where foreign investors are concerned, or when governments suddenly change the rules of the game halfway through the investment process, are likely to do their development prospects a great deal of harm. The interests of growth and development demand stability, predictability and low levels of uncertainty which can be accommodated by available risk-management mechanisms. That is one reason why developing or developed countries in which politics is polarized by parties with radically different economic policies and agendas are extremely off-putting to wealth-creators.

Increasingly, political competition in developing democracies has to be narrowed down to offering greater competence, probity and efficiency in the economic management of market systems, rather than oriented to the provision of radically different economic agendas to attract public interest.

International Relations with Other States and Global Interest Groups

By and large, except in the few very large countries of the world, most developing countries need to pursue foreign policies compatible with their development and trading interests. They also need to pursue good neighbourly policies in their immediate regions to encourage the formal and informal expansion of the market size and economic space in which their firms can freely operate. This should, of course, also be true of the very large countries, but it is not. And politicians in these countries, where they are democracies, have an unusual role and responsibility which they usually do not discharge very well.

The forces of globalization – in finance, technology transfer, the mobility of higher-level manpower (HLM), the mobility of production structures and the increasingly pervasive role of global media corporations and of global brands – pose major new challenges for foreign policy. Business and investment now drive foreign policy interests and regional policy interests in ways which are incomprehensible to most local politicians and to their foreign policy experts. Unless political leaders in these developing democracies begin to comprehend these dimensions, they are destined to focus on sub-optimal, defensive and reactive policies – inimical to their developmental interests – rather than to shape policies which safeguard the future developmental interests of their countries. Most politicians in developing countries are dangerously ignorant of international finance and basic macro-economics and of how the world is changing in ways which profoundly affect them. Political leaders and politicians in these countries will need to cope with the domestic fallout of interactions not only with global business interests but of global single-issue interest groups which will have a profound influence on the way in which their electorate thinks. An inability to accommodate and cope with that reality will severely disable growth and development prospects if this particular interface is badly mishandled.

Competitiveness Policies

Governments need to pursue policies which enhance and maintain national competitiveness in an increasingly integrated world. Basically, these policies comprise a combination of macro-, meso- and micro-economic policies which assist countries, industries and firms to compete effectively in the global market-place. The essence of competition and competitiveness lies in relative cost efficiency which is profoundly affected by exchange rate policies; the domestic and international cost of money; the relative real cost and productivity of labour and higher-level manpower (i.e. human capital costs); production process efficiency; a commitment to quality control approaching zero defect standards; the increasing relative cost of energy; transport and communications in production process; the diminishing relative cost of material inputs into the production process; the relative cost of transporting goods and services within and across markets; the relative real costs of doing business (i.e. explicit and implicit taxes, corruption costs, insecurity costs, etc.); and the relative cost of technological inputs.

Each of these areas is affected indirectly by other policies, such as fiscal and monetary policies, wage policies, social policies and the like. Governments which succeed in global competition, and therefore, by definition, succeed with development and growth, will be governments which understand the critical importance of these ingredients and which act decisively to lower the cost of production in all these areas. Governments and politicians who do not comprehend the fundamental importance of competitiveness will fail in the most basic task which justifies their existence in developing democracies, which is to deliver the goods.

It is often argued that democracies have been able to achieve non-disruptive, non-violent changes in an economic regime in ways that did not destabilize societies and polities. While the general philosophical and theoretical truth of the statement is attractive, there is in reality hardly any practical evidence. It is also argued that, in democracies, changes were likely to be slow but durable. The East Asian experience tells a different story, where changes have been more durable than elsewhere. Democracies, particularly the Westminster type, enable debate and discussion of problems but never solve them. The socialist measures adopted by several developing countries have not led them anywhere as regards economic development. Many of the leaders of developing countries did not have a good understanding and proper perspective of the economic imperatives for development. They followed policies which pushed their nations into economic chaos and entrapped them in a debt crisis. The political agenda frequently collided with the larger social good. Aided and abetted by a largely corrupt and bloated civil service, they prescribed their own policies of economic management which entrenched permeating corruption.

In many countries, the SOEs became symbols of the degeneration of the economy at the hands of the political class. Several countries, however, had to confront problems of a different nature. The lack of political stability, frequent changes in policy formulations, and threats posed by forces of terrorism and fundamentalism put a break on economic progress. Population explosion, depleting resources and infrastructure inadequacies hindered economic development in many societies.

In recent years, there has been a welcome change in policy approaches by developing countries worldwide, particularly in the context of emphasis on good governance by international funding agencies, financial institutions and donor countries. Many countries have embarked on economic reforms and structural adjustment programmes. The political leadership will have to take new policy initiatives to tackle the myriad crises facing the developing countries. The economies of small countries have problems unique to them which need to be addressed contextually. Politicians, particularly in the developing world, should realize that, at times, they also have to lead the people, rather than always pandering to them. There obviously cannot be global prescriptions which are equally applicable to all countries. Approaches have to be context-specific so that solutions come about to the satisfaction of all concerned. Is democracy an essential prerequisite for development? To some, the evidence seems to suggest that it is not, even though democracy may be desirable in its own right. They also underscore the point that a certain level of development is essential for democracies to be meaningful. All in all, creating an enabling environment conducive to economic development is an onerous task for political leadership worldwide.

3 Human Rights, Good Governance and Development

The protection and promotion of human rights have acquired new dimensions in today's global political order. The revolutionary developments in information technology, while paving the way for a global village, have also made it possible to easily survey the human rights situation worldwide. Thus, international organizations, human rights bodies and all others concerned are in a position to come to an objective understanding of the promotion or denial of natural rights by states to their citizens. Undoubtedly, human rights have become a major factor in the centre stage of international relations.

The origin of the natural rights philosophy is often traced to the 1776 American Declaration of Independence and the 1789 French Declaration of the Rights of Man and of the Citizen. However, many scholars in the realm of human rights are of the view that the primacy of the individual has been an inherent component of various religious philosophies which have evolved over the centuries. In 1945, the Charter of the United Nations stressed the 'faith in fundamental human rights'. The Universal Declaration of Human Rights, adopted by the UN General Assembly in 1948, enumerated the rights available to individuals. Nearly two decades later, recognizing the importance of human rights to the furtherance of the dignity of the individual, the UN proposed two International Covenants in 1966: the International Covenant on Civil and Political Rights and the International Covenant on Economic, Social and Cultural Rights. The latter was in recognition of the increasing prominence of these rights, particularly economic rights. The economic aspect of human rights – rather, the developmental factor – was further stressed when the United Nations Development Programme (UNDP) declared that the 'right to development' is also a fundamental right. The UN's efforts in this direction have led to the establishment of the

Development Decades. The relationship between human rights and development has been highlighted by the varied activities of both the UNDP and the UN Conference on Trade and Development (UNCTAD). The UN Commission on Human Rights, the International Labour Organization (ILO) and the Economic and Social Council (ECOSOC) have also been engaged in the task of promoting human rights everywhere. The developmental correlation with human rights was given a much-needed momentum when, in 1986, the UN Declaration on the Right to Development was proclaimed.

The Human Rights Scenario

It has increasingly been recognized that democracy, economic development and fundamental rights are basic to human development. In fact, the UN's appraisal report of the First Development Decade (1961–70) had delineated human rights and human welfare as integral parts of development policy. The dismantling of the erstwhile Soviet Union and the dramatic developments in Eastern Europe, resulting in the end of the Cold War, have offered new challenges and opportunities for democratization. However, there has been intense concern at the increasing incidence of overt and covert violations of human rights in many countries. In the developed world there has naturally been a greater understanding of the need for ensuring fundamental rights of citizens, even though in these countries there are also many instances of the basic tenets of human rights being violated, as is evident from media exposés and related studies by independent human rights bodies. However, in the case of the developing countries, because of socio-cultural and economic reasons, coupled with historical experiences, there is a lack of proper understanding of the larger ideals underlying human rights. The governments, in several cases authoritarian in some form or the other, trample upon human rights and values with impunity. The non-awareness of the rights of citizens is compounded by large-scale illiteracy, minimal access to the media, curbs placed on the media, inactive human rights bodies and judicial apathy. Incidentally, in almost all these countries, the constitutions provide for the promotion and protection of the rights of the citizens. Lately, of course, for a multiplicity of factors, there has been a welcome change in the attitudes of governments worldwide towards human rights.

Human Rights and Development

The human rights scenario in the developing countries is further complicated by the low level of economic development which has led to widening income disparities. There are, however, several countries which have recorded rapid strides in economic development, often achieving standards comparable with those of the developed world. There is nevertheless a question mark on the democratic credentials of these governments, as also their human rights records. The debate, then, is centred on a fundamental issue. Is enhanced protection of human rights a by-product of development or is it a prerequisite for development?

Countries' experience in this regard varies. Singapore, one of the 'miracle economies' of South-East Asia, has been successful in providing excellent standards of living for its citizens, and Malaysia, Indonesia and China have increased their economic growth substantially. Singapore would be rated high on the protection of the economic rights of the people but low on the civil rights front. The same holds true in the case of other countries too, but in varying degrees. There is a line of thought which emphasizes the 'Singapore model' of development to drive home the point that economic development cannot be attained without subordinating, at least for a time, the human rights of a substantial number of its citizens. In other words, one has to pay a price for economic development by voluntarily subjugating one's human rights to the larger interests of national welfare. Can the example of small city-states such as Singapore and Hong Kong be promoted as models for bigger states with complex problems? The arguments in favour of subordinating people's rights in the name of discipline for development has been seen to be misused by many countries where dictatorships of various hues have thrived to promote their vested interests at the cost of the national interests and human rights of their peoples. However, it is now recognized that upholding human rights is integral to development. One problem area is that economic and social rights are not justiciable, unlike civil and political rights. The 'growth first' strategy more often tends to sideline human rights development. As such, there is a need for investing in human rights.

According to the UN Declaration on the Right to Development, the human person is the central subject of development and should be an active participant and beneficiary of the right to development. The Declaration states:

> All human beings have a responsibility for development, individually and collectively, taking into account the need for full respect for their human rights and fundamental freedoms as well as their duties to the community, which alone can ensure the free and complete fulfilment of the human being, and they should therefore promote and protect an appropriate political, social and economic order for development.[1]

Emphasizing the role of the state in this process, the Declaration says:

States have the right and the duty to formulate appropriate national development policies that aim at the constant improvement of the well-being of the population and of all individuals, on the basis of their active, free and meaningful participation in development and in the fair distribution of the benefits resulting therefrom.[2]

The Declaration also underlines that all rights – civil, political, economic, social and cultural – are indivisible and interdependent. It goes on to add that the failure to observe these rights constitutes an obstacle to development. According to Neelan Tiruchelvam,[3] one of the more important innovations of the Declaration is the provision mandating states to remove 'obstacles' to development arising from the failure to respect rights and freedoms. This requires the states to observe and respect the rights and freedoms as embodied in the international human rights covenants and related instruments and to address the need to reform state structures, institutions and policies which are an obstacle to the realization of these rights.[4]

The development experience of many countries shows a haphazard pattern, making it difficult to identify models of development which can be emulated by others. The human rights aspect of development has further complicated the wider acceptance of any such models. As discussed earlier, many are of the view that the NICs of South-East Asia and the East Asian developmental models in general subordinated human rights to make way for economic growth. In several market economies, there is a clear-cut emphasis on consumption and material development. This aspect perhaps overshadows the promotion of human rights. According to the review and appraisal report of the first UN Development Decade:

> One of the greatest dangers in development policy lies in the tendency to give the more material aspects of growth an overriding and disproportionate emphasis. The end may be forgotten with the means. Human rights may be submerged and human beings seen only as instruments of production rather than as free entities for whose welfare and cultural advance the increased production is intended.[5]

In South-East Asia, the development process has marginalized many, including the indigenous people and the urban poor. There is also a 'dark underside' to development. There have been widespread violations of workers' rights linked to export-driven economies that are heavily dependent on low labour costs to attract investment. The denial of these rights could erode the very basis of economic development in the South-East Asian countries, where there has been a boom in export-oriented industries. The economic boom, combined with increasing education and awareness, has led to industrial unrest and stoppages by workers demanding higher wages and improved working conditions. Some of these countries have also discouraged freedom of association and the right to form trade unions. Human rights watchers feel that tight controls on freedom of association, along with mounting grievances, mean that some Asian countries are creating a 'pressure cooker' with the potential for causing greater damage than relaxing controls would do.[6] There is an imperative for reassessing the ground realities in view of the evolving situation and addressing issues in a more pragmatic manner. The crux of the matter is that the South-East and East Asian 'miracle economies' have their own approaches towards development, both economic and human. As one analyst puts it:

> Southeast Asian societies have formulated two major views when it comes to development. Firstly, development is a collective activity and primarily supplied by state agencies and other groups in society. Secondly, it is an economic and social process perhaps requiring in the short term the infraction of classical civil and political rights.[7]

But the political leadership in these countries would do well to take a fresh look at the overall human rights situation in the region and the mounting criticism from within and without.

Right to Development

In this context, it is worth re-emphasizing the relationship between economic development and human development, including human rights. A UN study has identified several aspects of the international dimension on the 'right to development' as part of the concept of development. These include:[8] the realization that the potentialities of the human person in harmony with community should be seen as the central purpose of development; the human person should be regarded as the subject and not the object of the development process; development requires the satisfaction of both material and non-material basic needs; respect for human rights is fundamental to the development process; human persons must be able to participate fully in shaping their own reality; respect for the principles of equality and non-discrimination is essential; the achievement of a degree of individual and collective self-reliance must be an integral part of the process.

The South Asian Experience

While countries of the South-East Asian region have gone a long way in giving their people better economic standards, in South Asia, however, the situation is vastly different. The record of the member countries of the Association of South-East Asian Nations (ASEAN) in human rights is often questioned by human rights watchers. The South Asian scenario is somewhat different. The region comprises enduring democracies such as India and Sri Lanka on the one hand and countries such as Pakistan and Bangladesh which had to confront successful military challenges to the civilian governments. However, in recent times, some form of representative institutions have come to the fore in most of the South Asian countries. Sociopolitical and economic management in the region has been a major source of problems for the leadership due to a host of factors. Historically, the South Asian region abounds with plurality and diversity. The problems are compounded by demographic and economic pressures. The region accounts for a mere 2 per cent of the global income while it accommodates 22 per cent of the global population! Nearly half the population lives below the poverty line. Annually, there is a 25 per cent increase in the population. Yet, as Tiruchelvam observes, South Asia remains a region which has the largest population committed to periodic elections, representative institutions, fundamental rights and democratic freedoms.[9] It is thus a region of considerable importance in terms of constitutional experimentation and institutional reappraisal and renewal, where issues of constitutionalism, human rights and democracy are at the centre of the political and intellectual aganda.[10] The South Asian system baffles many, especially in the wake of threats to political stability from forces of fundamentalism, terrorism and insurgency.

However, the economic development models being pursued by the countries in the region have been found wanting by many. In recent years, several South Asian countries, including India, have charted new courses in economic liberalization and restructuring of the financial sector. While the World Bank, the International Monetary Fund (IMF) and other multilateral financial institutions have advocated policies intended to favour private-sector development and privatization of state enterprises, opponents are wary of the end results of such policies which, they feel, will only widen inequality and disparity in the region. The likely centralization of authority resulting from these exercises would progressively exclude NGOs and other people's movements from the decision-making process. Trade union rights are bound to be adversely affected. In such a scenario, it is argued that there is every possibility of further impoverishment and marginalization of the poor and other disadvantaged groups.

What is important is that democratic experiments have succeeded in the South Asian context, even though (because of the accumulated problems faced by the countries in the region) they have lagged far behind in extending acceptable living standards to their populace. This, however, shows another picture of the unfolding 'Asian drama', especially with the ASEAN nations talking of 'Asian values' in their context. To human rights watchers like Mike Jendrzejczyk, it seems clear that, while economic development can be an important factor, it is not an automatic guarantor in Asia of improved human rights.[11] Other non-economic factors are equally important when it comes to protecting the rights of physical integrity, key social and economic rights, including the right of an adequate standard of living or decent working conditions, or fundamental civil rights such as freedom of expression and association.[12]

Good Governance and Aid

As discussed in the previous chapter, good governance is one of the crucial factors in economic management. Closely linked to the debate on human rights and development are the issues of good governance and aid. Much discussion has been going on in all concerned circles on these subjects, which are interrelated. Essential to an understanding of the complexity of the matter is a definition of good governance. This arises basically because aid has emerged as an important variable in international relations, particularly in the context of adherence to the principles of good governance and the practice of human rights in the aid receiving countries. In the words of Tiruchelvam:

> A question which has become central to the relationship between human rights and development is the issue of political conditionalities. This means that the continuance of developmental assistance would be dependent on the observance of political conditions such as 'good governance' and the observance of civil and political rights.[13]

What constitutes 'good governance' is itself a matter on which differences exist, particularly between the developed countries and the developing countries. The stand of the developed world has more or less coincided with that of the international financial and monetary institutions like the IMF and the World Bank, which are products of the Bretton Woods system. This primarily has led the developing world to articulate the need for a New International Economic Order (NIEO), which would necessitate the restructuring of these financial institutions to take into its domain the ground realities of the day. Their main argument is that these institutions today are essentially just pawns in the hands of the developed countries, the West particularly. As such, the Third World cannot expect any meaningful assistance from them. The developed world, on the other hand, dismisses these arguments and asserts that the international financial institutions also have a right to ensure that there is effective utilization of the huge assistance given by them to the developing countries. The thrust is on proper utilization of assistance and resources, effective financial and money management, restructuring of domestic financial institutions, structural adjustment programmes, liberalization of trade and the economy in general, and of protection of human rights in the larger context of good governance.

Good Governance

What is good government? Patrick Chabal observes:

> Admittedly, it is a concept more easily understood in theory than it is adjudged in practice. For when is a government good? Good in comparison to what? Good for what? Good for whom? Yet it is a fundamental concept, for what is the justification for politics, if not good government?[14]

John Dunn attempts a detailed analysis of the concept of good government. He says:

> As a concept good government is holistic and consequentialist rather than specific and procedural. It implies, *ceteris paribus*, and in relation to the policies that it actually pursues, a high level of organizational effectiveness; but it certainly does not imply the choice of a particular ideological model of state organization: a government of laws but not of men, a minimal state, or dictatorship of the proletariat. Good government is best defined ostensively rather than by semantic prescription. It is what Sweden and Singapore enjoy, and what Zaire and Ethiopia distressingly lack. In principle, heavily repressive regimes may on occasion exemplify good government. But they can do so only where there is a direct and palpable link between the effective contributions of their rulers to popular welfare, and the modes of repression which they employ – good government is not to be equated, for example, with ingratiating or virtuous government. Since any repressive regime in any public forum, national or international, is likely to justify its coercive activities by their putative contribution to popular welfare, the concept of good government is necessarily anti-ideological in intention. Its analytical purpose is precisely to distinguish the professed or actual self-understanding of ruling groups from their real causal contribution to the prosperity or misery of their subjects. The presence or absence of effectively guaranteed civil and political liberties does not in itself ensure the prevalence of good or bad government. But any set of repressive practices, as Jeremy Bentham salutarily noted, is in itself a direct contribution to human suffering.[15]

The World Bank, which is often in the eye of the storm in relation to economic management by countries, is credited with the view that governance means 'the manner in which power is exercised in the management of a country's economic and social resources for development'.[16] In the specific context of human rights, while there is debate about which rights are relevant to governance, and thus development, the World Bank has come up with some such rights: an objective and efficient judiciary (rule of law); freedom of association and organization (institutional pluralism); political and bureaucratic accountability; and freedom of information, including transparency of the decision-making process. Observance of these rights also enables the intended beneficiaries of the development activity to participate effectively in both political and economic life, and is closely correlated with another key governance concern, the legitimacy of the government.[17]

The European Council, in its Development Council Resolution on Human Rights, Democracy and Development adopted on 28 November 1991, emphasized that respect for human rights, the rule of law and the existence of political institutions which are effective, accountable and democratically legitimate are the basis for equitable development. The Resolution stressed that good governance should include democratic decision-making, adequate government transparency and financial accountability.[18]

The Standing Committee on External Affairs and International Trade of the Canadian House of Commons recommended in May 1987 that progress on human rights should be a central element of development assistance. The committee, however, recommended that where gross human rights violations prompted interruption of government-to-government assistance, alternative ways should be sought to channel such assistance to civil society, arguing further that emergency humanitarian assistance should never be denied.[19]

During the World Human Rights Conference in Vienna in 1993, the World Bank made a presentation in which it described the Bank's focus on governance within the constraints of its limited mandate. While noting that its charter explicitly prohibits the Bank from taking into account non-economic considerations, the paper acknowledged that

> the economic consequences of violations of political and civil human rights may, in certain circumstances, have significant effects which the Bank would need to take into account... . Human rights may ... become a relevant issue if their violation becomes so pervasive as to raise concerns relating to [economic] matters.[20]

In fact, the Bank had suspended financial assistance to Myanmar since the 1988 military takeover. In addition, at the aid consortium meetings with several Asian and African countries, the Bank has sent a clear message that progress in development is inextricably linked to progress in the protection of fundamental rights.

Japan, which is the world's largest bilateral foreign aid donor, in its 1992 Official Development Assistance Charter, has pointed out the link between development and human rights, saying: 'Full attention should be paid to efforts for promoting democratization and introduction of a market-oriented economy and the situation regarding the securing of basic human rights and freedoms in the recipient country.'[21] Major donor countries across the world have lately given explicit indications that the flow of aid and other terms of development assistance were contingent upon good governance and protection of human rights.

Human rights activists and human rights bodies have welcomed these initiatives by major donors and international financial institutions maintaining that such efforts would compel the deviant countries to mend their ways. They argue that the question of infringement of the sovereignty of nations do not come into the picture as human rights are universal in nature and indivisible. Many activists also draw attention to the fact that several impoverished countries have been diverting foreign assistance for the purchase of arms and building up their defence arsenal, and not for the developmental schemes for which the assistance was made available by the donor country.

Political Conditionalities and Sovereignty

Aid with strings has always been a sore point in the North–South relations, more so when concepts such as human rights and good governance come into the picture. The developing countries have always maintained that political conditionalities, or for that matter any string attached to aid, is an attack on the sovereignty of nations. They assert that it is for the people of a country to decide their future, what form of government they want, what model of development they should pursue, and what rights they have in their political framework. After all, these countries do have their constitutions, human rights commissions, judiciary and the media to take care of any aberrations. Why should someone else decide for them their requirements and their priorities? These arguments are then taken forward to stress that the socio-political and economic development of any country has to take into account its native realities, its history, its culture, its values. In view of this, imposing value systems from outside and trying to transplant ideas from elsewhere cannot be tolerated.

What should be kept in mind is that there are several aspects to intergovernmental relations in matters such as aid, human rights and good governance. The development relationship between the developing and the developed world has been substantially affected by the conditionalities attached to aid. The South feels that there cannot be global policemen or arbiters to decide on matters such as good governance, development and human rights. Such measures often invite the criticism of the imposition of 'Western values' and the resultant 'cultural hegemony' on the developing world. They also question the developed world on their record in human rights, pointing to alleged discrimination in their own societies, and asking how the South is treated by the North.

The developing countries also maintain that there is a need for credibility and consistency in the articulation of concerns by the developed countries. Very often, geopolitical considerations have forced the North to resort to selectivity while dealing with violations, the norms of which they themselves have proclaimed. Economic and other sanctions have been selectively used by the developed countries, always keeping in mind their national interests, which only goes to prove that the whole debate boils down to one's own interests and not the preservation of the higher principles as they are made out to be. The developed world has supported military governments and all forms of dictatorships when it suited their convenience, while at the same time preaching the inherent merit of democracy and political pluralism.

Denial of aid can often conflict with good governance. There is need to develop trade, rather than aid, and allow the developing countries to develop their infrastructure independently. In any case, recipient countries need a greater say as far as aid is concerned, more so because ultimately they only have to devise plans for programme implementation. Eventually, they are also answerable to the people. In recent years, however, the developing countries have been more accommodative of the donors' concerns, at the same time insisting that conditionalities cannot be imposed on them.

Unfortunately, in this ongoing debate, the crucial issue has been obscured. Kenneth Christie observes:

> The human rights issue is often politicized into a battle between the West and the developing world. From the latter's point of view, the West promotes a universal approach, forcing a single conception of human rights – the Western conception – upon the rest of the world. Western theorists, on the other hand, often argue that cultural relativism is an attempt by human rights violators to deflect criticism from their own record.[22]

There is another factor which is largely responsible for the diametrically opposed views of the North and the South. As Diane Mauzy argues,

> 'human rights' are generally divided into civil and political rights, on the one hand, and economic, social and cultural rights, on the other. However, the West normally places more importance on the former, whilst most of Asia sees them as equally important, and at times contradictory.[23]

To quote Christie again:

> Relativists offer two critiques of the universalist approach. First, they argue that, despite commonalities, circumstances vary widely enough among individual societies to require differing conceptions of human rights. The specific application of policy is therefore best left to each community to decide for itself... . Secondly, relativists charge the universalists with cultural imperialism.[24]

In any case, countries cutting across all barriers have now come to accept the imperative of ensuring human rights, including the right to development. As the Lawyers Committee for Human Rights underscores:

> The international community, both official and non-governmental, has increasingly come to understand that there are linkages between the respect for basic human rights, both civil and political and economic, social and cultural, and effective and sustainable development. In other words, human rights are not only worthy of protection in their own right, but as vehicles necessary to permit such development to occur.[25]

There are certain inevitable components required for the promotion and protection of human rights. These include representative institutions, an independent judiciary and a free and fair press. Imparting education to the people, particularly women and the weaker sections of society, and also educating the people on their rights are essential. Transparency in governmental actions is another must. The rights of women, children and the unemployed need special attention. In multi-ethnic systems and in highly pluralistic societies, the protection and promotion of human rights acquire added urgency. Alhaji Sir Dawda Kairaba Jawara's prescription for the Commonwealth has universal relevance. He says:

> The starting-point must be to reaffirm our strong commitment to the respect for human rights and the rule of law. These may be self-evident but in a world in which human rights' protection and the spreading of democracy still leaves much to be desired, they need to be stated and re-stated. If the basic human rights of our citizens are to remain inviolate then a firm knowledge of those same rights must become a vital element in the political ethos of our societies. The key elements in this regard are knowledge by the individual citizens of their basic rights and how to protect them.[26]

The NGOs and other such institutions can also play a prominent role in facilitating the advancement of human rights. The growth of NGOs in Asia has meant that demands for respect for human rights are increasingly linked directly to demands for economic development.[27] The number of NGOs in

Asia working in diverse fields has also increased substantially, which is indicative of a negation of the attempt by certain governments to brand the concern for human rights as a 'Western' concept. Regrettably, because of the political conditionalities attached to aid, the universal character of human rights has come to be questioned by many countries which try to counter these measures by asserting the primacy of their value systems in their own societies. Aung San Suu Kyi rightly stressed that 'if ideas and beliefs are to be denied validity outside the geographical and cultural bounds of their origins, Buddhism would be confined to north India, Christianity to a narrow tract in the Middle East and Islam to Arabia'. According to Tiruchelvam,

> A conspicuous failure of the human rights movement has been its inability to expand the base of support for secular, democratic and pluralistic values. The social imagination of an entire generation is being captured by the ideologies of ethno-populism, of exclusion, and intolerance.[28]

He also refers to the indigenous cultural and religious traditions in South Asia which emphasize communitarian conceptions of justice and conciliatory and consensual approaches to conflict resolution. There are other ideas such as *dharma* which are at the core of the Hindu–Buddhist theory of justice and define the moral limits which rulers may not transgress if they are to command the allegiance of their subjects.[29] The need of the times is to imaginatively build on such concepts to articulate the principles of good governance and democratic accountability while at the same time preserving and protecting human rights of the people the world over.

References

1 Declaration on the Right to Development, adopted by the United Nations General Assembly on 4 December 1986.
2 *Ibid.*
3 Neelan Tiruchelvam, in his presentation at the conference, *Parliamentary Democracy and Development: Allies or Adversaries?*, Wiston House, UK, 14 February 1996.
4 *Ibid.*
5 Cited in Theo Van Boven, 'Human Rights and Development: The UN Experience', in David Forsythe, *Human Rights and Development: International Views* (Basingstoke, 1989), p.126.
6 Mike Jendrzejczyk, in his presentation at the conference, *Parliamentary Democracy and Development: Allies or Adversaries?*, Wiston House UK, 14 February 1996.
7 Kenneth Christie, 'Regime Security and Human Rights in South East Asia', in David Beetham (ed.), *Politics and Human Rights* (Oxford, 1995), p.209.
8 Van Boven, *op. cit.*, pp.126–7.

9 Tiruchelvam, *op. cit.*
10 *Ibid.*
11 Jendrzejczyk, *op. cit.*
12 *Ibid.*
13 Tiruchelvam, *op. cit.*
14 Patrick Chabal, *Power in Africa: An Essay in Political Interpretation* (Basingstoke, 1994), p.166.
15 John Dunn, cited in *ibid.*, p.167.
16 Lawyers Committee for Human Rights, 'Linking Rights and Development' in *Human Rights: The New Consensus* (London: Regency Press, in association with the United Nations High Commissioner for Refugees (UNHCR), 1994), p.119.
17 *Ibid.*
18 Tiruchelvam, *op. cit.*
19 *Ibid.*
20 Jendrzejczyk, *op. cit.*
21 *Ibid.*
22 Christie, *op. cit.*, p.206.
23 Diane K. Mauzy, 'Human Rights in Indonesia, Malaysia and Singapore: Contrasting Views from ASEAN, Canada and Australia', *The Round Table*, no.335, July 1995, p.280.
24 Christie, *op. cit.*
25 Lawyers Committee for Human Rights, *op. cit.*
26 Alhaji Sir Dawda Kairaba Jawara, 'The Commonwealth and Human Rights', *The Round Table*, no.321, January 1992, p.40.
27 Jendrzejczyk, *op. cit.*
28 Tiruchelvam, *op. cit.*
29 *Ibid.*

4 Gender and Development

Human development as a concept has acquired wide acceptance the world over. This precept takes account of major aspects of the development of individuals and societies. The human development paradigm also emphasizes the concepts of gender equality and gender equity. As such, these principles have, over the last two decades, attained primacy in development planning. A glance at the national and international agenda reveals that the world is becoming increasingly gender aware. It is a fact, however, that the implementation process to achieve gender equality is proceeding at a slow pace due to historical, cultural and, to a certain extent, religious norms.[1]

The global community started paying particular attention to gender issues in the early 1970s. Before that, the United Nations and enlightened world citizens and groups had focused on this much-neglected sphere. Realizing the urgency of the situation in 1972, the United Nations proclaimed 1975 as the International Women's Year. Subsequently, the decade 1976–85 was declared the International Decade for Women. A significant development in this area was the First World Women's Conference held in Mexico City in 1975. Soon, gender-related issues became essential items on the global and national programmes of action.

From WID to GAD

It was in the 1970s that the concept of Women in Development (WID) acquired prominence. According to the framework drawn up by Caroline Moser, three WID policy approaches could be delineated.[2] These were: equity, anti-poverty and efficiency, although there has never been a strict chronological development or separation of these approaches. The main theme of the WID initiative was the integration of women, achievement of equality between the genders and increased socio-economic development of women. In subsequent years, three more World Women's Conferences have been held: in Copenhagen in 1980; in Nairobi in 1985 (which drafted the Forward-Looking Strategies); and in Beijing in 1995. During this period, the emphasis has moved away from WID of the 1970s. In the mid-1980s, the thrust area shifted from WID to Gender and Development (GAD). There was also a shift in focus from women to gender and from integration of women to mainstreaming women.[3]

Some Revealing Statistics

What has been the status of women during these two decades? According to the *Human Development Report 1995*, even though much progress has been achieved in developing women's capabilities, much more remained to be done.[4] The report showed that among the developing world's 900 million illiterate, women outnumbered men two to one. Girls constituted 60 per cent of the 130 million children without access to primary school. Of the 1.3 billion people in poverty, 70 per cent were women. There was high unemployment among women and they were earning less than their male counterparts. Even though there was a marginal rise in labour force participation of women, the rate of underemployment among them was very high. The health statistics of women and girls did not present a rosy picture. Illiteracy and school dropout rates were also high among girls. Netumbo Nandi-Ndaitwah[5] observes that, although there was an increase in employment opportunities for women, attempts to provide equal wages had not been successful. Because of legal barriers or family responsibilities, women tend to work shorter hours and were unavailable for overtime, night work and shift work. However, in several countries, women were found to be toiling in the farmlands and factories for longer hours than their male counterparts, besides attending to household chores.

Gender discrimination has also led to greater poverty among women. The low income level is basically because of lack of access to education. Culture and attitudes also have a negative effect on the advancement of women who are confined to the traditional roles of child-bearing and child-rearing. The inherent advantage man enjoys helps him to earn better incomes. Naturally, the contribution of men to economic productivity is higher than women. However, women are also engaged in work which promotes the economy and the well-being of the people. Regrettably, these activities do not appear in the statistics.[6] Within societies, the plight of women depends on their socio-economic status. Women in rural areas, with reduced access to educational facilities and where poverty is rampant, are found to be much more disadvantaged than their city counterparts. Migrant women are also victims of socio-economic deprivation.

Women in Decision-making

One of the critical factors identified as responsible for the prevalent state of affairs is the insufficient representation of women in decision-making levels and influential positions in national and international institutions. According to a UN Study,[7] as of 31 December 1994, only 24 women have been elected heads of state or government in the twentieth century. To date, the United Nations has not had a woman Secretary-General.

Another study of 178 parliaments conducted by the Inter-Parliamentary Union (IPU)[8] shows that, as at 30 June 1994, of the data available on 39,548 parliamentarians, 89.50 per cent were males. There were only 23 parliaments where the percentage of women members was equal to, or more than, 20 per cent of the members. In fact, according to the IPU, the participation of women in national parliaments has on average declined from 13 per cent in 1989 to 10.3 per cent in 1993.

Studies have also shown that, even where there are women ministers, they are found to be holding insignificant portfolios and not key positions such as defence, foreign affairs, or economic affairs. The representation of women in senior civil service and managerial positions is also significantly lower than that of their male counterparts. Thus, we see that although women form the backbone of the workforce and are the mainstay of the home, they have little say in public policies that affect them.[9] As such, they are not full participants in the public choices that affect their lives.

Barriers Preventing Women's Full Participation in Politics

What are the barriers preventing women's full participation in the political process? Eleni Stamiris identifies a host of factors responsible for the present situation. These include:[10]

- a historical philosophy and experience of politics as an interaction and competition between men, along with the conscious and subconscious perception, held by both men and women, of men as the rational political actors, and of masculine characteristic of leadership;
- the lack of a well-developed body of mainstream intellectual opinion and literature advocating women's participation in decision-making;
- implicit discrimination within the male-dominant culture of established political parties, institutions and organizations;
- the absence of women's perspective and positive contributions to society in the media;

- the pervasive use of sexist language in all forms of communication, including political commentaries;
- traditionally male-oriented assumptions regarding the nature and role of policy, and decision-making in terms of the selection system, electoral system and/or size of the constituency, timing, duration and location of meetings;
- the use of networking as a patronage system;
- the perception of politics as irrelevant or divorced from daily life;
- cultural values assigning specific roles and tasks to men and women, specifically women's dual roles;
- sexual harassment.

From another angle, the factors accounting for the negligible presence of women in parliaments and in the higher echelons of the decision-making structure the world over have to be seen in the larger context of the secondary role that society has unfortunately assigned to them since time immemorial. While the developed world has overcome some of these factors and encouraged greater participation of women in public life, the situation obtaining in the developing world is still deplorable. Women in these countries face too many barriers, very often insurmountable, on the road to a greater role in public affairs and politics.

As has been seen, despite the fact that women constitute half the electorate in most countries, relatively few of them reach the upper rungs of public decision-making processes. The reason for this lopsided picture of political reality is not due to an identity of interests between men and women, but to factors that are a direct result of the grossly unequal gender positioning in society. What, then, are those factors that perpetuate this seemingly universal tradition of masculine majority monopolizing public office?

In the process of civilization, most societies have evolved a gender-based role pattern which, over the years, became a permanent feature, much to the detriment of women because the gender-based division of labour has imposed a severe restriction on women's ability to participate in public affairs. It has tied them to dead-end jobs, thereby denying them a chance to realize the full worth of their personality. In some societies, this mind-set is reinforced by religious sanction. This has often been institutionalized in laws governing property and inheritance, and thus became a systemic barrier against the participation of women in spheres outside the home.

Often legal remedies are sought for social problems. This is a soft option and a short-cut method which does not produce results sustainable in the long run. For example, introducing a plethora of legislation to improve the well-being of women does not guarantee enforcement any more than granting them suffrage would guarantee their election to parliament. Unless a problem is properly understood and the need for its resolution internalized, laws by themselves would serve no useful purpose.

What is required, therefore, is a committed effort to change prevailing perceptions of prejudice about women stepping out of the stereotype role and entering such areas of activity that were hitherto denied to them. It is true that the modern woman is a symbol of confidence and assertiveness compared with what she was decades ago. Yet this is an urban phenomenon and has left rural people largely unaffected. It is here that much has to be accomplished by means of education, employment and elevation to elected office. The process has to begin, however, with education.

It is not possible to alter long-standing cultural prejudices of a society except through the medium of education. But unfortunately in most developing countries women's education has, until recently, not received the attention it deserves. If we study the literacy statistics of any country, men are found to be more literate than women. It is accepted in most traditional societies that the money spent on women's education is somehow unnecessary, as she would be married some day and would no longer be part of the labour force. On the other hand, the amount spent on boys' education is treated as a long-term investment. However, this scenario is fast changing, and women are taking to education with as much enthusiasm as men.

The key to women's realization of their self-worth, their rights and their role in society lies in first extending primary education to them, followed by higher education. This would not only liberate the mind from the cultural fetters inherited through the process of socialization, but would also inculcate a sense of self-confidence and assertiveness, the two prerequisites for a role in public affairs. In addition, female students should be encouraged to take a greater interest in the electoral arena at both college and university level. It is in this context that governments have to promote education among women by devising a system which enables the all-round development of the personality of the pupils, be they boys or girls.

This calls for a major change in the system. Educational institutions should not view political consciousness among students as indiscipline or deviation. Familiarity with the political process will create an added interest and break the traditional reluctance towards politics. In addition, education would create a better awareness among women about their rights – and politics, more often than not, is an assertion of rights and a claim to what is one's due.

This brings us to the next barrier, which is women's status in the world of work. Increased education would not only free the mind from the shackles imposed by cultural values and instill self-confidence in them, but would also make them economically independent. One of the chief reasons for the backwardness of women is because of their dependence on men for basic necessities. Once women enter the workforce with technical qualifications, they will not only be financially independent but will also have an opportunity to be part of the decision-making process in the corporate world. This would bring them in contact with a variety of situations and people. That could help a great deal for those interested in politics for, in a democracy, politics is nothing but an aggregation of various, often conflicting, interests.

However, in the world of work we rarely come across women taking an active part in the affairs of employees' associations and in trade union politics. There is a deep-rooted reluctance on the part of women to participate in the decision-making process due to traditional and cultural factors which have relegated them to behind-the-scene activities. This is reinforced by the absence of suitable female role models at local, provincial and national levels.

Last, but by no means least, are the political factors behind a lack of women's presence in legislatures. Women's access to elected office is often restricted by the way political parties in most countries operate. As Shirley Dysart says, 'While few women are restricted in law, a wide gap remains between women's *de jure* right to participate in the electoral process and their *de facto* actual participation.'[11] Winning the nomination to run in an election is a Herculean task in countries where there is no democratic method of nomination. There are countries where women are fielded in 'lost-cause ridings'. The selection process is often beset with too many problems. In most cases, women have no family connection or long association with political parties. While they are childbearing and rearing their children, their male counterparts may initially acquire valuable experience and useful skills through their involvement in local politics. By the time a woman is free from childbearing and its attendant health problems, much youthful time has been lost and she has virtually to start from scratch at a late stage, which places her at a distinct disadvantage *vis-à-vis* the male. This means that her struggle for political equality begins from a debilitatingly unequal footing.

One very important factor behind the dwindling presence of women in legislatures is that there is no location of women's power in society. They are everywhere and so cannot claim a particular constituency as theirs, unlike other interest groups who lobby for their own candidates in particular constituencies. It is presumably because of the lack of lobbying power with political parties that women are not fielded in respectable numbers in various elections. However, within the Commonwealth community, women appear to have done far better in general and in the South Asian region in particular. This part of the world has thrown up a galaxy of formidable women leaders. India, Pakistan, Bangladesh and Sri Lanka have been ruled by women at various times. Yet an analysis of women power in these countries would suggest that the position of women has not changed a great deal in the overall context. As the former prime minister of India, Mrs Indira Gandhi, once remarked: 'If a handful of women go forward, become ministers and judges, you should not think that women's status has gone up.'

Another reason why political parties are wary of fielding women candidates is because of the ever escalating cost of election and the inability of women to mobilize huge financial resources in the absence of any state funding of elections. In view of the handicaps suffered by women in this respect, the state could perhaps help to meet the election expenses of women candidates of major political parties. In addition, efforts could be made to encourage women's participation in the electoral process by reserving a certain percentage of seats for them. Several countries have initiated moves in this direction. In India, legislation has been enacted reserving 33 per cent of the seats for women in local bodies. Legislation similarly reserving 33 per cent of the seats for women in parliament and provincial legislatures is presently before parliament.

The UN Division for the Advancement of Women (UNDAW) has also identified some factors hampering women's participation in politics and which prevent them from reaching parliamentary and institutional positions which are more or less in conformity with the views expressed above. The factors identified by the UNDAW are:[12] the relatively short historical tradition of women's political participation and lack of experience in campaigning, public debate and exposure to the media; prevailing negative attitudes towards women's participation in public life, and lack of confidence and support for female candidates and politicians on the part of the electorate, including women; the difficulty women experience in combining a political career with the traditional role in the family and often in society; economic dependency or lack of financial means; insufficient education in general and political education in particular; and women's reluctance or diffidence to participate in politics, particularly at a high level.

The Human Development Report 1995 contained a Gender Empowerment Measure (GEM) and Gender Development Index (GDI). The Nordic countries lead in both, while some developing countries such as Thailand, the Bahamas, Barbados and Uruguay also stand high in the GDI rating.[13]

The International Conference on Population and Development, held in Cairo in 1994, saw a new consensus on two fundamentals:[14] empowering women and increasing their status are essential to realizing the full potential of economic, political and social development; and empowering women is an important end in itself. And 'as women acquire the same status, opportunities and social, economic and legal rights as men, as they acquire the right to reproductive health and the right to protection against gender-based violence, human well-being will be enhanced'.[15] Many activists feel that 'empowerment is a process of awareness and capacity-building leading to greater participation, to greater decision-making power and control, and to transformative action'.[16]

In what way can elected women representatives influence the gender agenda and the national agenda? Carolyn Pickles observes:

> I am sure that a new agenda will be set for politicians when women are properly and truly represented. Issues such as child-rearing, family life, mixing parenting and paid work responsibilities, and the struggle against violence will become correspondingly important to our politicians and our community as the number of women in parliament increases. The benefits will be there not just for women, but for the whole community.[17]

Norma Cox Astwood draws attention to another aspect of gender in politics. She writes:

> Those women who are able to overcome the hurdles of finance and social inequality, and who have the kind of personal characteristics that enable them to compete on an equal footing with males, are usually sufficiently assertive to compete successfully in the political arena. Politics will not attract the meek and submissive of either gender. It can be expected, therefore, that women who enter the race are confident, assertive, persuasive and psychologically strong. They are sensitive to people's needs and cognizant of the delicate balance that binds men and women in efforts to bring together – for the common good – those qualities and characteristics that contribute to the advancement and enhancement of the world which all of us share.[18]

J.T.R. Mujuru emphasizes the imperative for competent and qualified women in Parliament. She says:

> There is a need for more women of high calibre who can debate on the same wavelength as men. Women lawyers in parliament, for example, would be able to peruse the law and highlight those aspects of it which discriminate against women or militate against their emancipation. Women backbenchers who are prepared to conduct research would be effective in pushing women's concerns.[19]

Lynda Chalker points out that

> with 52 per cent of the human race full of talent, willing and ready to contribute, it would be a wanton waste not to educate and prepare women to take their rightful opportunity to contribute to politics and public life wherever they can.[20]

A helpful suggestion comes from Jan Brown:

We will have to learn how to build dependencies without being dependent, how to access currently underutilized resources without losing leverage and understand what is important to the various constituencies without being compromised. A tall order in a context that is constantly challenged by the agendas of those who roam the hallway.[21]

The IPU's *Plan of Action to Correct Present Imbalances in Participation of Men and Women in Political Life*, adopted as a resolution by the Inter-Parliamentary Council at its 154th Session in Paris on 26 March 1994, observes that an analysis of the various national realities would highlight the fact that all over the world, several conditions favour or hinder active participation of women in public life. According to the *Plan of Action*, wider community awareness of issues associated with such participation by women is an important aspect of correcting the present imbalances. Some of these factors include:[22]

The values of civilization and their transmission: with a view to enhancing women's dignity at the social level and allowing the emergence of a more balanced image of the capacity of men and women to participate in the management of both private and public affairs, without destabilizing cultures or imposing values foreign to the national culture, efforts may be made to develop the concept of parity and partnership; refrain from presenting activities outside and inside the home as conflicts; change the images and models to eliminate any suggestion that one sex is superior to the other; and harmonize customary and positive law to eliminate any kind of discrimination

Education: taking into account the importance of education in correcting gender imbalances, attempts may be made to provide for equality of access to schooling for boys and girls; establish an identical duration of schooling for boys and girls; draw up and implement adult literacy programmes; and reassess and reorient the educational content

Health: considering the importance of health in encouraging women's availability for participation in political life, stress should be laid on reinforcing the health systems; promoting family planning; and ensuring the moral and physical integrity of women through stringent legislation

Employment and participation in economic life: measures may be taken to promote the access of women to professional training and employment on equal conditions with men; steps may be taken to facilitate access to bank credits for those women capable of meeting the conditions laid down by the banks; and women without wages and with low income may be helped to increase their purchasing power by teaching them entrepreneurial principles and rules and by facilitating contact with national and international private aid organizations that help small-scale enterprises.

What happens to women elected to a predominantly male institution such as a legislature? Ann Symonds is credited with the view that if elected women representatives do not commit themselves to changing the status of women in society, liberating them by programmatic, legal and budgetary means, then they must be adjudged as 'collaborators' in the male system.[23] She cautions:

> It's fine to get women into parliament. But if women are adopting the male structure, processes and values, what are we doing for women? If those women who have decided to work within the male structures don't challenge the male structure, if they don't demand that, in accord with the rhetoric about the primacy of motherhood and families, we admit and give real value, societal value, to that role then we are not improving the lives of the majority of women in our society.[24]

Discussing women's movements and democratization in Latin America, Georgina Waylen has argued:[25]

> While it is difficult to generalize about the impact of democratization on women and women's movements, it is clear that some women's movements, often campaigning around practical gender interests, have become more marginal to the process of transition, as popular and social movements have been demobilized. This has occurred while other groups of women, who are often middle class and pressing more strategic gender-based political demands on the state, have had an impact (however limited) on the newly reconstituted competitive party politics and policy agendas.

The Commonwealth has been consistently active in creating the necessary enabling environment for women's participation in political life. The 1990 Commonwealth Heads of Government Meeting (CHOGM) held in Harare committed itself to defend and achieve the principle of 'equality for women so that they may exercise their full and equal rights'. The 1993 CHOGM in Malta 'expressed support for the proposal that special measures as appropriate be taken to increase women's position at all levels of political and decision-making processes at national level and in Commonwealth organizations'. The Fourth Meeting of the Commonwealth Ministers Responsible for Women's Affairs, held in Cyprus in 1993, recommended to member states: affirmative action which guarantees a percentage of seats to women; the promotion of women's economic development; education and training for women leaders; and the establishment of a roster of senior professional women to serve on national and Commonwealth decision-making bodies. The other areas highlighted for action were fostering institutional and organizational change, developing a mentor programme for young women in politics and establishing women's caucuses and pressure groups. The Commonwealth Heads approved the *1995 Commonwealth Plan of Action on Gender and Development* which represents a vision in which

> the Commonwealth works towards a world in which women and men have equal rights and opportunities at all stages of their lives to express their creativity in all fields of human endeavour, and in which women are respected and valued as equal and able partners in establishing values in social justice, equity, democracy and respect for human rights.[26]

It is thus established that women's empowerment is an important component of mainstreaming women. In today's world, women's rights are indeed human rights. The Beijing Platform of Action adopted at the Fourth World Women's Conference made many recommendations for action by governments, international institutions, non-governmental organizations and the private sector. The Beijing Declaration made specific mention of its renewed commitment to equal rights for all. The Declaration reaffirmed that women's rights are human rights and emphasized the significance of women's full participation in all spheres of society, including decision-making.

Some of the critical areas in gender and development identified by activists include: strengthening women's units, groups and organizations to ensure gender awareness, to act as pressure groups and to monitor the implementation of mainstreaming women; gender awareness and analysis training; building a critical mass of women inside development organizations; and lobbying and pressuring development institutions.[27]

The Human Development Report 1995 enumerates a five-point strategy for accelerating progress in women's development. These are:[28]

1 National and international efforts must be mobilized to win legal equality within a defined period, say the next 10 years.
2 Many economic and institutional arrangements may need revamping to extend more choices to women and men in the workplace.
3 A critical 30 per cent threshold should be regarded as a minimum share of decision-making positions held by women at the national level.
4 Key programmes should embrace universal female education, improved reproductive health and more credit for women.
5 National and international efforts should target programmes that enable people, particularly women, to gain greater access to economic and political opportunities.

Women have been victims of gender discrimination, overt and covert, for centuries. As we near the new millennium, it is essential that more than 50 per cent of the human race get their due share in all stages of development.

The Beijing Parliamentary Declaration adopted by consensus by participants in the Parliamentarian's Day organized by the IPU on the occasion of the Fourth World Conference on Women, says:[29]

> By transforming a mode of governance and management based upon a wrong hierarchy of gender, we shall not only let women use their ability to govern but also tap their particular creativity and values, while at the same time reflecting their realities, needs and aspirations in our policies. Such an integrated approach will make for more balanced access to resources and fairer distribution between men and women of both the cost and the benefits of an equitable, balanced and sustainable growth, which is the prime purpose of human development.

As such, gender and development is bound to be a focal point for action in national and international programmes. The success of these endeavours will be totally dependent on political will and the mobilization of public opinion in that behalf.

References

1. Netumbo Nandi-Ndaitwah, in her presentation at the conference, *Parliamentary Democracy and Development: Allies or Adversaries?*, Wiston House, UK, 15 February 1996.
2. Cited in Marilee Karl, *Women and Empowerment* (London, 1995), p.97.
3. *Ibid.*, p.102.
4. *Human Development Report 1995*, pp.3–6.
5. Nandi-Ndaitwah, *op. cit.*
6. *Ibid.*
7. *The World's Women: Trends and Statistics* (New York, 1995), p.151.
8. Inter-Parliamentary Union, *Distribution of Seats between Men and Women in the 178 National Parliaments Existing as at 30 June 1994* (Geneva, 1994).
9. Eleni Stamiris, in her presentation at the conference, *Parliamentary Democracy and Development: Allies or Adversaries?*, Wiston House, UK, 15 February 1996.
10. *Ibid.*
11. Shirley Dysart, 'Barriers to Women's Participation in Parliament', *Canadian Parliamentary Review*, vol.17, no.3, Autumn 1994, p.13.
12. Karl, *op. cit.*, pp.64–5.
13. *Human Development Report 1995*, *op. cit.*, pp.2–4.
14. *The World's Women 1995: Trends and Statistics*, *op. cit.*, p.xvii.
15. *Ibid.*
16. Karl, *op. cit.*, p.14.
17. Carolyn Pickles, 'Gender Equality: Barriers to Electing More Women to Parliament – And Some Solutions', *The Parliamentarian*, vol.LXXVI, no.4, October 1995, pp.292–3.
18. Norma Cox Astwood, 'Women in Politics: A Challenge to Tradition', *The Parliamentarian*, vol.LXXI, no.3, July 1990, p.156.

19 J.T.R. Mujuru, 'Women in Zimbabwe's Political Life', *The Parliamentarian*, vol.LXXI, no.3, July 1990, p.188.
20 Lynda Chalker, 'Women in Politics', *The Parliamentarian*, vol.LXXI, no.3, July 1990, p.159.
21 Jan Brown, 'Changing the Gender Agenda of Politics', *Canadian Parliamentary Review*, vol.17, no.2, Summer 1994, p.10.
22 Inter-Parliamentary Union, *Plan of Action to Correct Present Imbalances in the Participation of Men and Women in Political Life* (Geneva, 1994).
23 Ann Symonds, 'It's Still a Man's World: Women and Parliament', *The Parliamentarian*, vol.LXXII, no.4, October 1991, p.278.
24 *Ibid.*, p.280.
25 Georgina Waylen, 'Women's Movements and Democratization in Latin America', *Third World Quarterly*, vol.14, no.3, 1993, pp.584–5.
26 Eleni Stamiris, *op. cit.*
27 Karl, *op. cit.*, pp.102–3.
28 *Human Development Report 1995*, *op. cit.*, pp.8–10.
29 Cited in *Inter-Parliamentary Bulletin*, vol.75, no.3, 1995, p.156.

5 Freedom of the Press

One of the essential prerequisites for a successful democracy is a free press. An independent media can play a crucial role in building and even moulding public opinion which in turn can positively influence decision-making. The press is thus a vital link between the people and the government. Remarkable advancements in the field of science and technology have ushered in an information revolution, and today the emphasis is on an informed society. An informed society undoubtedly contributes substantially towards making an informed democracy. Perhaps never before have the media had such a critical task in shaping the future. As the high priest of modern mass communication Marshall McLuhan said, 'the medium is the message'.

Media and Politics

The relationship between the media and politicians has always been a subject of intense debate. As a vital link between the people and the administration, the media help the decision-makers to understand the pulse of society. On the one hand, the media convey to the people the policies and programmes of the government, and on the other, they act as a feedback mechanism by making the leadership aware of what society feels about specific programmes and policies. This is indeed a highly beneficial exercise for both parties. The government gains wide coverage for its developmental activities and also receives the views of the intended beneficiaries. The people obtain opportunities to convey their appreciation or apprehension concerning the proposed actions. Without free and fair media, there is every possibility that the administration may develop complacency, leading to stagnation, and the development process itself could be retarded. The media are effectively the interface between the people and the government. As a watchdog, the media keep a constant vigil on the executive, bringing to light its acts of omission and commission, and as the voice of the people, they safeguard their interests, rights and freedoms. It is thus that many observers have come to the view that there is a symbiotic relationship between the media and the government.

Media and Democratization

What is the role of the media in democratization? Primarily, the media help in furnishing better information, thus providing for an informed electorate or an informed democracy. In this information age, the media offer a proper political orientation for a democratic polity, for a successful democracy calls for informed participation of the people in the democratic process. The people require a factual account of developments, their background and causes, a forum for discussion and informed criticism whereby they can articulate their points of view or promote their interests. Naturally, the media are ideally placed to undertake this onerous task. A free media also enables free flow of information. Besides helping in creating efficient markets, the availability of objective and non-partisan socio-economic data can provide for accurate business planning and an informed public debate on various issues.

Educational Responsibility

A question often raised is whether the media have an educational responsibility. Linked to this is the much discussed theme of the social obligation of the media. These issues acquire added significance in the context of the developing countries where, on several occasions, the media have come into conflict with the ruling élite. In many developing countries, freedom of the press is a major issue, with newsmen having to work under trying circumstances. Governments in these countries often emphasize the role of the media in educating the people. They also stress the fact that the media should give sufficient coverage to the developmental activities of the state. The media, while accepting this responsibility with reservation on occasions because of inherent differences of opinion on the newsworthiness of these governmental efforts, are often critical of the impediments created by the government in the nature of official secrets acts and similar measures which are tantamount to gagging the press. However, the media in the developing world have, by and large, accepted that they have a social obligation too. As Bode Oyewole, a leading radio newsman and an official of the Nigerian Union of Journalists, observed at a conference of journalists in the Nigerian city of Ibadan:

So long as the journalist is aware of his responsibilities towards the community – principally that of helping development – so long as he realizes that his freedom has a bearing on what is good for the society and as such is not freedom without limits, then the traditional mistrust will be dissolved, and government and journalism will again become twin agents of socio-economic progress.[1]

The fact, however, remains that social or educational responsibility of the media means different things to different people. It is thus that there are differing perceptions on the role of the media in shaping the socio-political and economic agenda of a nation. All agree that the communication imperatives of developing countries are vastly different from those of the industrialized and developed world.

The media, in fact, have manifold responsibilities, especially in the present-day world where they have to walk a tightrope. To begin with, they have to keep the clientele happy. The media also have to be financially viable, or else their owners could be in trouble. They have frequently to confront the powers that be on matters of professional principles and ethics. Over and above all these, they have to help in creating an informed electorate. Michael Schudson, discussing the media in an American context, opines:

> I believe the news media *can* contribute to a more democratic society and should try to do so… . This is not to assume that the sole aim of the media is or should be to help create a better democracy. The media aim to make money for owners, provide jobs to employees, establish prestige among colleagues, entertain consumers … and these are all legitimate aims. But the media claim also to have a special mission of informing the citizenry to make democratic government possible, and the media claim special rights … and privileges … based on their unique status as the 'fourth branch of government'.[2]

Political Reporting

Ultimately, what matters is how the media are in a position to strike the right balance. This depends largely on the freedom they enjoy in society. Freedom of the press is certainly a controversial theme which attracts divergent views. Political reporting is one area where the media often come into direct conflict with the political leadership. There are two aspects of political reporting which can create problems for politicians and news coverage. It is observed that the media have the luxury of being able to pick up and discard ideals virtually at will. This permits the media to change their minds with impunity – extending support to a particular policy at one point and opposing it later. To a certain extent, even individuals also share this ability. Unfortunately, politicians are handicapped in this regard. One of the important roles played by the media is to expose reversals of policy positions by politicians. Politicians thus tend to be subjected to a barrage of criticism on charges of hypocrisy for championing a cause which they had earlier vehemently opposed.

One major problem area for the media, especially some segments of the press, is in the coverage of a politician's life – both private and public. In recent times, the private lives of many leaders have come in for closer scrutiny. Very few historical figures would have survived the personal grilling which today's leaderships are made to endure. One has to concede that the dividing line between the public and private life of a leader is indeed very thin. The electorate have every right to know the antecedents of an individual whom they are going to elect as their representative. It is clearly in the public interest, for example, to know that a politician who has campaigned publicly against drunken driving is himself subsequently charged with the same offence. However, other examples of private exposés regularly occur even when there is no discernible policy connection. Many feel that politicians should perhaps avoid issuing moral prescriptions for society so that the media are not tempted to judge the politician's morality.

Television in Politics

Several perceptive analysts are of the opinion that, in the political sphere, television is not a suitable medium for covering detailed information, analysis and debate on issues. However, it does bring voters closer to politics and politicians than ever before. The televising of parliamentary proceedings in many countries has helped in bringing the institution of parliament nearer to the people and removing several misconceptions about its functioning. More importantly, constituents now have the opportunity of seeing for themselves the role of their elected representatives in ventilating their grievances. Telecasting also enables the members of parliament to highlight to their constituents how they are doing their job. In such a scenario, it is natural that this has led to a preoccupation among politicians with their images and the image that will be created by a specific policy. The 'image' has thus become too strong a consideration, but there is hardly any way of avoiding it. Politicians should be wary of adopting policies designed merely to win a positive and favourable coverage. While there have not been many examples of the media being able to change government policy, there have nevertheless been several instances of politicians over-reacting to media campaigns.

Government and the Media

When the political leadership charges the media with operating irresponsibly or running out of control, they should remember that, in this information age, the media is at a distinct disadvantage in its daily dealings with the government public relations machinery. Hundreds of press officers constantly bombard the media with news releases and have immediate access to data not readily and easily available to the media.

Some governments will try to control their local media but the proliferation of other news sources, including the international media, tends to weaken this control. Moreover, people are now enlightened enough to know, on most occasions, when the government is lying to them. Many have described news as information. If information is power, there is every possibility that many governments will try to influence it, if not control it. Attempts at muzzling the media are made by limiting the availability of newsprint and other printing material, at times threatening mediamen and even shutting down outlets. What politicians should realize is that once the freedom of the media is jeopardized they would be losing the benefit of the mechanism through which their basic realities are reflected.

While the media and politicians need each other, they should nevertheless keep a distance between themselves and maintain positions of healthy mutual suspicion and even disdain. It is not the media's job to promote government policy, even though they do have an educational role. A sophisticated government will find ways to make use of the media, but it should not expect the media to help in the implementation of government policies.

Frequently, however, the media are not generally suspicious enough of interest groups. The media tend to be influenced by such groups and at times overreact to their campaigns without necessarily checking the groups' positions and claims carefully enough.

Politicians as Sources of Information

For the media, the politician is also a source of information. Parliament is one place where information or news is available in abundance. The member of parliament and the press can be said to have a shared constituency. Media coverage of parliament in several countries has declined over the years, possibly because the role of parliament itself in political life has diminished during the period. This is obvious from the fact that the coverage of politics as such has not decreased significantly. The most common complaint that British broadcasters receive from the public is that they are overly obsessed with politics. However, only a very active media preoccupied with politics can inform the citizenry of the goings-on which would help them make informed choices. Media outlets which ignore or trivialize politics do a disservice to the people.

The relationship between the media and the politician being a complex one, several issues crop up while debating this sensitive subject. Politicians in several countries complain about the extent to which the media, on many occasions, try to influence the political agenda, basically to protect the interests of the owners of particular media establishments which have their own political affiliations. They argue that there are many instances when the media would put a politician under the searchlight without the facts or his side of the story. Even if the politician concerned was later found to have done nothing illegal or dishonest, the media would confine that part of the story to some obscure corner. Meanwhile, the damage to the politician's stature and integrity is already done. Any number of corrections or apologies in the back pages would not help to retrieve it. Politicians also feel that the media are interested in a particular story only until the next surfaces, and that the media revel in sensationalism. In the process, the citizen is left with incomplete information, very often giving a distorted picture of reality.

Privileges

Privileges available to parliament and the media have also been the cause of friction in their relationship. In many instances, both call for codification of the privileges of the other so that digressions can be taken up effectively. It is a love–hate relationship that characterizes the interaction between the media and the politicians. In the words of Murumba Werunga:

> conflicts and disagreements do arise between the legislature and the press, primarily because of the shared constituency. The conflict arises due to lack of a united perception and interpretation of what is good for the people. It is also possible that both are sceptical of the underlying motives of one for the other. Mutual scepticism is exacerbated by the proven fact that their activities are like a double edged sword. As a result, each craves for an amiable portrayal 'to the people' of its activities.[3]

In this era of competition in every field, the media are hardly lagging behind. Every media agency tries to reach the scene of action first and wants to be the first to disseminate the news. In this competition, the politician often lands in trouble because the media wants his/her comments on the development to be conveyed to the public. Caught unawares, in many cases, politicians find themselves in unfamiliar territory, and make comments which they would not ordinarily have made. In this context, Sir Colin Shepherd is credited with the view that democracy would benefit by the insertion of a 'period of reflection' in today's fast-paced news.[4] There is a need for the media to exercise restraint so that leaders are not pressed into reacting instantly to developments. As Sir Colin Shepherd argues, the rush of global news puts enormous pressure on politicians to make snap decisions without time to reflect. On several occasions, these hasty reactions added an unfortunate element to good governance.[5]

However, political leaderships in all countries have also made use of the media to project their achievements. In several developing countries where the electronic media is under the control of the government, the executive has taken recourse to television to highlight its achievements, often inviting criticism from opposition parties who charge that it is a blatant misuse of the medium. Charismatic leaders across the world have manipulated the media to focus attention on their achievements and further their electoral prospects. The media's position becomes all the more critical at the time of general elections. In fact, criticism is rife that the media has come to influence election outcomes, particularly by way of public opinion surveys. Psephology, in recent times, has become very much a part of elections.

The power and influence of the media cannot be overemphasized. Whereas Kennedy, Reagan and Thatcher successfully cultivated their images, thanks to the media, Nixon had to make an unceremonious exit following his trial by the media in the wake of the Watergate scandal. The media coverage of the Vietnam War is still a watershed in media history. Many politicians are critical of certain aspects of investigative journalism which they feel does not do justice to the individual concerned. But, publicly at least, they profess wholehearted support for the independence of the media.

Arthur C. Clarke said long ago that freedom of information will be determined not by governments but by technology. The free flow of information is vital for the successful functioning of a democracy. The developing countries frequently complain about the invasion of their territory by media moguls from the developed world and their 'cultural imperialism'. In this context, they have repeatedly called for a New International Information Order. At the threshold of a new millennium, and with a shrinking world, we are entering the age of the 'global village'. Competition and cooperation in news-gathering and news dissemination could go a long way to address the problem.

In the final analysis, it is obvious that freedom of the press is a very important adjunct of a successful democracy. An informed society is better equipped when it goes to the polling booth. The media are one of the instruments which can facilitate the protection of human rights and the rule of law. By highlighting acts of omission and commission, the media make the executive accountable to the people at large, though the media themselves frequently come in for criticism for their coverage. Truthfulness of news published or broadcast is always a matter intensely discussed. In this context, Walter Lippmann observes in his celebrated treatise *Public Opinion*:

> The hypothesis, which seems to be the most fertile, is that news and truth are not the same thing, and must be clearly distinguished. The function of news is to signalize an event, the function of truth is to bring to light the hidden facts, to set them into relation with each other, and make a picture of reality on which men can act. Only at these points, where social conditions take recognizable and measurable shape, do the body of truth and the body of news coincide. That is a comparatively small part of the whole field of human interest.[6]

Once this aspect is clear in one's mind, the task of assessing the role of the media becomes somewhat easier. The next question often raised is about what constitutes news. To quote Lippmann again:

> In the first instance ... the news is not a mirror of social conditions, but the report of an aspect that has obtruded itself. The news does not tell you how the seed is germinating in the ground, but it may tell you when the first sprout breaks through the surface. It may even tell you that the sprout did not come up at the time it was expected. The more points, then, at which any happening can be fixed, objectified, measured, named, the more points there are at which news can occur.[7]

Yet another complaint is that, in so many cases, the media report only negative news or disaster news while failing to report 'developmental news'. Professionals in media circles do agree that there is an element of truth in this charge, but they counter it by arguing that news has to sustain human interest or it ceases to be news. Media managers assert that they have to first assess the 'newsworthiness' of a particular event before it is conveyed to the public. What is it that makes one thing worth reporting and another not? Graham Murdock offers an answer:

> It has to be an event. It has to be something that has happened, rather than a long process that's been unfolding over time. It has to have happened recently. It almost always involves élite figures.... News is not about what ordinary people do, it's about what the powerful people do.... It has to be an event that has some significance for the country as a whole ... and that means that our map of the world which we get through news is highly partial.... There are whole areas of the world ... which are very sporadically covered in the news. The other criterion would be human interest: something like a disaster would be automatically news.[8]

As is evident, the complexity of media management in a highly competitive world in this information age is mind-boggling. The daily interaction between the media and politicians is bound to generate some friction at some point. Both the media and the political leadership should have a proper understanding of the constraints under which they operate. Even if the quality of the media is not up to one's expectations, it is for that institution itself to come up with corrective measures. In several countries, the print media have their own ombudsmen who investigate allegations of unfair reporting. The political class also needs to undertake introspection and self-assessment about its own actions and performance. Lippmann wrote over seven decades ago:

> The press is no substitute for institutions. It is like the beam of a searchlight that moves restlessly about, bringing one episode and then another out of darkness into vision. Men cannot do the work of the world by this light alone. They cannot govern society by episodes, incidents, and eruptions. It is only when they work by a steady light of their own, that the press, when it is turned upon them, reveals a situation intelligible enough for a popular decision. The trouble lies deeper than the press, and so does the remedy.[9]

As such, a free, fair and enlightened media can supplement and complement a responsible and responsive political class. The success of democratic governance would be greatly facilitated if these two influential branches had a perceptive appreciation of each other's role in the national endeavour.

References

1. Cited in Herbert Altschull, *Agents of Power: The Media and Public Policy* (New York, 1995), p.236.
2. Michael Schudson, *The Power of News* (Cambridge, Mass., 1995), pp.204–5.
3. Murumba Werunga, 'Legislatures and the Mass Media', *The Parliamentarian*, vol.LXXI, no.2, April 1990, p.119.
4. Colin Shepherd cited in *The Parliamentarian*, vol.LXXIII, no.4, October 1992, p.254.
5. *Ibid.*
6. Walter Lippmann, cited in Doris A. Graber, *Media Power in Politics* (2nd edn) (New Delhi, 1990), p.41.
7. *Ibid.*, pp.37–8.
8. Graham Murdock, cited in Andrew Hart, *Understanding the Media: A Practical Guide* (London, 1991), pp.100–1.
9. Lippmann, *op. cit.*, p.43.

6 Promoting an Efficient and Independent Public Administration*

Development is a process aimed at the all-round well-being of society, at the core of which lies economic growth and prosperity. This is a process usually accompanied by a host of factors such as the size of the population, the quality of manpower, the availability of natural resources, the cultural ethos of the people and, last but not least, the political organization of the society.

If the given political organization is a parliamentary democracy, then the need to promote an efficient and independent public administration assumes a special significance because parliamentary democracy is also a responsive system of governance. If the system aims to be responsive, then it has to devise an efficient method to deal with the needs of the people. Public administration is one such organ that remains amid the public to administer the policies of the government for the benefit of the people. To be precise, public administration involves the planning, organizing, co-ordinating and controlling multifarious governmental activities. A society moving on the path of socio-economic development needs an efficient and independent public administration. The government, the people and the public administration are the key factors involved in an enlightened nation-building endeavour. What is markedly required is a harmonious interplay of these entities.

When one talks about public administration, what comes to mind is the institution of bureaucracy that mans the various channels of public administration – be it at the national, provincial, county or sheriff level or even below that. If we have a bureaucracy committed to accomplish development, it will function as an instrument of socio-economic change. This

---

* This discussion has benefited from the presentations by Bertram Tittewella and Giles Radice at the conference, *Parliamentary Democracy and Development: Allies or Adversaries?*, Wiston House, UK, 13 February 1996.

aspect of the functioning of bureaucracy is vital in a parliamentary democracy. In democracies especially, government is an abstract notion while public administration is a palpable reality. Governments may come and go after every election but what goes on for ever and lends an aura of continuity to governance is the bureaucracy which is the permanent executive. While the elected executive formulates a broad framework of policies and programmes, it is the bureaucracy which provides the nitty-gritty and brings the policies to the people in a concrete form. These policies are formulated on the basis of the actual needs of the people in various sectors of national life. But there is a need for an efficient apparatus to implement them, and that apparatus is public administration. It should be efficient enough to provide a stimulus to enterprising individuals to come forward with initiatives to undertake productive ventures. This is particularly so since the modern state plays a key role in accelerating and sustaining the process of development.

Development is a complex process which cannot be achieved overnight. If a country has to develop industrially, it should have the necessary infrastructure such as an efficient communications network, transport facilities, energy, trained manpower, and so on. These are core sectors which cannot be managed entirely by private enterprise without some kind of state involvement. And state involvement means a clear-cut policy prescription that guides the direction of development. Thus comes public administration into the picture, on whose efficiency and commitment depends the successful implementation of development policies and welfare schemes. As a natural corollary, promoting an efficient public administration is of vital importance for the successful functioning of democracy. It is imperative that public administration should not only be efficient but also be independent. As has been stated earlier, policies are formulated by the elected executive, namely, the government which is formed by the party that wins the election. Therefore, the policies are, to a certain extent, coloured by the ideological preferences of the party in power. But parties obtain and lose power after elections while public administration is unaffected by the political process. It is therefore essential that the permanent executive should not show any preference or loyalty to any party, and should remain completely independent in its character. It should steer clear of political prejudices and remain committed to achieving economic development, social progress and political stability.

Democracy in its classical sense is a system of government of the people, for the people and by the people. Since it is a government for the people, it has to respond constantly to the concerns of the people with concrete actions, and this responsibility percolates down to the public administration which is entrusted with the task of implementing the policies and programmes formulated for the benefit of the society.

Every society aspires to prosperity by achieving economic growth and development. But mere aspiration is not enough. Those at the helm of affairs have to give the necessary direction and create conditions conducive to achieving development. Since the rulers in a democracy are bound to lose power if they do not deliver the goods, it is more probable that development will be accomplished in an enlightened democratic environment. For that, an efficient and independent public administration is of paramount importance.

Development of Public Administration

Public administration systems across the world have several things in common, even as they have definitive features native to the societies in which they operate. Political systems the world over are engaged in the task of administrative reforms to cope with emerging challenges. Public administration in developing countries has in particular to confront such situations where it is to function as a vehicle of social change. A stagnant, inertia-ridden bureaucracy is itself an obstacle in the path of economic development. In the early years of decolonization, soon after the Second World War, many nascent societies advocated the cause of a welfare state in which the bureaucracy had a critical role to play. Soon, the concept of development administration caught the attention of political leaderships. As an analyst observes:

> Development goals were usually referred to as 'nation-building and socio-economic development'. Also, development administration was seen as concerned with the will to develop the mobilization of existing and new resources, and the cultivation of appropriate capabilities to achieve the developmental goals. Development administration was not only supposed to retool the foreign inputs in terms of both funds and ideas, but as a spearhead of modernization was also to act as a main instrument of nation-building and socio-economic development.[1]

The developing countries gave a special thrust to providing an independent and efficient public administration system. Most of these countries had inherited a strong bureaucratic structure from their colonial masters. The primary task of the then prevalent set-up was the collection of taxes and a few regulatory services in the socio-economic sphere. The post-independence imperatives called for a thorough restructuring of the establishment with a view to making it sensitive to the aspirations of the people, as also to expanding trade and inviting foreign investments. The ultimate goal was enabling better standards of living and generating fuller employment. It was in this context that development administration acquired an added significance. The process also saw several countries discarding the orthodox method of public administration. Several Asian societies resorted to rejection of the traditional approaches to achieve high standards of living, notwithstanding the fact that this invited criticism, especially from Western nations. To these developing societies, the sacrifice of some democratic practices was a small price to pay in the larger cause of rapid economic development. However, several practising democracies in Asia could not match the great strides made by their brethren. While a country such as Singapore achieved remarkable economic growth (though at the cost of disparaging remarks about its democratic credentials), well-entrenched democracies such as India lagged far behind in providing decent standards of living to its people.

Socio-political Stability

One of the essential prerequisites for the success of these efforts is political and social stability. The political leadership in Singapore could provide the much-required stability, though not within the classical democratic framework. However, in several practising democracies in Asia, factors such as national disasters and terrorism threatened internal stability and so public administration achieved only marginal success. Another prerequisite is the continuity of a political ideology. Public administration functioned successfully and improved over the years in some Asian countries, which encouraged a free-market economy with active private-sector participation. This policy was also sustained by successive governments. On the other hand, in Sri Lanka, which has a history of changing governments democratically and where the two principal political parties were alternately returned to power in the elections, the public administration apparatus suffered since the rival parties had diametrically opposite strategies for achieving economic growth. Thus, even when people have abiding faith in the democratic process, unless there is a continuity in policy formulations and strategies, economic growth could well suffer.

Recognizing the importance of the interdependence of economies, several Asian countries have formed regional and trade alliances. The emphasis is on interregional investment, free-market enterprise and expansion and diversion of international trade. Naturally, a revamped public administration making use of the most modern management techniques is an important element in this exercise.

Several Asian countries have been able to withstand the repercussions of serious international crises – the oil crisis of 1973, the recession of the 1980s, the disintegration of the Soviet Union, transformation in Eastern Europe and protectionist trends in the West – basically because of sensible policies and supportive institutional mechanisms through their public administration systems. In the South-East Asian region, the ASEAN countries initiated several reforms for economic co-operation. They came up with enlightened policy decisions supportive of one another and created the necessary infrastructure and personnel in the administration working in close harmony with the private sector. In the area of trade and economic co-operation, the Preferential Trade Agreement envisaged liberalization of intra-Asian trade. The ASEAN Industrial Project visualized assigning priority industries to each member country. The ASEAN Industrial Complementation was another novel first step. The ASEAN Free Trade Zone was launched in 1992. Furthermore, the ASEAN decision-makers were looking eastwards to develop their economies, independent of the West.

Human Resources Development

Stress was laid on human resources development. Several Asian countries set up training institutions, administrative staff colleges, service improvement units and administrative reforms commissions. They also developed in-service training programmes and courses in management training. Imparting expert training in advanced technology has received special attention. Emphasis has been given to attendant problems such as high absenteeism, indiscipline, low morale, apathy and indifference to work. Simultaneously, the skilled and the talented have been given bonus and other incentives. Workers' participation in management has been encouraged. Recruitment procedures have been streamlined. In addition, archaic rules and regulations have been simplified.

The Civil Service and Politics

When one discusses the role of public administration in the development endeavour, one has to bear in mind the fact that the bureaucracy basically operates in an environment permeated by politics. In any society, the civil service is expected to be both civil and in the service of the people. Countries the world over have advocated an impartial, honest and non-partisan civil service. The debate has been on how to preserve the key civil service values. In several countries, civil service codes have been enacted by laying down broad parameters for the bureaucracy.

Why is it that there has been extensive discussion on the role of bureaucracy in a democracy? As we have seen, various countries have a very different experience, which has largely depended on domestic factors. But in many developing countries the bureaucracy, for many reasons, has come to be identified with the political class as being responsible for the ills afflicting the society. Bureaucratic power is equated with political power, basically because the civil service, in many cases, has become a tool in the hands of the party in power. While the blame should go to a large extent to the politicians, the civil servants are also responsible for this sorry state of affairs. Once the bureaucracy developed vested interests, the seeds of degeneration were sown. Highly regulated economies offered increased scope for corruption, nepotism, red-tape and maladministration. The growth of government saw a corresponding growth in the civil service and the bureaucracy became a leviathan, crushing under its weight the expectations society had on the public administration. Shortsighted political leaders called for a committed bureaucracy, which to them meant subservient officialdom. Instead of a responsive bureaucracy, nations were confronted with repressive bureaucracies, frequently invoking sarcastic comments on the sorry state of these 'bureaucratic democracies'. It was government by bureaucracy, with the 'faceless bureaucrat' running the show. In matters of recruitment, patronage won over merit. The lack of an informed and enlightened political class meant that the bureaucracy could manipulate them for personal aggrandizement. The centralization of power in a few hands added to the problem. The politicizing of the civil service was not far away, though the worst victim of the experience was open government. Even where parliaments tried to ensure accountability, it became a question of ministerial accountability to parliament as opposed to ministerial responsibility for the actions of civil servants. Parliaments were frequently given inaccurate information or no information at all. In such instances, the politician became a tool in the hands of the permanent executive, making a mockery of the institution of parliament. As Max Weber says:

> The prime interest of bureaucracy in power, however, is efficacious far beyond those areas where purely functional interests make for secrecy... . [I]n facing a parliament, a bureaucracy, out of a sure power instinct, fights every attempt of the parliament to gain knowledge by means of its own experts or from interest groups ... bureaucracy naturally welcomes a poorly informed and hence a powerless parliament – at least in so far as ignorance somehow agrees with the bureaucracy's interests.[2]

However, many countries have come out of this quagmire, with both the bureaucracy and the political leadership realizing the adverse impact in the people's minds on their role in nation-building. Globalization and liberalization have considerably influenced their powers. Structural adjustment programmes and other economic reforms have led to the dismantling of control regimes. The new emphasis is on the delegation of power, decentralization and democratization of the decision-making process. The redefined responsibilities of the public sector have led to a downsizing of the bureaucracy. There has been a rationalization and streamlining of the bureaucracy in many countries. Technological advancements have also made way for a 'techno-bureaucracy', and special attention is being given to modern management methods. Civil servants are being made increasingly aware of their role in nation-building and the need for remaining above party politics. As a result, public administration is constantly improving. Integrity, honesty and uprightness have been stressed as the hallmarks of the civil servant. It is important that the permanent civil service should be provided with a good salary and other necessary perquisites to ensure that they are not swayed by monetary or other temptations for underhand or illegal dealings.

As discussed earlier, a public administrator has to tender unbiased and truthful advice to the political leadership. If, however, his advice is rejected, it is incumbent on him to initiate legitimate steps to implement the very same policy which he had earlier opposed. In order to preserve job security for honest and efficient administrators, disciplinary control should vest in an independent body not subject to political pressure. All those found guilty of malpractice should face exemplary punishment.

Several countries have resorted to modern methods of staff management. Australia has devised means whereby short-term contracts are made for the completion of specific jobs. In the United States, the 'hire and fire' system is widely prevalent; a change in government is followed by a change in the administrative apparatus. 'Adhocracy' or recruiting people for specific tasks, however, raises the issue of ensuring accountability.

Public servants are the instruments of government in carrying out its policies. Changing times have, however, redefined the role of the permanent civil service, which has necessitated a change in the approach of the modern as opposed to the traditional civil servant. Constitutional guarantees provide for continuity in the civil service. While civil service codes are acceptable in the light of experience, the question is whether we can bind future administrators who will have to operate in entirely different environments. There are competing conceptions, just as there are also competing managerial styles. However, at the core of the matter is the underlying imperative of an independent and efficient public administration in the larger cause of national development.

References

1 R.B. Jain, 'Nature and Problems of Structural Adjustment: Emerging Critical Issues in Developing Societies', in R.B. Jain and Heinz Bongartz (eds), *Structural Adjustment, Public Policy and Bureaucracy in Developing Societies* (New Delhi, 1984), p.37.
2 Cited in Nicholas Henry, *Public Administration and Public Affairs* (6th edn), (Englewood Cliffs, 1995), p.16.

7 The Relationship between Government and the Military

The relationship between government and the military has always been a matter of serious concern. It is widely felt that military interference in civilian administration is anathema to democratic development. All successful democratic polities have in-built mechanisms to ensure that the armed forces are subject to civilian authority. Enduring democracies have been capable of keeping the armed forces in the barracks even when their political systems are confronted with socio-economic and political turmoil. This has not been the case with countries which do not have a strong democratic base. Fragile democracies and polities which do not have entrenched representative institutions have had to contend with repeated and frequently successful usurpations of power by the military.

It is thus obvious that there is a direct relationship between the level of democratic culture of a country and the threat of military takeover. Samuel Huntington is of the view that 'the most important causes of military intervention in politics are not military but political and reflect not the social and organizational characteristics of the military establishment, but the political and institutional structure of the society'.[1] Huntington also observes that: 'The causes which produce military interventions in politics ... lie not in the nature of the group but in the structure of society. In particular, they lie in the absence or weakness of effective political institutions in the society.'[2]

The African Experience

In addition to the extent of democracy prevalent in a society, a variety of other factors have also been identified as encouraging potential military interference in politics.[3] To understand the complexities involved, one only has to consider the way in which the military has played a prominent role in several African, Latin American and Asian countries. The African continent particularly has been a haven for the politically virile military establishment. Claude Welch points out that between 1958 and mid-1985, there were 65 successful seizures of power in Africa, the overwhelming majority of which were carried out by soldiers.[4] It was as if praetorianism was the order of the day in large parts of the African continent.

What is it that led to this anomalous situation where the military was in control of so many states? George Ayittey has identified several factors responsible for this in Africa.[5] According to Ayittey, there had been an increasing recognition of the role of the military in pan-Africanism that was directly attributable to Kwame Nkrumah of Ghana who wanted to create an All African Command Guard. The Command Guard was expected to liberate the other African colonies and also to fight the forces of imperialism and racism throughout the continent. Secondly, the ruling élite in the African states was intent on self-preservation. There were widespread human rights abuses and violations, and naturally these provoked an adverse reaction from the people. With a view to bolstering political legitimacy, recognition and credibility, governments increased the military expenditure and strengthened the military presence in the political arena to intimidate or deter their political opponents and opposition. Thirdly, the performance of the post-independence leadership in Africa in the economic and political spheres was lacklustre and even scandalous. The polity was witness to the degeneration of political parties, and the politics of patronage became the order of the day. Mismanagement of various sectors of national life, particularly the economy, became endemic, and leaderships were interested only on personal aggrandizement. Finally, the personal ambition of the military establishment was also a contributing factor. The armed forces, acting like any other politically active and vocal group, sought to increase its own share of government largesse through intimidation, blackmail and frequently the forceful takeover of the government itself.

While Ayittey's analysis is contextually specific to the African continent, one can discern a commonality in most cases where there have been military *coups* and interventions, though of course, the immediate provocation or the precipitating component may have varied from country to country. Interestingly, the militarization of African politics in the 1960s, at least in several cases, was welcomed by populations which had become weary of the utter mismanagement of their political élites. Ayittey is of the view[6] that in the 1960s the men who led the forces were professional soldiers who did not tolerate inefficiency, waste and corruption. They strove to clear the mess and inject a sense of discipline and then returned to the barracks. However, human rights violations continued even during this period. The 1970s saw a reversal of sorts with the military leaderships themselves becoming corrupt, incompetent and tyrannical, even worse than the civilian administrations which they replaced. The scenario was even more dismal in the 1980s when the military became increasingly obsessed with political power *per se*. By the late 1980s and early 1990s, it was rule by 'uniformed buzzards'[7] in Africa.

Modes of Intervention

What has been the mode of intervention by the military in politics? Samuel Finer,[8] who has conducted extensive studies of civil–military relationships, locates four levels as far as intervention is concerned: influence, blackmail, displacement, supplantation. These methods are employed alone or in conjunction with one another. How do the military go about usurping political power? Finer delineates different methods in this regard.[9] At times, the military reach positions of power through normal constitutional channels. At other times, it is through collusion and/or competition with the civilian authorities. The military frequently intervene through the intimidation of the civilian authorities. In some cases, the *modus operandi* is the threat of non-co-operation with, or violence towards, the civilian authorities. In other cases, the military facilitate the process of coming to power through their failure to defend the civilian authorities from violence. In certain cases, they themselves resort to violence against the civilian leadership.

All military regimes begin with the handicap of lack of legitimacy. Initially, many of them make attempts to derive some sort of legitimacy but they soon get sucked into the vortex of politics. There is a line of thought that the military succeed in coming to power because of their discipline, command structure and organizational hierarchy, and pride in their profession. Countering this, another argument is that these very same factors can also be hindrances in reaching out to the people. Once the people are alienated, the acquisition of legitimacy becomes a casualty. Slowly but steadily, opposition to the military begins to build up. This is a crucial stage in the military–people relationship because the junta is never in a position to reconcile to opposition. The result is large-scale suppression of the fundamental rights of the citizenry. The quest for legitimacy continues, however, with the military looking for props, internal or external, to sustain its rule. In most cases, as has been experienced in large parts of Africa, Latin America and several parts of Asia, the military fail to deliver the goods and drive the country to abysmal depths of want and privation. Eventually, the inexorable march of popular antipathy forces the junta from power, though this may take many years.

The military, when they are waiting in the wings to gain power, are aided and abetted by several aspects of civilian management. In many countries, the military are called upon to perform civilian operations such as controlling insurgency, helping the administration in tackling the ravages of natural calamities, restoring law and order and managing domestic conflicts. Civilian leadership which lacks popular support may call on the armed forces to put down political opposition. In many cases, the military may be enjoined by the ruling élite to wage war with weaker neighbours to bring temporary relief to the leadership. All these give the military a taste of power. However, once in power they succumb to the inevitable. Military rulers always emphasize the role of the armed forces as the political guardian, which is a very convenient concept for them. As a guardian, they do not take any responsibility of their own. On the contrary, they shift the blame to the civilians if and when things go wrong.

Disengagement

Once the armed forces are compelled to hand over the reins of power to the civilian authority the country is faced with problems of a different nature, as has been experienced by most of the re-civilianized polities. Not only the political parties but also the military find it difficult to cope with emerging realities. This is particularly so in the case of the military, which have first to find their bearings. The people who were victims of brutalization under the junta would indubitably be clamouring for exemplary punishment of the military leaders for their wanton disregard of human rights. On the other hand, the political leadership which had just taken over would generally prefer to follow a more cautious path where the perpetrators of only the most blatant violations of fundamental rights would be brought to book, at the same time taking a more lenient view of other transgressions. Furthermore, the state has to guard against remilitarization and conspiracies by service officers at various levels to thwart disengagement efforts. The military also have to be assuaged so that the morale of the forces is not altogether destroyed. All in all, the task is undoubtedly formidable. To understand the complexities of these endeavours, we attempt an analysis of the relationship between the government and the military in Argentina.

Argentina – a Case Study[10]

The people of Argentina have been victims of protracted authoritarianism which tyrannized them and left deep scars on the nation's body politic. For long, Argentina suffered from various forms of dictatorship which isolated the country from the rest of the world. This imposed isolation denied the country any economic and political interaction with other advanced economies. The authoritarian regimes were also characterized by an isolated artificial environment favourable to increased trade union power, state protection for uncompetitive enterprises and unproductive employment, billion dollar deficit public enterprises and three-figure inflation. When the military usurped power during the period 1976–83, Argentina witnessed the worst form of brutalization in its history.

Military Rule

Military rule, besides resulting in indiscriminate human rights violations, also pauperized the Argentine economy as never before. People's discontent with the junta reached unimaginable levels. Then came the fiasco of the South Atlantic (Falklands) War of 1982 which was the beginning of the end of military rule in Argentina, and it was only a question of time before democracy triumphed. Beginning in 1983, democratically elected governments transformed the face of the nation with radical economic reforms, unquestioned civilian control of the armed forces and well-entrenched guarantees of long-term democratic stability. There has been a radical shift towards democracy to an extent which is so far unknown in other post-authoritarian experience. Any attempt at endangering the democratic structure, especially by ascribing a political role to the military, has been roundly rejected by the people stoutly defending democracy.

How did a polity so badly mauled by the military dictatorship achieve this ideal? The 'social ejection of authoritarianism' as is seen in today's Argentina unambiguously disallows any role for the military in politics. In fact, within the military institutions themselves, there has been a change in values and perceptions. The military earlier had to contend with hostile feelings among the people at large and certain political groups and the intelligentsia in particular. The defeat in the South Atlantic War led to considerable introspection within the armed forces, particularly the younger officers. All these contributed to a new professionalist orientation, akin to democracy within the military set-up.

The Military under Civilian Control

Simultaneously, the elected government initiated several measures to bring the military under civilian control. To begin with, in 1984, the government cut the military budget by over 50 per cent. Between 1984 and 1986, the elected president took over as commander-in-chief of the armed forces, and some military powers were delegated to the minister of defence. The ministry of defence was entrusted with the charge of the 34 military enterprises, most of which were subsequently privatized. In 1988 a defence law was passed which put an end to all internal functions of the armed forces and which stressed that their role was to deal with external security threats. In 1994 conscription was abolished and in its place an all-volunteer professional armed service system was established.

In the intervening period, during 1984–5, Raul Alfonsin's government carried out an exercise to mete out punishment for human rights violations to former members of the successive military juntas. The prosecution of the younger officers led to two rebellions. While the first rebellion had widespread support, the passage of the Due Obedience Law in 1987 put an end to the revolt. The second rebellion of early 1988 could not succeed because by then the armed forces were completely subordinated to the civil authority.

Reform Measures

In addition, several other reforms aimed at civilianizing the armed forces were set in motion. For example, officers were promoted and encouraged to undertake undergraduate and graduate studies in public and private universities. It was even proposed that such studies be financed by the respective service, which was earlier an impossible proposition. Taking another step forward, the military profession was opened up to women. The Argentine military saw a complete about-turn when, in 1995, the chief of the defence staff stressed in a television programme that anyone who *gave* an immoral order committed a crime as much as anyone who *obeyed* such an order.

The Military in UN Endeavours

On another front, the armed forces have supported several programmes undertaken by the elected governments in promoting international peace and security. Thus, when President Carlos Menem decided to participate in the Gulf War in 1990, in pursuance of United Nations Security Council Resolutions, the armed forces were in support of that decision. Starting with this, there has been an active Argentine commitment to UN principles. Since 1991, Argentina has participated in the United Nations Protection Force (UNPROFOR), United Nations Peace Keeping Force in Cyprus (UNFICYP) and several other UN peace-keeping activities. Interestingly, the number of Argentine officers who have participated in UN peace operations is now probably close to one-half of the army.

Global and Regional Co-operation

In line with its new policies, Argentina has been an active proponent of nuclear non-proliferation and a member of the Nuclear Non-Proliferation Treaty (NPT) regime. Argentina has also signed a series of agreements with Brazil on the peaceful uses of nuclear energy. With Brazil and Chile, Argentina has campaigned for a nuclear weapons-free Latin America. It is also a member of the Missile Technology Control Regime (MTCR). In addition, it is committed not to develop or use any chemical or bacteriological weapons. Argentina has been contributing to regional security and the strengthening of the Organization of American States (OAS). It has promoted harmonious relationships with Brazil and Chile, and normalized relations with the United Kingdom which had suffered in the wake of the South Atlantic imbroglio. All these endeavours have given a substantive redefinition of the role of the armed forces in the international context as also in the imperatives of a democratic society. There is thus an increasing 'routinization' of civil–military interaction in the sphere of an active process of policy-making. This has led to a new professionalist orientation of the armed forces which has opened up a channel for a military role at the operational level, with objectives linked to peace, co-operative security and preventive diplomacy. More significantly, the interaction with the armed forces of other countries has helped to reinforce the change of values and perceptions of the post-1982 Argentine armed forces. Initially, Argentina benefited by going global. Efforts should now be directed more towards national and regional issues. Regional currents should be stressed and emphasized, rather than internationalizing local issues.

However, certain problem areas remained, especially during the 1980s and early 1990s. The reduction of over 50 per cent in the military budget was not followed by a reform of the size and structure of the armed forces. A redefinition of the military's role in the new democratic set-up and a changing global scenario was not completed. Neither was 'civilian empowerment' of the state administration achieved. In Argentina, a generation of officers have been caught in a situation where they find it difficult to cope with the changed realities.

Overall, the disengagement process has been peaceful and its effects long-standing. There are, however, analysts who caution the government on the need to address problems effectively. As Wendy Hunter says:

> In the absence of military-centered methods of control, keeping the military at bay in Argentina has come to depend largely on the ability of civilians to preside over effective and legitimate governments. Strong economic performance accounts in no small measure for the Menem government's current success in

containing the military. If civilian governance begins to falter, however, the armed forces may begin to reconsider their subordinate role. They could well take advantage of governmental weakness by demanding greater resources and expanded activities, at the very least to help restore corporate autonomy and pride.[11]

The political and economic reforms ushered in by democratic governments have improved the Argentine economy substantially, at the same time providing political stability in the country. This has narrowed the scope for remilitarization in Argentina. According to Hunter, the 'political and economic constraints on the armed forces have been highest in Argentina. These constraints, coupled with the military leadership's basic acceptance of civilian authority, have drastically narrowed the military's sphere of operation, both political and professional.'[12] By and large, Argentina's current democratic strength is based on profound domestic changes – a less 'state dependent' society and also a shift in foreign policy leading to the re-entry of the country into the international system and to regional integration.

Civil–Military Relationship

As discussed above, the relationship between the military and the government is indeed tenuous. The chances of military takeover of governments are high in those countries which have limited experience in democracy and where the democratic ethos have not struck deep roots. Axel Hadenius is credited with the view that large armed forces, with a potential for intervention that this confers, have an adverse effect on democracy.[13] Some studies have also demonstrated that countries where a high proportion of the resources are assigned to the armed forces tend to have a low level of democracy.[14] There are, in addition, several socio-economic factors which are responsible for possible military intervention, as is evident from the experience of several African, Latin American and Asian countries. However, where countries have an inherent democratic culture and where civil–military relations are well demarcated constitutionally or otherwise, as in the case of India, there is less possibility of military interference.

The dynamics of a civil–military relationship is a crucial aspect in any society. In the case of countries such as Pakistan, Sudan and Nigeria, there have been strong local factors responsible for military interference with the civil administration. The issue of development in a country is also a contributing factor. Many countries had to endure the vicious cycle of militarization, then demilitarization and again remilitarization. During the Cold War era, the thrust of international relations was drastically different from the emphasis in the post-Cold War scene of the 1990s. In the Cold War phase, military regimes were often propped up by external factors, due to the compulsions of the then prevalent international relations.

Once in power, military regimes adopt several populist measures, primarily with a view to achieving some sort of legitimacy. A former Nigerian ruler, Mohammed Buhari, has even propounded the concept of 'military democracy'. After the first flush of enthusiasm and change, military regimes degenerate into 'governments at war with their own people'. As defence spending increases, there is a corresponding degeneration of the economy, leading to manifold problems for the people. This also indicates that there is an intrinsic relationship between democracy, demilitarization, disarmament and development. The huge sums of money wasted on militarization, if diverted for developmental purposes, could go a long way to ameliorating the lot of the people. To add to their distress, the ruling juntas unleash a terror campaign to quell any form of protest against their rule. Eventually, dictatorships are forced to abandon power, giving way to representative governments (at least in the late 1980s and 1990s). What is evident is that, wherever the military came to power, they could not tackle the problems faced by the people. In some cases they might have been able to provide a façade of stability and progress for some time, but in no case could they ensure all-round socio-economic and political achievement.

There has been a demand in many quarters that institutions, including military institutions, need thorough transformation. Many women activists feel that the military is one of the most sexist institutions which promote characteristic male values.

On another front, there has been an underlying animosity in many societies towards the military. There is an imperative for a new thinking on security norms. Of course, there have been significant efforts towards reforming military institutions. Several countries have abolished conscription since it was felt that it facilitated the possibility of a military *coup*. Trends towards globalization and liberalization can promote more democracy everywhere. The more advanced and the more developed that societies are, the fewer are the chances of military intervention and vice versa. The protection of people within their own boundaries has acquired new dimensions, especially in the context of military rule. If the people are more involved and familiarized with the military, there are fewer chances of military intervention. Civilian control of the military and the prevention of military *coups* need not, however, necessarily go together. Conflicts have become less international and more inter-state. The international community is now in a better position to bring pressure on military juntas. In many instances, however, vested interests, particularly economic interests, have thwarted international pressure on military regimes. When a country has to offer something in the nature of precious natural resources, international pressure on a junta is greater. On the contrary, there will be no major pressure on a country lacking in vital resources. The case of Nigeria and Somalia prove this point. An unreliable international system with vested interests could surreptitiously aid and abet military regimes.

To sum up, what is needed to prevent military takeovers is the enrichment of representative institutions and the prevention of the decay of the political structures. If the political leadership lacks legitimacy and is devoid of farsightedness in enabling socio-economic advancement of the society, there is the likelihood of the military interfering in the civilian administration. Eternal vigilance is thus called for to prevent rule by the armed forces. Additionally, in those countries where the military are removed from power, there is every need to facilitate proper disengagement and civilianization of the military and prevent remilitarization which could pose a threat in the future.

References

1. Samuel P. Huntington, *Political Order in Changing Societies* (New York, 1968), p.194.
2. *Ibid.*, p.198.
3. For detailed analyses of civil–military relationship, see Harold Lasswell, 'The Garrison State', *American Journal of Sociology*, vol.46, January 1941, pp.455–68; Samuel E. Finer, *The Man on Horseback: The Role of the Military in Politics* (2nd enlarged edn), (Boulder, Colorado, 1988); Samuel P. Huntington, *Political Order in Changing Societies* (New Haven, 1968); Claude Welch, *Military Role and Rule* (N. Scituate, Mass., 1974); Claude E. Welch, Jr, *No Farewell to Arms? Military Disengagement from Politics in Africa and Latin America* (Boulder, Colorado, 1988); Samuel Decalo, *Coups and Army Rule in Africa* (New Haven, 1990); Morris Janowitz, *Military Institutions and Coercion in Developing Nations* (Chicago, 1977); Morris Janowitz (ed.), *Civil–Military Relations: Regional Perspectives* (Beverly Hills, 1981); Bengt Abrahamsson, *Military, Professionalization and Political Order* (Beverly Hills, 1972); Eric A. Nordlinger, *Soldiers in Politics: Military Coups and Governments* (Englewood Cliffs, NJ, 1977).
4. Claude E. Welch Jr, 'The Military and the State in Africa: Problems of Political Transition', in Zaki Ergas (ed.), *The African State in Transition* (Basingstoke, 1987), p.191.
5. George B.N. Ayittey, *Africa Betrayed* (New York, 1992), pp.136–7.
6. *Ibid.*, pp.137–9.
7. *Ibid.*, p.139.
8. Samuel E. Finer, *The Man on Horseback: The Role of the Military in Politics* (Boulder, Colorado, 1988), p.127.
9. *Ibid.*
10. This discussion is based on the presentation by Andres Fontana at the conference, *Parliamentary Democracy and Development: Allies or Adversaries?*, Wiston House, UK, 13 February 1996.
11. Wendy Hunter, 'Contradictions of Civilian Control: Argentina, Brazil and Chile in the 1990s', *Third World Quarterly*, vol.15, no.4, 1994, p.641.

12 *Ibid.*, p.633.
13 Axel Hadenius, *Democracy and Development* (Cambridge, 1992), p.141.
14 *Ibid.*, p.148.

8 The Singapore Model

The remarkably rapid strides that the Singapore economy has achieved has drawn global attention to this South-East Asian nation and led to animated debates on the 'Singapore model' of development. Singapore, which became a self-governing state in 1959, joined Malaysia as a constituent state in 1963. However, it withdrew from the Federation in 1965. At the time of independence in 1965, Singapore was just another low per capita income country with limited physical resources and surplus labour force. There was hardly any major domestic industry, and naturally the rate of unemployment was very high. In the next few decades, however, Singapore emerged as a 'miracle economy' whose human development standards matched, if not excelled, those of the developed world.

According to the *World Development Report 1996*, the per capita gross national product (GNP) of Singapore in 1994 was $22,500. The average annual growth of GNP per capita during the period 1985–94 was 6.1 per cent. The average annual growth of gross domestic product (GDP) 1980–90 was 6.4 per cent while 1990–4, it grew by 8.3 per cent.

The *Asian Development Outlook 1995 and 1996* shows that, in 1994, Singapore's GDP grew by 10 per cent. Private consumption rose by 5 per cent and public consumption by 12.5 per cent above its 1993 level. Labour productivity in the manufacturing sector grew at 11.5 per cent. The current account surplus in 1994 was $6.5 billion, equivalent to a healthy 9.6 per cent of the GDP. In 1994, the unemployment rate averaged 1.9 per cent. During the period 1970–80 the average annual rate of inflation was 5.9 per cent, while during 1980–93 it fell to 2.5 per cent. Consumer price inflation in 1994 was 3.8 per cent.

The *Human Development Report 1995* ranks Singapore at 35 in its Human Development Index. According to this report, between 1985 and 1995, the population with access to health services was 100 per cent. Similarly, during 1988–93, the population with access to safe water was also 100 per cent and with access to sanitation was 99 per cent. The infant mortality rate per 1000 births, which was 36 in 1960, dropped to six by 1992. The *World*

Development Report 1995 shows that life expectancy at birth was 75 years in 1993. Illiteracy was less than 5 per cent (UNESCO). These are exemplary achievements by any standards.[1]

The Early Years

How is it that an underdeveloped economy reached these dizzy heights of development in such a short time, and what has been the price that Singapore had to pay for this? Perceptions have varied and opinions have differed on these crucial questions. However, both the admirers and critics of the 'Singapore model' of development have one view which shows convergence – that the socio-economic and political policies pursued by the ruling People's Action Party (PAP) were mainly responsible for this sterling performance. In the formative years after independence, particularly after separation from the Malaysian Federation and once they overcame several challenges to their authority, the PAP and its leader Lee Kuan Yew set out clear-cut goals and policies before the people in a nation-building endeavour. These goals and programmes were pursued and implemented with a missionary zeal, sweeping aside all opposition, inviting in the process international criticism, particularly from Western countries. Over these years of agony and ecstasy, the PAP tried to inculcate among Singaporeans certain 'shared values', imparted moral education, and laid stress on certain aspects of Confucianism. According to some observers,[2] the basic tenets of the PAP philosophy have been pragmatism, multiracialism and meritocracy. Bearing in mind the complex plurality of Singaporean society, the government came up with the '4 Ms' policy, which underlined multiracialism, multilingualism, multiculturalism and multireligiosity.[3] This was most definitely a very pragmatic approach, since Singapore had people with different origins: Chinese, Malays and Indians speaking Chinese, Malay, Tamil and English languages. The religious identities of these groups also varied. Hence, it was essential that attempts were made to forge a commonality of purpose among them, which was the building of a nation economically sound and politically stable, where people could pursue their ideals within a structured order. Particular emphasis was laid on welfare activities aimed at social development: access to education, medical facilities and a hygienic environment. A public housing programme was launched to provide shelter for the people. The planning process was constantly monitored to cater for emerging needs: 'The experience of planning in Singapore started from a formal basis in the 1960s to a more *ad hoc* and indicative basis in the 1970s and 1980s. The change-over was dictated by pragmatic and eclectic considerations.'[4] The purpose behind all these efforts was to enlist the support of the people to the PAP programmes and policies. Simultaneously, the government also took many practical measures towards restructuring the economy, developing the infrastructure and generating employment. The results soon began to appear, with impressive performance in diverse sectors.

The Political Spectrum

How was this achieved? The political component of the entire process has been a matter of extensive debate the world over. The PAP has managed to retain a stranglehold on power throughout these critical years, using means which, to many, have been far from democratic. Critics claim that democracy has been mortgaged in Singapore, that human rights violations are many and that democratic institutions are not permitted to flourish. Draconian laws are enacted to prevent any opposition to the ruling party from gaining ground. International opinion, particularly in the West, has not been in favour of the undemocratic character of the PAP government. However, even opponents of these policies have been compelled to welcome the dramatic progress the 'Singapore model' has brought to its people.

The Singapore School

The proponents of the 'Singapore school' have a different perspective on these developments. The 'Singapore school' is credited with the view that, in order to achieve all-round development, a country needs discipline rather than democracy, and that democracy may actually stand in the way of orderly development. They are also of the opinion that human rights are not universal, but differ according to cultural factors. They assert that Singaporean society is a mature expression of democracy with 'Asian values'. They contend that the society produced by this 'model' is apparently very ordered, clean and safe, with a vibrant economy.

Asian Values

Developments in Singapore since 1965 show that the policy-makers had all these matters in mind when they went about their tasks in a systematic manner. As some analysts suggest:

> In common with other aspects of nation-building in Singapore, the search for a common symbolic core in the form of shared values dates from the mid-1970s,

after the initial period of economic consolidation had been successfully completed ... from the mid-1970s there was an expanding concern with what were labelled as 'Asian values'.... . In the 1980s the concern with 'Asian values' was largely transmuted into a consideration of the positive elements in Confucianism, which were seen to be an encouragement of collective orientation and social discipline.[5]

In particular, the PAP government has underscored the concept of 'Asian values'. The emphasis on communitarianism in Singaporean society has to be seen in this light. Beng-Huat Chua is of the view that central to communitarianism, is the idea that collective interests are placed above those of the individual.[6] The emphasis on 'Asian values' laid by the Singapore government, to several observers, had to be seen in the larger context of Western criticism of political management in Singapore. They feel that this was more in the nature of a reaction, seen especially against the backdrop of the PAP in drawing the Singapore people's attention towards 'degeneration' of family values, societal violence and criminalization and lack of discipline in the West. The PAP ideologists, while repeatedly lambasting 'decadent' Western values, sought to promote the common features of Asian cultures. Some scholars describe the essential features of Asian societies as including collectivism (loyalty to the group, a prime virtue); consensus (harmonious unity, a desired goal); hierarchy (reciprocal obligations of superior and inferior); and power as status (a traditional reverence towards power as the necessary component for generating order and civilization out of chaos and barbarism).[7]

Shared Values

While promoting the concept of 'Asian values', the PAP government also set in motion efforts at building value consensus. These attempts at shaping values, which had earlier been tried through religious institutions, took concrete shape in 1988 when a government committee was set up to draft a set of values. The following year, the president of Singapore, in his opening address to parliament, presented four such values: community over self; upholding the family as the basic building block of society; resolving major issues through consensus instead of contention; and stressing racial and religious tolerance and harmony.[8] Subsequently, a study group on the subject proposed two additional values: honest government and compassion for the less fortunate. In January 1991 the government issued the White Paper on Shared Values, which enumerated five components: nation before community and society above self; family as the basic unit of society; regard and community support for the individual; consensus instead of contention; and racial and religious harmony.

It is thus seen that the PAP government has ever been conscious of the need to promote certain basic values in society while at the same time pursuing an economic strategy which would give the people better standards of living. However, observers (especially Western analysts) have been concerned that the 'Singapore model' has created a greater acceptance of a hierarchically structured society, and a situation where the ruling party could retain power for a long time. They are also highly critical of the intrusion of the PAP in all activities of national life. Singapore being a small island, the power of the state is considerable and magnified. As Erik Paul notes:

> The party controls the executive, legislative and judicial branches of government. The party leadership, through senior cadres and clients, controls the key decision-making areas in the civil service, military and the state business sector. The party has gained strength over the years because of its policy to recruit into its ranks talented and compliant individuals..... The power of the PAP resides in a wide range of state instrumentalities which the party uses to ascertain compliance with its will and maintain political power.[9]

Human Rights in Singapore

The PAP government has been under attack from various quarters for its muzzling of the opposition. The Internal Security Department is a powerful agency of the government, and keeps track of people's activities. The Internal Security Act has been widely criticized for detention without trial, even though in recent years this has been rarely used. Opponents also focus attention on the coercion of government critics and opposition leaders and various constraints on the freedom of the press, which even includes censorship extending to the reading lists in the Singapore National University. *Asia Watch*, in a report in 1989, said that in the previous two years, the Singapore government had been engaged in what appeared to be 'a systematic campaign to destroy both civil society and the rule of law'. The Singapore authorities were also alleged to have harassed and abused the Catholic Church, welfare groups linked to the Church, the Law Society, the National University, domestic and foreign media and opposition political parties.[10]

Communitarianism

On the issue of communitarianism there are different viewpoints. Some observers point out that the consensus model in Singapore is not genuine or true communitarianism as all obligations are imposed from above. Commenting on the political implications of communitarianism, Beng-Huat Chua says that the 'technical difficulties of soliciting opinions from every interested and affected party tends to be resolved, in practice, by a conflation of state/society, in which the elected political leadership assumes the position of defining both the consensus and the national interests by fiat'.[11] Futhermore:

> Politically, this communitarianism makes it ideologically possible to rationalize the conflation of state/government/society, which in turn justifies state interventions in social life as pre-emptive measures for 'ensuring' the collective well-being; thus, as measures of 'good government' rather than abuses of individual rights. The closed ideological logic of communitarianism makes it difficult to think beyond it; consequently, even members of the opposition parties have difficulty constructing alternative scenarios to the PAP's ideological constructions of the 'national interests' of the whole society.[12]

Other criticisms centre on the perception that Singapore's economic success has emanated essentially from its illiberal political structures. Critics also complain that the emphasis on the 'Chineseness' of its citizenry has often been overstressed to the detriment of other communities in the country, particularly Malays, Indians and guest workers whose rights are reportedly often violated. There is definitely an income disparity among the ethnic populations, with the Chinese on top.

The larger question is whether aspirations and values are the same the world over or whether there are beliefs and qualities which are peculiar to a particular nation or region. Naturally, there cannot be any consensus on this issue; while some assert that this is so, others argue that even as common values may exist, there are numerous manifestations of them. In the Singaporean context, the lack of democracy is seen by some as an intelligent trade-off made by individuals in order that they might progress economically. People are not the centre-piece of democracy but only a component of democracy. Citizens have many fundamental rights, including the right to life, property and freedom of movement. They have, however, willingly surrendered some other freedoms for pragmatic reasons. Supporters of this school of thought point out that many Singaporean students who go abroad to study choose to return to their country and not settle elsewhere. Similarly, many people are wealthy enough to leave Singapore. If the situation in the country is so intolerable as it is made out to be, why is it that they do not prefer to exercise their option of migrating to and settling down in other countries where there are no restrictions? Critics are quick to point out that it is not as simple as that. If dictatorships were to make countries rich, then many countries in Africa and Latin America should have been economic colossuses.

The supporters of the 'Singapore school' assert that some enduring democratic countries were unable to provide their citizens with even the basic necessities of life. In contrast, the 'authoritarian' Singapore regime provided a good standard of living for its people, with ample access to health care, education and other necessities. If democracy as a system of government results in the suppression of the majority by keeping them poor for ever, then it should be questioned. The people of Singapore had the right to choose a system that delivered their avowed goals, even if that involved relinquishing certain rights. The fact that several countries wanted to emulate the 'Singapore model' indicates that the system in Singapore had wide appeal. Many are particularly attracted by the high standards of hygiene and cleanliness and the efficiency of bureaucracy. Several countries have similar laws to Singapore regarding litter and graffiti, but failed to enforce them. Singaporean society is a disciplined one, which is the crucial point. While the 'Singapore model' is not intended to be transitory, change is inevitable. Many petty restrictions such as the prohibition against the chewing of gum, the playing of loud rock music and long hairstyle would eventually be corrected. The wealthy children of once poor and, therefore, more passive parents will not tolerate such ridiculous restrictions for ever.

Does this signify that the non-democratic route is the best way to achieve development? After all, is not Singapore only a city state which cannot be recommended as a 'model' of development? Are 'soft authoritarianism' and 'soft dictatorship' the best prescriptions for economic development? Orderly development is possible even within a democratic framework, as is evident from the history of Western societies. The collapse of the erstwhile Soviet Union and the turn of events in Eastern Europe point towards the non-viability of the 'models' of development practised in those countries, as also the rejection of political ideologies practised by regimes which lacked popular participation. The information revolution has reduced the globe, and the winds of democratic change are sweeping across the continents. What does the future hold for Singapore in this emerging scenario?

The Future of the PAP

The political base of the PAP has been eroded to a considerable extent, as is evident from the election results of 1991. As discussed, the success of PAP's vision for the Singapore of the twenty-first century is conditioned by several factors. Erik Paul feels that liberalization would threaten the fulfilment of this vision because foreign capital would interpret political change towards a more open society as a major political risk and, therefore, alter their strategies in regard to the island. The growing middle class would not compromise their benefits with a sudden shift away from their political allegiance.[13] The swing away from the PAP in the 1991 elections is not a manifestation of their urge for democracy but for greater economic entitlement.[14] As such, the PAP is experimenting with ways to open up the political process without revising the fundamental principles of governance nurtured by the founding fathers.[15] The PAP will have to be very introspective in properly assessing its role in the years ahead. There is bound to be greater pressure on Singapore to further democratize, particularly in the context of the thesis put forward by Francis Fukuyama on the end of the Cold War.[16] The success of the 'Singapore model' has been largely due to an enlightened health and social security policy and one of the most advanced programmes of social distribution in Asia and the world. Chan Heng Chee writes: 'Even with the evolution towards greater democratization as a result of economic development, what may evolve in Asia is a democracy that is quite unlike liberal democracy. Democracy perhaps, but an Asian Democracy.'[17] Fukuyama, who first emphasized the triumph of the liberal idea and the inevitability of liberal democracy, was to write in July 1992: 'Asian politics could take an autonomous turn if Asians are to believe more strongly that continued economic modernization in the post-industrial world requires a re-emphasis of traditional Asian values at the expense of Western democratic norms.'[18]

Lee Kuan Yew, when asked whether being a democracy is a help, a hindrance or irrelevant to how fast Asian countries can grow, said:

> I would say that democracy is not conducive to rapid growth when you are in an agricultural society.... But once you reach a certain level of industrial progress, you've got an educated workforce, an urban population, you have managers and engineers. Then you must have participation because these are educated, rational people. If you carry on with an authoritarian system, you will run into all kinds of logjams. You must devise some representative system. That will ease the next stage to becoming industrialized. Then you may get the beginnings of a civic society, with people forming their own groups.... Then only do you have the beginnings of what I would call an active grassroots democracy.[19]

The 'Singapore model' continues to invite both admiration and antagonism, though all are fascinated by the level of socio-economic advancement that the country has achieved in recent times.

References

1   All figures cited have been compiled from the *World Development Report 1996*; the *Human Development Report 1995*; and the *Asian Development Outlook 1995 and 1996*.
2   Michael Hill and Lian Kwen Fee, *The Politics of Nation Building and Citizenship in Singapore* (London, 1995), pp.246–7.
3   Cited in Vera Simone and Anne Thompson Feraru, *The Asian Pacific: Political and Economic Development in a Global Context* (New York, 1995), p.239.
4   Somsak Tambunlertchai and S.P. Gupta (ed.), *Development Planning in Asia* (Kuala Lumpur, 1993), p.248.
5   Hill and Lian Kwen Fee, *op. cit.*, pp.8–9.
6   Beng-Huat Chua, *Communitarian Ideology and Democracy in Singapore* (London, 1995), p.191.
7   Simone and Feraru, *op. cit.*, pp.219–24.
8   For details, see Hill and Lian Kwen Fee, *op. cit.*, pp.210–19.
9   Erik Paul, 'Prospects for Liberalization in Singapore', *Journal of Contemporary Asia*, vol.23, no.3, 1993, p.295.
10 'Singapore after Lee', *The Economist*, vol.317, no.7678, 27 October 1990, p.20.
11 Beng-Huat Chua, *op. cit.*
12 *Ibid.*, p.210.
13 Paul, *op. cit.*, p.294.
14 *Ibid.*
15 Chan Heng Chee, 'Democracy, Human Rights and Social Justice as Key Factors in Balanced Economic Development', *The Round Table*, no.329, January 1994, p.31.
16 Cited in Paul, *op. cit.*, p.301.
17 Chan Heng Chee, *op. cit.*, p.32.
18 Cited in *ibid.*
19 Interview in *The Economist*, vol.318, no.7713, 29 June 1991, p.16.

9 Development and Democracy in the Island States of the Caribbean

As discussed earlier, native realities and regional compulsions have substantially influenced the growth of democratic culture in different parts of the world. This is equally true concerning the nature and content of development in countries across the globe. The Caribbean region has been no exception to this general rule. The evolution of democratic politics and the stage of development in the Caribbean countries have a distinct regional stamp to them. Despite several similarities within the countries of the region, there are also marked diversities among them which have surfaced over time. Thus, there are commonalities among the Spanish-speaking countries of the region and the Commonwealth Caribbean, as well as distinctive differences among them. In the words of Colin Clarke:

> Caribbean coherence and distinctiveness hinge on a combination of four features, one of them geographical and three historical. The geographical feature is insularity, which intersects with the three historical themes of colonialism, sugar plantation and slavery. Not all Caribbean societies have experienced true insularity, nor do they share a synchronized chronology; however, all have reacted vigorously against the deeply entrenched pattern of inequality which was their character in the late eighteenth century, and most have now thrown off colonialism, sugar monoculture and the most blatant forms of racial hierarchy and discrimination.[1]

Within the Caribbean region, the island states of the English-speaking Caribbean, with Guyana, could be considered a distinctive region because of a variety of factors. These include the geographical location, similarities in historical background, colonial association with the United Kingdom, political and constitutional evolution and the common bond of slavery and the sugar plantation system.² However, the fact remains that there are wide variations among them in area, size, natural resources, ethnic composition and population distribution. Significant differences in the growth of party systems and trade union movements have contributed towards the emergence of differing patterns of behaviour in socio-economic and political spheres.³

The Commonwealth Caribbean

The political development in the English-speaking Caribbean has naturally been greatly influenced by the Westminster system. The island states of the Caribbean subscribe to the basic tenets of democracy, including regular, free and fair elections based on universal suffrage; constitutional multi-party regimes; extensive civil liberties; and the separation of powers among the various organs of government. In the wake of the decolonization process, the Caribbean states embarked on the path of nation building which was indeed a hard task, considering the fragile state of their economies. The endeavour was further inhibited by the peculiar geographical location of these countries. As Jean Grugel says:

> The Caribbean Basin was one of the first parts of the globe to experience colonization and the region where British imperialism survived longest; it remains an area which the most powerful nation in the contemporary system, the US, defines as crucial for its national security; and as a region made up of small peripheral states, it is vulnerable to a variety of outside pressures in policy-making. These factors combine to give external agents an unusual degree of influence over politics in the region and to raise doubts about the sovereignty in the area.⁴

The adoption and subsequent adaptation of the Westminster model by the island states displayed a strong urge of the people for representative institutions. Over a period, multi-party systems have been institutionalized in the small states. An analysis of Caribbean politics shows that the political parties are conservative, in the process reflecting the social structure of which they are a part. The political parties also accept existing societal values and are willing to work within the limits of these values. Wherever possible, parties have by and large worked towards a sensible political centre, and avoided class and racial cleavages. In the recent past there have, of course, been aberrations when racial issues emerged prominently in national politics. On the whole, there has been relative political stability, which is conducive to the enhancement of human potential.⁵

Economic Development

The debate whether democracy is a precondition for development or whether it is the other way round is not essentially important in the case of the island states of the Caribbean. This is primarily because significant changes in the social, political and economic fields have taken place in the wake of the transplanting of the Westminster constitutional and institutional framework. The question whether democracy is an inhibiting factor or a positively contributing component in the development of small island states, however, merits serious attention.[6] Economic developments in the Caribbean region have been major features in discussions on dependency theory.

Native and regional pulls and pressures have also had their impact on economic and political development in the Caribbean. Anthony Rolle points out that the island states are small, open, developing countries whose economies are founded on primary production and import–export activities, with a high ratio of foreign trade to GDP and dependence on a small number of primary export products. These products are highly vulnerable to fluctuations in world prices and market conditions. The 1960s and 1970s witnessed uneven economic development in the region, and the consequent income concentration in certain sections of the population naturally led to social and political tension. The 1980s were marked by an unprecedented recession which affected the socio-economic conditions of the people at large. A new policy orientation later emerged which emphasized the liberalization of trade, export promotion and fiscal authority. Grugel has identified the most important characteristics of the Caribbean model of development as the smallness of their economies; their acute economic vulnerability; their location on the periphery of the international system; the excessive influence of external agents; and a tendency towards extreme concentration of power internally.[7]

Over the decades, the Caribbean region has achieved a level of development which places it in an intermediate position between the developed world and the developing countries. The rate of literacy and of infant mortality and other indicators of human development are particularly good in Barbados and the Bahamas, and in several other cases compare favourably with the developed world. On the other hand, the areas of weakness are mostly functions of size and scale – shortage of skills and high per capita costs of providing government services. The region is also beset with an external debt crisis, inflation and a low proportion of world trade.

The enhanced level of development has also brought attendant problems. The middle and upper classes particularly are greatly influenced by the trends in the North Atlantic states, and naturally expectations and life styles have undergone considerable change. As a natural corollary, there is a heavy emphasis on consumerism, most of which comes from outside the region. When aspirations for improved standards of living are high and when the system is not able to deliver the goods because of meagre resources, tensions are aggravated. These trends impose constraints on the government's ability to plan realistically for socio-economic development. Westminster-style electoral politics also poses a problem because the politician, with an eye on votes, promises populist improvements in the metropolitan-determined standards of living. Inevitably, all these impose an added strain on the democratic process.

It is, however, a fact the the transplanting of the Westminster system has been accepted by the small island states. But people are left wondering whether it is good or best suited to native requirements. There is a general feeling that the Westminster model is very expensive in running all organs of government in the smaller states. The problem, however, is that alternative models of governance are unfamiliar to the Caribbeans. Several English-speaking Caribbean countries have in the past faced occasional threats of military intervention, such as Trinidad, Barbados, St Vincent and Grenada. The debate continues on whether successful political concepts from foreign shores should be transplanted in societies which cherish substantially different cultures and values. Caribbean politics has thrown up several charismatic leaders who could galvanize people to action, though time and again, criticism has been levelled against strong-man politics in small states. There is a general feeling that politics is more concerned with the personality of the leader than genuine political issues. Analysts of Caribbean politics have been found to lay emphasis on the need for developing native traditions of democracy rather than mimicking the political structures of other countries.

The role of subaltern social groups has also been quite significant in the Caribbean system. As Grugel observes:

> Traditionally, the state in the Caribbean Basin operated as an instrument of domination for powerful local socio-economic groups or the metropolis. However, élite groups have not always been able to exercise uncontested domination. Subaltern social groups have been able to challenge the ruling élite at a number of critical historical moments, though generally in an unorganized and spontaneous fashion. In fact, struggles to broaden participation and to construct polities representative of all its citizens are a feature of contemporary politics in the region.[8]

The achievement of administrative rationalization and bureaucratic efficiency continues to be thwarted by the constraints of imitating the formal structures of the Westminster model and the temptation and opportunities for political patronage which it provides. In the process, small island societies are forced to bear an inefficient administrative structure with adverse consequences for the general viability of the states.

In many of the small states in the Caribbean, tourism is the single most important source of foreign exchange and employment. These states offer a friendly atmosphere of safety and stability and a consensual belief in the sacredness of democracy. The extensive civil liberties prevalent in these countries make for a welcoming populace which is an added attraction for tourists. Even if downturns in tourism are experienced, this is attributable more to the economic situation in the sending country rather than the political situation of the host country. In this limited context at least, parliamentary democracy is seen to be more than an ally in development, but a prerequisite.

One of the related problems – in the wake of the boom in tourism – faced by the Caribbean states is the drug menace and drug trafficking which have acquired threatening dimensions in recent years. A country such as the Bahamas has been affected by the refugees who have been using its territory as a stop-over and transhipment point to the United States. However, there have been concerted efforts to check drug abuse and drug trafficking. For instance, the Bahamas and the United States launched a joint exercise to check drug trafficking, a drive which has met with considerable success.

Regional Co-operation and Integration

The commonalities in the history and politics of the small states in the Caribbean have also thrown up lively debate and discussion on the need for viable regional co-operation and integration. In the past, the region experimented with the West Indies Federation and the Caribbean Free Trade Association (CARIFTA). An institutional arrangement for regional co-operation was realised with the setting up of the Caribbean Common Market and Community (CARICOM) in 1973. Earlier attempts at Caribbean co-operation had not met with much success since the nation states, irrespective of size, were against any delimitation or surrender of political autonomy, with each of them wanting to possess all the organs of government.

There are differing perceptions about the need for regional co-operation in the Caribbean. While the results of attempts towards co-operation in the region were not entirely to the satisfaction of the states, recent efforts in the area of trade and the 'successes' of CARICOM and the Organization of American States (OAS) have been encouraging. The setting up of the North American Free Trade Agreement (NAFTA) offers another opportunity for the Caribbean Community. There is a prevalent view that efforts at regional co-operation have been more in the area of trade than in politics, though the emphasis on trade is understandable when one considers the geographical realities.

What is integration supposed to achieve? Trevor Harker[9] feels that there are both qualitative and quantitative aspects of integration. Qualitative factors include elements of culture, ethnicity, common legal and constitutional modes, and the strengthening of affinities and kinship. At the material level, integration could be a mechanism for accelerating the rate of growth. Integration could help to create a larger market, and could also facilitate the achievement of intrastate and intrasectoral linkages to make a more rational use of factor endowments. The benefits from institutional rationalization could also be substantial. Further, integration could help in co-ordinating foreign policy, thus leading to better bargaining power for the region as a whole. Observers of the Caribbean system are credited with the view that institutional arrangements like CARICOM should devote more attention to devising workable and practicable propositions with a view to addressing the problems of development in the region. Winston Dookeran says:

> Caricom has been stigmatized as a body that announces, decides and slowly or never implements. Unless Caricom is perceived as offering workable solutions that would deliver the fruits of economic development, there will continue to be inertia in implementation and an unflattering performance.[10]

There is, however, support in large measure for the concept of regional co-operation in the Caribbean. Differences there may be as to how to proceed, what should be the nature of the institutional arrangements and the like, but the success of regional co-operation elsewhere has given further emphasis to the need for effective co-operation in the Caribbean too. Needless to say, free trade is an important factor in all the measures that are discussed. Harker stresses:

> Whatever model the region selects, it will be of little value unless the integration being considered is seen as a process that will ultimately lead the Caribbean into some form of hemispheric association, as a precursor to freer trade. For whatever the global and regional tendencies, the logic of cooperation among small island countries, having as they do similar characteristics, interests, and problems, is inexorable.[11]

The politics of the English-speaking Caribbean has been largely conditioned by native realities and its close association with the Westminster system. After decolonization, the region endeavoured to achieve socio-economic progress mostly within a democratic framework. The level of economic development achieved by the Commonwealth Caribbean has been acclaimed, lending credibility to the policies followed. To quote Grugel:

Development and Democracy in the Caribbean   105

The imperial legacy in the English-speaking Caribbean stresses the supremacy of civil society, links democracy with a tradition of popular participation through trade unions, and delegates to the state some limited but key functions in the provision of welfare services and in the redistribution of income. Democracy could be said to deliver moderate material gains in the Commonwealth Caribbean, and this fact has served to legitimize the system.[12]

The region is, however, confronted by several developmental issues which also have a bearing on the polity. As one perceptive analyst emphasizes:

> The major developmental issue facing the Caribbean economies in the 1990s is the prospect and outcome of switching to a new generation of export products and services. A policy environment supportive of international competitiveness and capturing international markets that are skill-management and knowledge-intensive may be a point of departure, as the region prepares for a new world economic order. The premise of future economic strategy must be the acceptance of a vibrant export sector that is sustainable without trade preferences. This sustainability, while push-started by negotiated treaties, must be founded on market forces. In order to facilitate this use of new resources, some critical policy instruments will be exchange rate regimes, technology application and political consensus-building.[13]

These are major concerns for the Caribbean Community. The political system has a pivotal role in the emerging scenario, especially in the context of economic development. The strains imposed on the governments by electoral compulsions are often found to hinder balanced development. The five-year imperative for elections is a time horizon not supportive of a planning ideology. The transformation of societies through long-term inflexible plans with practically no input from the electorate is certainly an unsatisfactory model of development and has been rejected by almost all the Caribbean states. The system, though inefficient in the sense that it does not allow for long-range, rational and comprehensive plans of socio-economic development, is tolerated because peace and happiness is best achieved in a democratic polity.[14] The Caribbean Community needs to look to overcoming deficiencies in its polity so as to sustain and also to further economic development in the region.

References

1 Colin Clarke, 'Sovereignty, Dependency and Social Change in the Caribbean', in *South America, Central America and the Caribbean, 1986* (London, 1985), p.20.
2 Anthony Rolle, in his presentation at the conference, *Parliamentary Democracy and Development: Allies or Adversaries?*, Wiston House, UK, 13 February 1996.

3   *Ibid.*
4   Jean Grugel, *Politics and Development in the Caribbean Basin: Central America and the Caribbean in the New World Order* (Basingstoke, 1995), pp.83–4.
5   Rolle, *op. cit.*
6   *Ibid.*
7   Grugel, *op. cit.*, p.3.
8   *Ibid.*, p.62.
9   Trevor Harker, 'Caribbean Economic Performance in the 1980s: Implications for Future Policy', in Hilbourne A. Watson (ed.), *The Caribbean in the Global Political Economy* (Boulder, Col., 1994), pp.12–13.
10 Winston Dookeran, 'Caribbean Integration: An Agenda for Open Regionalism', *The Round Table*, no.330, April 1994, p.205.
11 Harker, *op. cit.*, p.26.
12 Grugel, *op. cit.*, p.97.
13 Dookeran, 'NAFTA, the EC and the Uruguay Round: Does the Caribbean have a Place in the New Economic Order?', *The Round Table*, no.326, April 1993, p.154.
14 Rolle, *op. cit.*

10 Indirect Democracy in Uganda

The travails of democratic experiments worldwide have, in some ways, brought to the fore the inherent but inhibited democratic aspirations of the people in general. In the African continent, country after country had to contend, time and again, with forces inimical to representative government. Dictatorships of different hues thrived in the continent, crushing popular desires for a government elected by the people under universal adult suffrage. The history of African attempts at democracy is very much reflected in the trials and tribulations the Ugandan political system has undergone in recent decades.

Background

To understand the present state of government and politics in Uganda, one has to have some knowledge of the evolution of its polity since independence.[1] Uganda, which became a British protectorate in 1894, passed through several critical phases of political activity before it eventually gained freedom in 1962. The strong content of tribalism in national politics, which has a distinct African stamp, has been very much in evidence in the Ugandan system. As Kenneth Ingham says, 'if one is seeking for examples of the influence of tribalism on political development one could scarcely do better than to look first at Uganda'.[2] During British rule, Uganda witnessed strenuous efforts towards the protection and promotion of tribal interests. As early as 1891, the British entered into a treaty with the Kabaka (king) of Buganda, the principal kingdom. Later, in 1894, Buganda was declared a protectorate. Two years later, Ankole, Bugosa, Bunyoro and Toro received the same status.

Independence Movement

The freedom struggle in Uganda was characterized by intense political differences over several issues, particularly the role of Buganda in a future state. The first of the several political parties which came into existence was the Uganda National Congress (UNC), established in 1952. This was followed by the Democratic Party (DP) in 1956. Then came the Ugandan Peoples Congress (UPC) led by Milton Obote in 1958. The independence movement thus suffered because there was no unified leadership. The suspicion and mistrust of the Bugandan leaders, who wanted to protect their privileged position, led them to set up the *Kabaka Yekka* (KY – King Alone). In the first countrywide elections held in 1961, the Democratic Party won a majority of the seats. However, the leadership was not acceptable to the KY. Self-government was granted to Uganda in March 1962.

Post-independence Politics

Before full independence in October 1962, Uganda went to the polls in April 1962 to elect members to the National Assembly. The UPC emerged victorious and its leader Milton Obote took over as prime minister. The major problem confronting the country was the form of the federation, which was tackled by granting semi-autonomous status to Buganda, Ankole, Bunyoro and Toro. The Kabaka of Buganda, Mutesa II, was elected president in October 1963, though this peace was short-lived. Obote, who advocated centralism, could not come to terms with President Mutesa, who was widely identified as a symbol of Bugandan hegemony. In February 1966 Obote deposed the president and the vice-president. The constitution was suspended, and all executive powers were taken over by the prime minister. Two months later Obote introduced an interim constitution, cancelling the provision for regional autonomy and ushering in executive presidency, and Obote became the head of state. Soon, the Bugandans were up in arms demanding restoration of their autonomy. However, government forces led by Idi Amin attempted to crush the agitation, which led to the kabaka fleeing the country. In the meantime, the National Assembly voted Obote a five-year term as president in April 1966. In September 1967 a new constitution was enacted which allowed for a unitary republic. It also abolished all traditional rulers and legislatures. The country entered a new phase when, in December 1969, Obote imposed a ban on all political parties and established a one-party state.

The Reign of Amin

Two years later, in January 1971, Idi Amin seized power when Obote was abroad attending the Commonwealth Heads of Government meeting. Amin terrorized the country as never before: corruption became rampant; the economy was derailed; and human rights violations became the order of the day. The National Assembly was dissolved and parts of the constitution dealing with executive and legislative powers were suspended. President Amin ruled by decree.

Political Turmoil

Ugandans had to suffer the Amin tyranny for eight years before help arrived. In April 1979 Ugandan exiles under the banner of the Uganda National Liberation Army, aided and assisted by Tanzanian forces, toppled Amin who fled the country. Following the capture of Kampala, Yusuf Lule was installed as president. Lule, however, was replaced by Godfrey Binaisa in June 1979 and Binaisa himself made way for Paulo Muwanga in May 1980.

The Return of Obote

Uganda went to the polls in December 1980, and Milton Obote of the UPC returned as president amid complaints of large-scale rigging of the elections. While the Democratic Party chose to take its seats in the National Assembly, the Uganda Patriotic Movement of former President Yusuf Lule and his defence minister, Yoweri Museveni, declined to accept the single seat it had won. The two then established the National Resistance Movement (NRM) which soon started a guerrilla campaign under the banner of the National Resistance Army (NRA). There were also other guerrilla factions active against the Obote regime.

President Obote was overthrown by a military *coup* in July 1985 and army commander Tito Okello became the head of the ruling Military Council. Meanwhile, Yoweri Museveni had consolidated his position. In January 1986 the NRA succeeded in overthrowing the Okello regime, and Museveni was sworn in as president on 29 January 1986.

Differing Perceptions

The evolution of the political system in Uganda reflects the stresses and strains which democracy as a system of governance had to confront in the African continent as a whole. The march of democracy was indeed an obstacle race; tribal loyalties, despotic rulers and aggressive military establishments placed major hurdles in the path of proper constitutional development. The challenge to the African leadership started in the latter half of the 1970s, which Jean François Bayart has described as the 'revenge of the African societies'.[3] The movement for change attained greater impetus in the late 1980s, with Africa witnessing a political upheaval during which several authoritarian regimes were overthrown.

African countries, over the decades, have experimented with different systems of governance with varying degrees of success. But the urge for democracy has always been clearly discernible, even if somewhat latent. The question is, what form of democracy is good for society? There cannot be any universal prescription for the malaise afflicting individual countries. Every country has to develop its own model of polity to suit its native requirements within the broad parameters of a democracy which are well recognized. As some scholars have pointed out:

> democracy is not an export commodity; it cannot be shipped from one society to another... . It is an internal process, rooted in a country's history, institutions and values... . It is an extremely complex task, the most important parts of which must take place within the nation itself.[4]

Leopold Senghor has referred to the African idea of democracy as involving the *palaver*, a dialogue or discussion, followed by unanimity of decisions.[5] Stephen Riley draws attention to contemporary analyses which point to the positive effects of ethnic heterogeneity and the surprising resilience of a democratic political culture or a democratic ethos underlying the authoritarian model.[6]

How does one describe the form of democracy presently prevalent in Uganda – guided democracy, indirect democracy, one-party democracy? Over the last decade Uganda, under President Museveni, has moved in the direction of a new brand of democracy which many feel run counter to the widely preferred form of multi-party democracy that permits the coexistence of differing ideologies and contending perceptions. A survey of Ugandan politics since colonial times shows that the country always had elements of both direct and indirect elections in its constitutional history.[7] As long ago as 1958, the colonial administration had set up an advisory legislative body which was composed of people appointed by the British governor and those indirectly elected by the district councils. However, in the case of Buganda, the kabaka had a dominant say in choosing the members. In 1962, when the country became independent, there was already a precedent for continuing with the practice of indirect elections. Thus, indirect elections to the new National Assembly brought in representatives from the traditional Buganda kingdom who joined the directly elected members from various political parties. Under the 1967 constitution, elections to the district and urban councils (direct and indirect) were abolished, with the government appointing all the councillors. Parliament was to be elected by universal suffrage through a secret ballot, but the president was to be elected indirectly. It was written into the constitution that the leader of the party which obtained 40 per cent or more of the seats in parliament automatically became the president, whether or not the person was a member of parliament.[8]

There are differences of opinion among political activists and scholars concerning the way in which the Ugandan polity developed immediately after independence. One school of thought believes that the parties evolved along religious lines and had therefore become a divisive force. Others, contesting this view, observe that a political system with a strong element of tribalism in it was bound to have divergent approaches and as such could not be taken as a divisive element. However, there is unanimity in the view that Uganda was a victim of nearly two decades of authoritarianism – under Milton Obote, Idi Amin and then 'Obote 2'. The repression let loose by these dictatorships had no parallels in Ugandan history. Worst of all, they systematically undermined all democratic structures, either abusing them for ulterior motives or abolishing them altogether. The tragedy of Uganda continued unmitigated, and eventually led to a civil war. It was the assumption of power by President Museveni's NRM that put a halt to death and destruction in the country.

Uganda then saw a relatively consensual era when the political leadership strived to set aside partisan politics in order to heal the wounds of protracted civil war. This was necessary to restore peace and security, which was the prime need. In addition, the economy, which had been severely impaired, could be brought back on track only if all energies were concentrated for that purpose. It was imperative to rebuild the infrastructure, which had been totally neglected by successive regimes. Above all, democratic institutions had to be revived and the democratic culture, which was badly bruised during the tyrannical regimes, had to be re-established.

The Museveni Regime

On assuming office, President Museveni announced several major decisions, one of which was the setting up of a National Resistance Council with representation from both the military and the civilian sectors. The cabinet consisted of leaders of different shades of political opinion, and a policy of national reconciliation was set in motion. The president declared that human rights would be safeguarded, and established a commission to investigate allegations of human rights violations. Emphasis was also laid on a mixed economy with a view to improving the country's faltering financial system.

President Museveni, over the last decade, has attempted to strengthen his position politically by introducing several measures. His invitation to the leaders of major political parties to join the government was widely welcomed by Ugandans, who had until then experienced only factional politics. This approach of consensus was supplemented by an effective use of the NRM to further Museveni's political ambitions. The NRM extended its military presence to a substantial part of the country. The government, however, barred campaigning by political parties, though political parties as such were not banned.[9] The ostensible reason for this was explained as the need to provide for an interim period of reconciliation and reconstruction.

The Resistance Councils

At the time of the guerrilla war during the period 1981–6, village committees known as Resistance Councils had been set up by the local people to manage the affairs of the liberated areas. Drawing on this, the Museveni government introduced an intricate structure of Resistance Councils from village to district levels. In February 1989 the Military Council was dissolved. In its place, a new structure of government was introduced, built on the Resistance Councils. The six-tier Resistance Council system had the Village Resistance Councils as the lowest tier. Above that was the Parish Councils, to be followed by the Gombolola Councils, County Councils and District Councils. At the top was the National Resistance Council or the national parliament.

Under Museveni's scheme, only the Village Councils were to be elected directly by way of a queueing system. The other councils were to be elected from one council up to the next. Candidates for elections to the Village Councils stood on their own merits rather than on party tickets as party-based political activity had been suspended for four years, which was later extended to nine years. In the meantime, in July 1993, Ronald Mutebi was crowned kabaka, though it was merely a ceremonial post.

Constitutional Commission

A sixteen-member Constitutional Commission, headed by Justice Benjamin Odoki, was appointed in February 1989 to draw up a new constitution for the country. The commission was expected to complete its work by 1991. In February 1989 elections were held for various councils at the lowest level, which was followed by indirect elections to the higher councils. The Constitutional Commission toured the country extensively hearing submissions, and was given a year's extension to submit its report. In the meantime, the Museveni government was granted a five-year extension from 25 January 1990. The first interim report of the Constitutional Commission was published soon after. Elections to local and lower-level Resistance Councils were held in February 1992. The second interim report of the Constitutional Commission recommended the election of a separate Constituent Assembly. The commission produced a draft constitution in March 1993. Among other things, the draft constitution recommended the continued suspension of political parties for at least five more years. It also recommended that the office of the president should be restricted to only two terms.

There was pervasive criticism of the Constitutional Commission for the delay in finalizing its report. In fact, several of Museveni's cabinet colleagues wanted the 1962 independence constitution to be adopted after deleting all the amendments made by Idi Amin and Milton Obote. The delay was also attributed to the undue influence of the army in the process.[10] The most severe criticism regarded the ban on party activities. While supporters of political pluralism wanted the immediate lifting of the ban, the Museveni regime argued that multi-partyism would plunge the country into chaos which it could not again afford. The latter also wholeheartedly welcomed the Constitutional Commission's stand on extending the NRM's rule to 1999.

The Constituent Assembly was elected in March 1994 by a system of direct voting in non-party elections in what was widely reported as 'the most free and fair of Uganda's nationwide elections since independence'.[11] Observers were of the view that the results of the Constituent Assembly elections reflected an overwhelming endorsement of the government, but they also displayed a voting pattern based on ethnic differences, with the Bantu people of Buganda and the western region of the country voting for pro-NRM candidates, while the Nilotic north and north-east favoured multi-party candidates opposed to the Museveni regime.[12]

It was felt that though candidates contested the Constituent Assembly elections as individuals rather than as party members, their party preferences were widely known. After the results were announced, it was obvious that 'no-party democracy' supporters outnumbered the advocates of an early resumption of multi-party politics in the country by roughly two to one.[13] Observers pointed out that Museveni's decision to allow the restoration of the tribal kingdom of Buganda had earned him votes in that populous province.[14]

There have, however, been dissenting voices regarding the elections to the Constituent Assembly. Dr Paul Ssemogerere, a former second deputy prime minister and minister of foreign affairs in the Museveni government, who is also the president of the Democratic Party, has been a critic of certain aspects of the constitution. In fact, Ssemogerere left the Museveni government because of his opposition to some elements of the new constitution. As regards the elections and constitution of the new Constituent Assembly, he points out that those directly elected were elected under a system where political parties were prohibited from sponsoring or in any way promoting any candidate. It was, however, clear that the president, the NRA secretariat and the office of the Central Government Representative did much to promote and assist certain candidates who were regarded as belonging to the NRA. Furthermore, while the political parties whose followers were in millions were given only a token representation of two seats, the president was empowered to nominate ten members.[15]

The Constituent Assembly then drafted the provisions of the constitution, always considering the representations they had received from various quarters. The new constitution retains an element of indirect election, providing for the representation of varied groups such as women, the disabled and young people. It is, however, widely felt that this provision is basically a token representation for groups other than women.

The constitution provides for direct elections by universal adult suffrage and secret ballot for the office of the president and parliament. Election to parliament will be by the first-past-the-post system to represent single-member constituencies. Considering the fact that some of the Ugandan leaders were uneducated (most notably Idi Amin), a restriction has been placed on the electoral system – candidates for the presidency and parliament will thus have to be high school graduates or hold an equivalent qualification. This latter condition, however, has not yet been defined for a society which lacks universal mandatory secondary education.

The constitution permits the continuation of political parties, though it extends for another five years the ban on certain party activities. Interestingly, the NRM is not considered to be a political party. Some party activities not permitted under the constitution include holding conferences to elect new leaders or formulate policies, holding public rallies, opening or operating party branches or sponsoring candidates in elections. New parties cannot be established for another two years, pending enabling legislation by parliament. The ban on some political activities was prompted by widespread public opposition to adversarial politics which many feared would be divisive and would lead to the return of violence and instability. However, critics are of the view that these restrictions will make parties lifeless, leading to political frustration among those who are not associated with the NRM. They also express the fear that such frustration would again embroil the country in turbulence.

Under the constitution, candidates for parliamentary elections cannot campaign on party tickets, nor can they organize into parties once they are elected. The elected members of parliament will have the power to legislate, scrutinize and approve the budget and question the executive. Ministers do not have to be members of parliament. However, all ministerial and other senior public appointments will be subject to parliamentary approval.

Intense debate on the absence of political parties in parliament has taken place in the country. Many feel that without political representation, parliament will have no meaning. It will also be contrary to the concept of constructive opposition to the government which is the bedrock of democracy. Opponents of non-party democracy stress that the continued suspension of functional party politics was made a constitutional provision at the insistence of President Museveni. There are others who emphasize that the vast majority of Ugandans are supportive of the emerging constitutional arrangements. Many are also of the view that the absence of a disciplined back bench will mean that ministers must win parliamentary support for policy and legislation rather than being able to rely on whips issued by the party.

Interestingly, the constitution envisages an open debate to be held in three years' time on the question of the resumption of adversarial party politics. A year later, a referendum will be held on the subject. Proponents of this scheme argue that it would give the political leadership ample time to demonstrate to a cautious electorate that there would be no recurrence of the excesses and distortions of the past. Countering this, others point out that Uganda, after 33 years of independence and an even longer history of advanced political culture, need not undertake such experimentation, which is totally unwarranted and which would only help further entrench the Museveni government. In this context, they feel that Uganda is being governed by an intimidating personality cult the performance of which leaves much to be desired. Challenging this line of thought, Museveni's supporters maintain that ministers now fear a hostile parliament where they have no guarantee that their programmes will be approved.

According to Paul Ssemogerere, another perspective from which the constitution may be evaluated and found deficient and retrogressive is in the threat to constitutionalism and, underlying it, the concept of government by consent.[16] He is also of the view that the constitution has a built-in bias against, even condemnation of, political parties.[17]

Political Developments

The Constituent Assembly held extensive deliberations spread over a period of 18 months. The new constitution was eventually adopted on 8 October 1995. The election to the office of the president was held on 9 May 1996, when Yoweri Museveni was elected president securing 74.2 per cent of the votes cast. His main rival, Dr Paul Ssemogerere, contested the election in his individual capacity and not as the president of the Democratic Party, as required by the constitution. The third candidate was Professor M. Mayanja Kibirige, an academic at Makerere University, Kampala. An analysis of the electoral performance indicated[18] that President Museveni secured overwhelming support in most of the 39 districts; he failed to secure more than 50 per cent of the votes in only six districts. While Kibirige secured over 5 per cent of the votes in only one district, Ssemogerere polled more than 20 per cent of the votes in 11 districts, and in six of them he polled more votes than Museveni.

Indirect democracy has been a striking characteristic of the Ugandan polity at different stages of its evolution. However, as with several other African countries, Uganda too was a victim of repeated repression. The subjugation of the democratic aspirations of the people by successive dictatorships could not, however, crush the will of the people. It needs reiteration that whoever was at the helm of affairs, be it Obote or Idi Amin or Obote in his second incarnation, manipulated the representative institutions to suit his own ends and to consolidate his position. The result was that the country was bedevilled by civil wars and fragmentation on regional, religious and ethnic lines, which inevitably had an adverse impact on the economy. When President Museveni assumed control in 1986, he tried to re-implant indirect democracy, consistent with Uganda's tradition. His efforts towards healing the wounds of the past and ushering in socio-political and economic reforms have won approbation, though there has been criticism of some of his political actions. The embargo on political parties and political activity has not found favour outside the NRM even though many people, embittered by the experience of the past, have reportedly welcomed the move. Museveni's critics are especially wary of his political promotion of the NRA at the cost of other political parties which, they feel, goes against the very foundations of democracy. In spite of these differing views and perceptions, there is a consensus that the ability of the Ugandan people to discuss and debate their differences openly and in a parliamentary manner augurs well for the future of the country in its efforts to emerge as a fully democratic member of the Commonwealth community.

References

1 For a detailed history of the political developments in Uganda, *see* Rita M. Byrnes (ed.), *Uganda: A Country Study* (Washington, 1992); *see also*, *Africa: South of the Sahara, 1994; Africa Review, 1995* and *Political Handbook of the World 1994–95*.
2 Kenneth Ingham, *Politics in Modern Africa: The Uneven Tribal Dimension* (London, 1990), p.11.
3 Jean Francois Bayart, cited in Christopher Clapham, 'Democratization in Africa: Obstacles and Prospects', in *Third World Quarterly*, vol.14, no.3, 1993, p.430.
4 A.F. Lowenthal (ed.), *Exporting Democracy: The United States and Latin America*, cited in Sahr J. Kpundeh and Stephen P. Riley, 'Political Choice and the New Democratic Politics in Africa', *The Round Table*, no.323, July 1992, p.268.
5 Stephen P. Riley, 'Political Adjustment or Domestic Pressure: Democratic Politics and Political Choice in Africa', *Third World Quarterly*, vol.13, no.3, 1992, p.540.
6 *Ibid.*
7 J.F. Wapakabulo in his presentation at the conference, *Parliamentary Democracy and Development: Adversaries or Allies?*, Wiston House, UK, 14 February 1996.
8 *Ibid.*
9 Holger Bernt Hansen and Michael Twaddle, 'Uganda: The Advent of No-Party Democracy', in John A. Wiseman (ed.), *Democracy and Political Change in Sub-Saharan Africa* (London, 1995), p.142.
10 *Ibid.*, p.141.
11 *Ibid.*, p.149.
12 Joseph Ochieng, 'Uganda', *Africa Review 1995*, p.205.
13 Hansen and Twaddle, *op. cit.*
14 Ochieng, *op. cit.*
15 Paul K. Ssemogerere, 'Reflections of the New Uganda Constitution', p.2.
16 *Ibid.*, p.5.
17 *Ibid.*, p.6.
18 M.S. Prabhakara, 'Better Times for Uganda', *The Hindu* (Delhi), 19 May 1996.

11 The Role of Parliamentary Associations in Facilitating the Proper Functioning of Parliaments

The new thrust to democratic experiments the world over in recent times has brought into sharper focus the relevance of parliamentary institutions in further promoting the cause of a representative political system. Today, Alcuin's assertion *Vox populi vox Dei* finds acceptance in more countries than ever before. The inherent resilience of democracy derives its sustenance from the people at large. The representatives of the people have at all times to bear in mind this cardinal principle of democracy.

Discussion and debate constitute the spirit and soul of democracy. Parliamentarians have often been described as opinion moulders, opinion makers and opinion leaders. The problems faced by them differ from people to people, country to country, region to region. Nevertheless, the issues with which they are confronted have many things in common, in spite of the differences in political systems and socio-economic backgrounds. The resurgence of democracy in recent times offers new challenges and opportunities to parliaments and parliamentarians. Accordingly, international organizations and associations engaged in the task of strengthening democratic ideals have an added responsibility to cope with the demands of the emerging scenario.

Parliamentary Associations

There are many parliamentary associations around the world actively involved in promoting parliamentary democratic standards. While some of them, such as the Commonwealth Parliamentary Association (CPA) and the

Inter-Parliamentary Union (IPU), have global membership, there are others representing common interests or regional concerns. In the latter category fall the Union of African Parliaments, the Arab Inter-Parliamentary Union, the Asian and Pacific Parliamentarians Union, the ASEAN Inter-Parliamentary Organization, the International Assembly of the French-speaking Parliamentarians and the Association of SAARC Speakers and Parliamentarians. An overview of the various activities of the CPA, the IPU and the Association of SAARC Speakers and Parliamentarians makes clear the sweep and scope of their potential in fostering democratic principles as well as inter-parliamentary co-operation.

The Commonwealth Parliamentary Association

The Commonwealth, over the decades, has evolved into a multiracial, multicultural and multilingual association of independent sovereign states. Spread across the continents and the oceans, the member states of the Commonwealth are united in holding dear the noble ideals of universal peace and prosperity, the rule of law, the freedom of the individual and, above all, a democratic form of government. The Commonwealth today is perhaps the best repository of the rich legacy of parliamentary democracy which has struck deep roots all over the Commonwealth community. More importantly, parliamentarians in the member countries have strongly felt the imperative for consultation and co-operation to share one another's experiences and thus further advance the Commonwealth ideals which they cherish. It is in this context that the Commonwealth Parliamentary Association has come to play a crucial role in promoting the cause of parliamentary democracy the world over.

The CPA, which is among the oldest of the Commonwealth organizations, was founded in 1911[1] as the Empire Parliamentary Association with six members – Australia, Canada, Newfoundland, New Zealand, South Africa and the United Kingdom. In the years that followed, the CPA grew with the Commonwealth and, following the phenomenal decolonization process in the late 1940s, adapted itself to the new milieu.[2] Thus, in 1948, the Empire Parliamentary Association became the Commonwealth Parliamentary Association, reflecting the emerging realities.

Today, CPA branches exist in 126 national, state, provincial and territorial parliaments, with a membership exceeding 13 000. The essential prerequisite for membership in the CPA is a democratically elected functioning parliament. As well as the national parliament, branches of the association may be formed at state or provincial level. Legislatures of dependent territories can also opt to become members of the CPA. The membership of the

CPA is open to parliamentarians belonging to the ruling party, the opposition and the minority parties in member parliaments. This has proved to be an asset to the CPA as the association has benefited from differing perceptions on issues and situations presented by members belonging to divergent shades of political opinion. In the words of Colin Shepherd:

> The *strength* of our Association is that we are made up of individual parliamentarians representing the parliaments of our countries, not the governments; that we draw our membership from governing, opposition and minority parties. The *force* of our contribution to parliamentary democracy is derived from the recognition of our strength and integrity by governments who will want our mark of approval and by other international forces who recognize our commitment and even-handed expertise.[3]

Organization

In its endeavour towards promoting parliamentary democracy, the CPA acts as a forum for an exchange of views among parliamentarians from the Commonwealth community. This is achieved through conferences, seminars, meetings, exchange of parliamentary delegations and various publications. The principal governing body of the CPA is the General Assembly which meets every year during the Commonwealth Parliamentary Conference. Delegates to the conference constitute the membership of the General Assembly which elects an executive committee entrusted with the management of the affairs of the Association.

Conferences

The plenary conferences of the CPA were biennial from 1948 to 1959, though from 1961 onwards these conferences have been held annually. Deliberations at the conferences are not bound by rigid norms, rules or regulations. As a former secretary-general of the CPA has observed:

> Members find that by exchanging details of procedures and comparing experiences, they learn more about the parliamentary process and the underlying principles of parliamentary democracy. They also learn more about each other and all the things they have in common, and this is the other main objective of the Association. By providing opportunities for the parliamentarians of the Commonwealth to come together to share their views and experiences and to know each other better, the CPA promotes the understanding, tolerance, mutual respect and friendship which are fundamental to membership of the Commonwealth family.[4]

In addition, as the current secretary-general, Arthur Donahoe says, the CPA meetings provide an excellent vehicle for professional development of new members as well as a means by which new and veteran members are able to familiarize themselves with the issues and individuals in Commonwealth legislatures.[5]

The CPA discusses topical issues of global concern and subjects related to parliamentary practice and procedure at its conferences. The CPA's concerns can be gauged from the subjects discussed at some of its recent conferences. At the 40th Conference held in Banff, Canada, in October 1994, the following subjects were discussed: parliament and people – making democratic institutions more representative, responsible and relevant; what contribution can parliamentarians make to the development of the United Nations, the Commonwealth and regional organizations and the prevention and resolution of international disputes?; what practical steps can be taken to enhance relations between Commonwealth countries with regard to trade, debt repayment and deficit-reduction problems and resist the tendency towards a widening of the inequality between developed and developing countries, and how can parliamentarians assist these efforts?; how can Commonwealth parliaments develop practical and innovative processes to achieve full equality for women?; how can parliamentarians contribute to the understanding of environmental protection problems and their implications for development and the need for effective legislation to deal with them?; how can parliamentarians help in achieving a better understanding of the worldwide problems of unemployment, drug abuse and AIDS, and encourage the acceptance of ideas for combating them?; and what steps can be taken to enhance the public perception of parliaments and the legislative process?

The forty-first conference, held in October 1995 in Colombo, Sri Lanka, discussed the following subjects: democracy and development – adversaries or allies?; how can parliamentarians and elected local representatives collaborate in support of the Commonwealth goal of democracy and good governance?; how can present imbalances in the participation of men and women in political life be redressed?; how can parliamentarians improve standards of human rights?; does religious extremism pose a threat to democracy?; how can social, economic, political and parliamentary programmes involve young people in development?; and what is the role of parliamentarians in the matter of sustainable development?

At the forty-second conference held in Kuala Lumpur in August 1996, the following subjects were discussed by the delegates: facilitating consensus-building in dealing with global issues – the role of the Commonwealth and its parliamentarians; educating the Commonwealth about the Commonwealth; is there an effective democratic deterrent to terrorism?; the protection of women and children exposed to violence, exploitation and abuse; how can the improvement in the world economy be more equitably shared?; and how can barriers to the participation of women in political life be overcome?

It may thus be seen that the Commonwealth Parliamentary Conferences provide significant opportunities for parliamentarians from across the Community to have meaningful discussions on a host of contemporary issues of common concern. Interestingly, no resolutions are adopted at the CPA Conference; rather, delegates are completely free to discuss issues, without being limited by any constraints imposed by their national policies or party ties. Bernard Braine once described the CPA as 'a powerhouse of ideas rather than an anvil upon which policies are hammered out'. Arthur Donahoe is of the view that the association is a solution-seeking rather than a decision-making body.[6] However, there has been a lively debate in CPA circles on the issue of resolutions. To quote Secretary-General Donahoe again:

> This is a long-standing debate in the Association at the policy level. The present practice is to have wide-ranging discussions rather than try to make people accept or reject a given point of view or resolution. We meet as a parliamentary organization and not as representatives of governments or countries.... . I think we have functioned fairly well without resolutions and any move in that direction would probably have fairly profound consequences for the Association.[7]

Conference for Small Countries

Following requests from branches in small countries for a forum to discuss problems peculiar to them in view of their size, the CPA introduced a separate Commonwealth Parliamentary Conference for Small Countries in 1981. The conference is held annually, immediately preceding the main conference. This meeting is for branches serving populations of up to 400 000, and is normally held at the same venue as the plenary conference.

Women Parliamentarians Group

During the thirty-fifth Commonwealth Parliamentary Conference held in Barbados in 1989, a group of women delegates met separately with a view to discussing issues relating to women and the Commonwealth response. Since then, the Commonwealth Women Parliamentarians Group (CWPG) has met regularly alongside the plenary conference, articulated problems confronting women and explored Commonwealth action to tackle them, as well as discussing issues of topical concern.

Regional Conferences

Alongside these conferences and meetings, several regional conferences are held under the aegis of the CPA. The African, British Isles, Mediterranean, Canadian, Caribbean, American and Atlantic regions organize conferences of branches in their respective regions and the Australian and the Pacific regions hold joint conferences. Naturally, the subjects for discussion in these Conferences lay stress on regional issues and interests which are better deliberated at regional conferences rather than at the Commonwealth Parliamentary Conferences.

Seminars

Under the auspices of the CPA, several seminars are organized regularly for the benefit of its members. Since 1951 the Association, in conjunction with its United Kingdom Branch, has hosted a seminar on Parliamentary Practice and Procedure. The seminar, held annually at Westminster, is open to all branches.

The CPA also annually jointly hosts another Commonwealth Parliamentary Seminar where, again, issues of parliamentary interest are discussed. The first such seminar was hosted by Zambia in 1989. This was followed by Canada in 1990, the Isle of Man in 1991, Trinidad and Tobago in 1992, Western Australia in 1993, India in 1994, Papua New Guinea in 1995 and Hong Kong in 1996.

Additionally, regional CPA seminars on practice and procedure are held in the Australian and Pacific regions as also in the Asian, Canadian and South-East Asian regions.

Publications

The CPA, through its various publications, keeps members informed of developments of constitutional, parliamentary and political interest. The quarterly CPA journal *The Parliamentarian* is a vast reservoir of information for seasoned parliamentarians and students of parliamentary political science. The association also publishes newsletters, books, reports and specialist studies. The CPA maintains at its headquarters secretariat in London a Parliamentary Information and Reference Centre.

In its work towards presenting a parliamentary perspective on global issues in the inter-governmental community, the CPA sponsors groups of eminent parliamentarians to undertake in-depth studies on parliamentary subjects. In 1994, the association, along with Wilton Park, an international policy assessment agency of the British Foreign and Commonwealth Office, sponsored a week-long conference, 'Strengthening Democracy Throughout the World: Electoral Systems, Election Monitoring and Good Government'. The conference was attended by representatives from Commonwealth countries, the European Union, and civil servants and diplomats. Encouraged by the success of this venture, in 1995 the CPA and Wilton Park co-hosted another conference, 'Parliament and People: Making Democratic Institutions More Representative, Responsible and Relevant'. In February 1996 the CPA and Wilton Park co-hosted another conference 'Parliamentary Democracy and Development: Allies or Adversaries?' (the proceedings of which are the subject-matter of this volume).

Election Monitoring

In another significant domain, the CPA has been co-operating with the Commonwealth Secretariat in constituting Election Observer Groups. A register of current and former members is maintained so that experienced politicians can be nominated to serve on Commonwealth missions. The CPA has also extended administrative support on several occasions. In the post-election scene, the CPA organizes seminars for newly elected legislators with a view to familiarizing them with the nuances of rules, practices and procedures. The association's efforts have led to the compilation of a Guide for Election Observers which has been very well received.[8]

Women in Public Life

The CPA has also made a detailed study of factors responsible for the limited participation of women in public life. The study entitled *Barriers to Women's Participation in Parliament*, was published in 1996.

Training of Parliamentary Staff

The association has embarked on another notable venture in the field of training parliamentary staff. In a welcome initiative, an Expert Group on 'Training of Parliamentary Staff' was set up by the secretary-general. The group met in New Delhi in February–March 1996 and surveyed a wide range of training methods available to legislatures and considered them in making their recommendations on the development of a curriculum for parliamentary training. It agreed that a guide should be published summarizing those recommendations in a form that would be of immediate practical use to all Commonwealth legislatures. The group specifically recommended that attention should be paid to creating an information database of training availability, to ensure that Commonwealth legislatures are aware of what could be provided for them. In addition to the existing provision of attachments at other legislatures, there was strong support for further development of workshops, the provision of resource people to assist with staff training, and the training of trainers. The group suggested to the secretary-general that it would be useful to consult colleagues in the Society of Clerks-at-the-Table during the course of the Kuala Lumpur Commonwealth Parliamentary Conference in August 1996. The secretary-general agreed that this would be of assistance in receiving comments and suggestions on the draft guide and its future use, in advance of the finalization of the text for publication. Accordingly, the first draft of *The Guidelines for the Training of Parliamentary Staff*, compiled by the group, was circulated among members of the society in July 1996 prior to the Kuala Lumpur meetings. While the endeavour was acclaimed by all at one of the society's sessions held on 22 August 1996, an extension of time until mid-October was given at the request of some members to send in their views. At its meeting the next day, the group decided to make modifications to the draft in the light of the discussions held among its own members as well as with members of the society. *Guidelines* was published in July 1997.

Future Role of the Association

Within the association, considerable thought is given to the future role of the CPA. Special emphasis is being laid on the need to implement the recommendations of the working paper prepared by the CPA in the early 1990s, which laid stress on establishing study groups; producing authoritative study papers and reference documents; developing expertise and availability for more active parliamentary seminars; being involved in election monitoring; and doing whatever is needed to be a positive force in strengthening and sustaining parliamentary democracy.[9]

In this age of the communication revolution, there have also been demands from members for the networking of databases and developing new resource bases. Many parliamentarians feel that there is immense potential for communication linkage among legislators throughout the Commonwealth.[10] As David Warner points out,

> tying existing networks in legislatures together or using existing bulletin-boards to share information of interest to individual legislators even where there are not

extensive computer resources might be investigated by the CPA as providing a cost-effective means of sharing information among all members of the association.[11]

Many have also called for greater branch-to-branch interaction so that parliamentarians can interact more easily, thereby contributing greatly towards inter-parliamentary co-operation. In fact, parliamentary diplomacy has acquired newer dimensions in this context. This aspect is being seriously looked into within the association. An exchange of views at individual and branch levels could go a long way towards fostering good relations in the community. The provincial politician needs such exposure to blossom into an effective parliamentarian with a wider perspective on national and international issues. Joan Sawicki rightly points out that the 'evolution from politician to parliamentarian takes a lot more hard work and that is why we need the CPA'.[12] Several parliamentarians also believe that the association could think about inviting guest speakers and experts to the seminars and conferences. As Sawicki suggests:

> With more active branches, regular annual activities and programmes, above and beyond attendances at conferences and seminars, and with guest speakers and workshops, we will be better able to move beyond the partisanship that can so often dominate, in a very negative way, our parliamentary institutions.[13]

The changing global situation warrants new concepts and fresh ideas, especially from the parliamentarians' perspective. The CPA could play a leading role in such a context. Addressing the delegates to the thirty-eighth Commonwealth Parliamentary Conference at Nassau, Commonwealth Secretary-General Chief Emeka Anyaoku voiced the aspirations the Community has on the association when he said:

> The CPA is not just another Commonwealth non-governmental organization. It is a living embodiment and testimony to what the Commonwealth is ultimately about. For the Commonwealth is either about the advocacy and promotion of its citizens or it is nothing. That is why the health of the CPA matters so much to us; for your strength is our strength.[14]

Fully realizing the responsibility it shoulders, the association has embarked on new initiatives to further its goals and enhance its role in the community. As Secretary-General Arthur Donahoe emphasizes, 'within the Commonwealth, the CPA will continue to play an increasingly important role in what has been described by many as the resurgence of democracy or the democratic renaissance which has developed since the end of the Cold War'.[15]

The Inter-Parliamentary Union

The Inter-Parliamentary Union (IPU) was founded in 1889 and is recognized as the first international organization committed to promoting the concept of peace and international arbitration.[16] When delegates from nine countries and three continents gathered in Paris in 1889 at the first Parliamentary Arbitration Conference, their basic purpose was to set up an arbitration court to settle disputes between states.[17] In 1892, the conference, meeting at Berne, as the Inter-Parliamentary Conference for International Arbitration, envisaged the constitution of an Inter-Parliamentary Bureau for International Arbitration. However, it was as late as 1908 that the present title of the Inter-Parliamentary Union eventually appeared in the statutes. Over the decades, the union has undergone profound changes, especially after the Second World War. In the process, the IPU has transformed itself from an association of individual parliamentarians into an international organization of parliaments, a focal point for dialogue and parliamentary diplomacy among legislators representing divergent political systems.

Aims and Objectives

In its multifarious activities, the union works for peace and co-operation among peoples and nations and for the establishment of representative institutions. With that in view, the IPU fosters contacts, co-ordination and the exchange of experience among parliaments and parliamentarians; considers questions of common interest and expresses its views on such issues to facilitate action by parliaments and parliamentarians; contributes to the defence and promotion of human rights, an essential factor of parliamentary democracy and development; and also contributes to better knowledge of the working of representative institutions and the strengthening of their means of action.[18] The IPU has also been an active supporter of the objectives of the United Nations. The union brings together the representatives of national parliaments for the objective study of political, economic, social and cultural problems of global significance. The members then submit to their respective parliaments and governments the resolutions adopted at the conferences and promote their implementation. With a total membership of 134 national parliaments and three associate members, the IPU is the largest worldwide parliamentary organization.

Inter-Parliamentary Conferences

The Inter-Parliamentary Conference, which is the principal statutory organ of the union, examines and studies problems placed on the agenda by the Inter-Parliamentary Council and makes recommendations representing the views of the organization as a whole. Alongside topical issues of a political nature often concerning local or regional conflicts, recent conferences – held twice a year since 1984 – have adopted resolutions on issues such as disarmament, development, health, population, environment, human rights and humanitarian law. At present, there are four committees which assist the conference in its work. These committees, set up by the Inter-Parliamentary Council, are those on Political Questions, International Security and Disarmament; on Parliamentary, Juridical and Human Rights Questions; on Economic and Social Questions; and on Education, Science, Culture and the Environment.

The IPU's global concern comes sharply into focus if one surveys the subjects that are taken up for discussion at the Inter-Parliamentary Conferences. Besides the mandatory general debate on the political, economic and social situation in the world, each conference discusses several other important larger issues of immediate concern. For instance, the ninety-third Inter-Parliamentary Conference held in Madrid in April 1995 discussed the following items on the agenda: the international community in the face of the challenges posed by calamities arising from armed conflict and by natural or man-made disasters: the need for a coherent and effective response through political and humanitarian assistance – means and mechanisms adapted to the situation; bioethics and its implications worldwide for human rights protection; and parliamentary action for women's access to, and participation in, decision-making structures aimed at achieving true equality for women.

The following subjects were discussed by delegates to the ninety-fourth Conference held in Bucharest in October 1995: parliamentary action to fight corruption and the need for international co-operation in this field; strategies for effective implementation of national and international commitments adopted at the world summit for social development in Copenhagen; and to comprehensively ban nuclear weapons testing and halt present nuclear weapon tests.

The ninety-fifth conference, held in Istanbul in April 1996, discussed the following items: the protection of minorities as a global issue and a prerequisite for stability, security and peace; conservation of the world's fish stock in order to provide an important source of protein and to ensure the continued viability and economic stability of fishing around the world; and fighting terrorism, an international phenomenon which threatens democracy and human rights as well as international peace and security and which hampers development – measures needed on national and international levels to prevent acts of terrorism.

It is clear that the union has been actively pursuing various global issues covering the political, economic and social spheres.

Regional Conferences

As well as the meetings of its statutory organs, the IPU organizes specialized worldwide and regional conferences and symposia bringing together parliamentarians and experts for the study of specific problems of international co-operation, development, human rights, the environment, and so on.

In the field of international security and *rapprochement*, the union has been involved in the holding of several Inter-Parliamentary Conferences on European Co-operation and Security. The union has also conducted two Inter-Parliamentary Conferences on Security and Co-operation in the Mediterranean. In collaboration with the United Nations, the union organized a symposium on Disarmament relating to Conventional Weapons as well as a conference on disarmament. It has held conferences covering the environment, population and development, human development, health, employment, agricultural development and food security, economic co-operation, drug abuse, human rights, rights of the child, participation of women in the political and parliamentary decision-making process and promotion of tourism. The union is also actively involved in election monitoring.

IPU and Women Parliamentarians

The IPU regularly conducts studies on the participation of women in political life and the distribution of seats between men and women in national parliaments. As in the case of the Commonwealth Parliamentary Conferences, women parliamentarians attending the Inter-Parliamentary Conferences also meet separately and debate issues confronting them and other topical issues.

Other Endeavours

The union launched a Technical Programme in 1973 through which international support and funding are mobilized for the purpose of strengthening the national parliaments of new and developing countries. It extends expert advice on the structure and working methods of legislatures and the organization of staff training courses and the provision of technical equipment and other material resources. It has periodically organized international symposia for parliamentarians, senior parliamentary officials and civil servants, scholars and experts on the functioning of parliamentary institutions. Information seminars covering all aspects of the IPU programmes and activities are also arranged.

Information Dissemination

Through its programmes for the study and promotion of representative institutions, the union gathers and disseminates information on the constitutional powers, structure and working methods of parliaments, on the status of their members, on electoral systems and on parliamentary elections and their results. It also publishes comparative studies on parliaments and electoral systems, periodicals, monographs and reference material for the use of parliamentarians, research scholars and the general public. The International Centre for Parliamentary Documentation (CIDP), set up in Geneva in 1965, promotes parliamentary research and serves as a repository of comparative parliamentary information.

IPU and the United Nations

The IPU works in close co-operation with the United Nations and its agencies, as also with various international organizations and inter-parliamentary bodies. Often described as the 'Parliament of Parliaments', the union has extended wholehearted support to the United Nations. This led to a Memorandum of Understanding between the United Nations and the IPU.[19] Working hand in hand with the United Nations, the union has long espoused the cause of preventive diplomacy and parliamentary diplomacy.

In conformity with the decision taken at its session in Madrid in March–April 1995, the Inter-Parliamentary Council held a special session at the headquarters of the United Nations in New York in August–September 1995 on the occasion of the fiftieth anniversary of the United Nations. The general theme of the session was 'The Parliamentary Vision for International Co-operation into the Twenty-first Century'. The deliberations concentrated mainly on two subjects: Agenda for Democracy, Peace and Sustainable Development; and Reinforcing and Democratizing the Structures for International Co-operation. At the end of the session, the participants adopted a declaration and a set of comprehensive findings and recommendations in which they laid out their parliamentary vision for international co-operation into the twenty-first century.

Parliamentary Diplomacy

In February 1992 the executive committee of the IPU issued a declaration on the 'Special Role of Parliamentary Diplomacy in Peacemaking and Peacekeeping', which assured the UN secretary-general of the union's support for UN activities.[20] Some instances of the union's initiatives in parliamentary diplomacy[21] include a resolution at the IPU conference in Mexico in 1986 unanimously condemning the Iran–Iraq conflict, which led to moves to end the war, and a resolution on human rights at the 1989 Budapest conference which resolved a deadlock at the Conference on Security and Co-operation in Europe (CSCE) in Madrid. The gradual *rapprochement* witnessed in the early 1990s between North and South Korea followed the IPU conference in Pyongyang in 1991, and the conference in Santiago the same year emphasized the Chilean people's yearning for democracy. The first contact between Argentina and the UK, following the Falklands (Malvinas) conflict, took place at the seventy-first conference in Geneva in 1984. Subsequent contact was maintained at successive Inter-Parliamentary Conferences which led directly to the resumption of diplomatic relations in 1990.

The Association of SAARC Speakers and Parliamentarians[22]

The nations and peoples of the South Asian subcontinent are bound by lasting ties of history and culture. The South Asian Association for Regional Co-operation (SAARC) was set up in 1985 with the avowed purpose of promoting peace, stability, amity and progress among the member states, namely Bangladesh, Bhutan, India, the Maldives, Nepal, Pakistan and Sri Lanka.

The success of any effort towards fostering greater co-operation depends to a large extent on the involvement of the people of the region and their commitment to support and strengthen institutional arrangements. In pursuance of the decision of successive SAARC summits stressing the importance of a greater degree of people-to-people co-operation, the speakers of the parliaments of SAARC countries, at a meeting held in Kathmandu in 1992, resolved to establish the Association of SAARC Speakers and Parliamentarians.

The charter of the association endeavours, among other things, to promote, co-ordinate and exchange experiences among member parliaments and to supplement and complement the work of SAARC and enhance knowledge of its principles and activities among parliamentarians; to provide a forum for the exchange of ideas and information on parliamentary practices and procedures and for making suggestions; and to co-operate in international forums on matters of common interest.

The first conference of the Association of SAARC Speakers and Parliamentarians was held in New Delhi on 22–4 July 1995. The conference was attended by 84 delegates – 26 from India and 58 from the other member parliaments. Forty-three observers from the Indian parliament and the state legislatures also attended the conference. The conference discussed two items: SAARC parliaments – their relations with the executive and the judiciary; and the committee system in SAARC parliaments. The New Delhi conference was a great success in bringing about greater understanding and goodwill among the parliamentarians of the South Asian region.

Parliamentarians, as representatives of the people, have a pivotal role in moulding public opinion and influencing policy decisions at governmental level. The opportunities that come their way at the inter-parliamentary conferences enable them to widen their horizons and look at issues from a broader perspective, rather than from a purely nationalistic viewpoint. They also stand to benefit from the exchange of views and experiences on the working of parliamentary institutions. Inter-parliamentary co-operation has been a major factor in promoting a better understanding of issues and situations by decision-makers. The personal contacts and professional relations developed at the conferences, seminars and symposia facilitate greater appreciation and awareness among the parliamentary community. Parliamentary organizations committed to the task of nurturing and furthering parliamentary ideals and espousing peace and prosperity everywhere have a challenging mission ahead of them in the years to come.

References

1 For a detailed history of the CPA, *see* Ian Grey, *The Parliamentarians: The History of the Commonwealth Parliamentary Association, 1911–1985* (Aldershot), 1986.
2 This section has drawn information from *Commonwealth Parliamentary Association: Aims, Organization, Activities* (London, 1996).
3 Colin Shepherd, 'The Chairman's View', in *The Parliamentarian*, vol.LXXIV, no.4, October 1993, p.191.
4 David Tonkin, 'The Commonwealth Parliamentary Association', in *Commonwealth Parliaments: A Commemorative Souvenir* (New Delhi, 1991), p.3.
5 Arthur Donahoe, in an interview for *Canadian Parliamentary Review*, vol.15, no.4, Winter 1992-3, p.46.
6 Arthur Donahoe, in his presentation at the conference, *Parliamentary Democracy and Development: Allies or Adversaries?*, Wiston House, UK, 15 February 1996.

7   Donahoe, *op. cit.*, Interview for *Canadian Parliamentary Review*, p.47.
8   For details, *see* Ron Gould, Christine Jackson and Loren Wills, *Strengthening Democracy: A Parliamentary Perspective* (Aldershot, 1995).
9   Joan Sawicki, 'CPA and the Parliamentary Profession', in *Canadian Parliamentary Review*, vol.15, no.3, Autumn 1992, p.13.
10 David Warner, 'CPA, Commonwealth Parliamentary Aid: Responding to World Changes', in *The Parliamentarian*, vol.LXXIV, no.4, October 1993, p.195.
11 *Ibid.*
12 Sawicki, *op. cit.*, p.12.
13 *Ibid.*, p.13.
14 Address by the Commonwealth Secretary-General, Chief Emeka Anyaoku, to the 38th Commonwealth Parliamentary Conference, 7 October 1992, *The Parliamentarian*, vol. LXXIV, no.1, January 1993, p.37.
15 Donahoe, *op. cit.*, in his presentation at the conference, *Parliamentary Democracy and Development: Adversaries or Allies?*
16 This section has drawn information from Inter-Parliamentary Union, *Inter-Parliamentary Union, 1993* (Geneva, 1993).
17 For a detailed history of the Inter-Parliamentary Union, *see* Yefime Zarjevski, *The People Have the Floor: A History of the Inter-Parliamentary Union* (Aldershot, 1989).
18 R.C. Bhardwaj (ed.), *The 89th Inter-Parliamentary Conference, New Delhi, April 1993 – A Report* (New Delhi, 1994), pp.1–5.
19 Michael Marshall, lecture, 'The Role of the IPU and the CPA in International Affairs', New Delhi, 29 February 1996.
20 Michael Marshall, 'Parliamentary Diplomacy: The IPU and the UN', in C.K. Jain (ed.), *Triumph of Democracy: An Overview of World Parliaments* (New Delhi, 1993), p.8.
21 *Ibid.*, pp.8–9.
22 This section is drawn from R.C. Bhardwaj, 'The First Conference of the Association of SAARC Speakers and Parliamentarians: An Overview', *Journal of Parliamentary Information*, vol.XLI, no.3, September 1995, pp.234–46.

APPENDICES

Appendix 1 List of Conference Participants

Aasland, Tertit von Hanno	Norway
Consultant, Ministry of Foreign Affairs, Oslo

Allen, Harold	Guernsey
Member of Parliament, St Peter Port

Berendsen, Bernard
(Speaker)	Netherlands
Director for Development Co-operation with Africa and the Middle East, Ministry of Foreign Affairs, The Hague

Bhardwaj, Romesh Chander
(Rapporteur)	India
Honorary Officer; former Secretary-General, Lok Sabha, New Delhi

Brandt, David	Montserrat
Member, Legislative Council for the Leeward District, Plymouth

Braun, Harald	Germany
Head, Parliament and Cabinet Division, Ministry of Foreign Affairs, Bonn

Broad, David	United Kingdom
Head, Commonwealth
Co-ordination Department, Foreign
and Commonwealth Office, London

Cichucka, Malgorzata	Poland
Council of Europe Desk Officer,
Department of European
Institutions, Ministry of Foreign
Affairs, Warsaw

Cody, Veronica	European Union
Administrator, Council of the
European Union, Brussels

Donahoe, Arthur
(Speaker)	Commonwealth Parliamentary
Association
Secretary-General, Commonwealth
Parliamentary Association, London

Dookeran, Winston	Trinidad and Tobago
Economic Adviser to the
Government, Port of Spain

Dorey, Jeremy	Jersey
Member of Parliament, St Helier

Ducklau, Volkere	Germany
Director, Policy Planning, Federal
Ministry of Economic Co-operation
and Development, Bonn

Faulkner, Greg
(Session Participant)	United Kingdom
Latin America Department, Foreign
and Commonwealth Office, London

Fontana, Andres
(Speaker)	Argentina
Director, International Security
Studies, Simon Rodriguez
Foundation, Buenos Aires

Appendix 1   139

Galanis, Philip	Bahamas Senator, Progressive Liberal Party, Nassau
Georges, Elton	Virgin Islands Deputy Governor, Tortola
Greene, Christopher	United Kingdom Head, Vietnamese Section, BBC World Service, London
Grove, Russell	Australia Clerk, Legislative Assembly, Sydney, New South Wales
Healey, John (Visiting Speaker)	United Kingdom Research Associate, Overseas Development Institute, London
Henry, Martin	Jamaica Consultant, Citizen's Charter Unit, Office of the Prime Minister, Kingston
Hopkinson, Nicholas	United Kingdom Senior Associate Director, Wilton Park, Steyning
Imlach, Andrew	Commonwealth Parliamentary Association Editor of Publications, Commonwealth Parliamentary Association Secretariat, London
Jendrzejczyk, Mike (Visiting Speaker)	United States of America Washington Director, Human Rights Watch/Asia, Washington
Judd, Lord Frank (Visiting Speaker)	United Kingdom House of Lords, London

Ligale, Andrew　　　　　　　　Kenya
　　　　　　　　　　　　　　　　Assistant Minister for Reclamation,
　　　　　　　　　　　　　　　　Regional and Water Development,
　　　　　　　　　　　　　　　　Nairobi

Lowey, Edmund　　　　　　　Isle of Man
　　　　　　　　　　　　　　　　Minister of Industry, Douglas

Lyon, Peter　　　　　　　　　United Kingdom
　　　　　　　　　　　　　　　　Academic Secretary, Institute of
　　　　　　　　　　　　　　　　Commonwealth Studies, London

Marshall, Sir Michael　　　　Inter-Parliamentary Union
(Visiting Speaker)　　　　　　　Former President, Inter-
　　　　　　　　　　　　　　　　Parliamentary Council; former
　　　　　　　　　　　　　　　　Chairman, British IPU Group,
　　　　　　　　　　　　　　　　House of Commons, London

May, Kyi Kyi　　　　　　　　Burma
　　　　　　　　　　　　　　　　Burmese Section, British
　　　　　　　　　　　　　　　　Broadcasting Corporation, London

McLaughlin, Audrey　　　　　Canada
　　　　　　　　　　　　　　　　Member of Parliament, House of
　　　　　　　　　　　　　　　　Commons, Ottawa

Medalinskas, Alvydas　　　　Lithuania
　　　　　　　　　　　　　　　　Embassy of Lithuania, United
　　　　　　　　　　　　　　　　Kingdom

Mistry, Percy　　　　　　　　India
(Speaker)　　　　　　　　　　　Chairman, Oxford International,
　　　　　　　　　　　　　　　　Oxford

Mtintso, Thenjiwe　　　　　　South Africa
　　　　　　　　　　　　　　　　ANC Member, Parliament of the
　　　　　　　　　　　　　　　　Republic of South Africa, Cape
　　　　　　　　　　　　　　　　Town

Nandi-Ndaitwah, Netumbo　　Namibia
(Speaker)　　　　　　　　　　　Deputy Minister of Foreign Affairs,
　　　　　　　　　　　　　　　　Windhoek

Paukku, Jorma	Finland Deputy Director-General, Ministry of Foreign Affairs, Helsinki
Paxman, Jeremy (Visiting Speaker)	United Kingdom Journalist, author and broadcaster; Presenter, *Newsnight*, British Broadcasting Corporation, Television Centre, London
Pelletier, Eric	Canada Desk Officer, Peace-building and Democratic Development Division, Department for Foreign Affairs and International Trade, Ottawa
Perton, Victor (Speaker)	Australia Member of Parliament, Legislative Assembly, East Doncaster, Victoria
Phumamphi, Johannah-Joy	Botswana Member of Parliament, National Assembly, Gaborone
Poley, Johannes	Netherlands Sociologist, Ministry of Foreign Affairs, The Hague
Puna, Ngereteina	Cook Islands Minister of Education and Cultural Development responsible for Legislative Service Vote and Ombudsman's Office, Rarotonga
Radice, Giles (Visiting Speaker)	United Kingdom Labour Member for Durham North, House of Commons, London
Ranchod, Bhadra	South Africa Deputy Speaker, National Assembly, Parliament of the Republic of South Africa, Cape Town

Reynolds, Diana
Commonwealth Parliamentary Association
Assistant Editor, Information Officer, Commonwealth Parliamentary Association Secretariat, London

Rolle, Anthony
(Speaker)
Bahamas
Minister of State for Health Services, Nassau

Sakalas, Aloyzas
Lithuania
Deputy Speaker, Head, Social Democratic Party, Seimas, Vilnius

Shepherd, Sir Colin
Commonwealth Parliamentary Association
Chairman, International Executive Committee, Commonwealth Parliamentary Association, London

Sivakova, Danica
Slovakia
Special Adviser, Department of Information and Analysis, National Council of the Slovak Republic, Bratislava

Ssemogerere, Paul
(Speaker)
Uganda
President-General, Democratic Party, Kampala

Stamiris, Eleni
(Visiting Speaker)
Commonwealth Secretariat
Director, Women's and Youth Affairs Division, London

Steffen, Thomas
Germany
Ministry of Finance, Bonn

Swaraj, Sushma
India
General Secretary and Spokesman, Bharatiya Janata Party, Lok Sabha, New Delhi

Timmer, Boris
Netherlands
Lecturer in International Relations, Royal Netherlands Army, Breda

Tiruchelvam, Neelan
(Speaker)
Sri Lanka
Member of Parliament, Parliament of Sri Lanka, Sri Jayewardenepura Kotte

Tittewella, Bertram
(Speaker)
Sri Lanka
Secretary-General of Parliament, Parliament of Sri Lanka, Sri Jayewardenepura Kotte

Vijayakrishnan, Keshav Chandran
(Rapporteur)
India
Joint Director, Lok Sabha Secretariat, New Delhi

Wapakabulo, James
(Speaker)
Uganda
Minister without Portfolio, Kampala

Wilkens, Ann
Sweden
Ambassador, Special Adviser to the Minister, Ministry of Foreign Affairs, Stockholm

Appendix 2 Conference Programme and Presenters

Presentations

The Contribution of Democracy to Economic Development: Is There a Correlation?

Dr John Healey
Research Associate, Overseas Development Institute, London

Parliamentary Democracy and Development: Allies or Adversaries?

The Rt Hon. the Lord Judd of Portsea
House of Lords,
United Kingdom

Development and Democracy in the Island States of the Caribbean

The Hon. Anthony C. Rolle, MP
Minister of State, Ministry of Health and Environment,
Bahamas

Promoting an Efficient and Independent Public Administration

Bertram Tittewella
Secretary-General,
Parliament of Sri Lanka

146 *Democracy and Development*

and

Giles Radice, MP
Labour Member for Durham North, House of Commons,
United Kingdom

The Relationship Between Government and the Military

Dr Andres Fontana
Director, International Security Research Programme,
Simon Rodriguez Foundation,
Buenos Aires

Development and Human Rights

Dr Neelan Tiruchelvam
Member of Parliament,
Sri Lanka

and

Mike Jendrzejczyk
Washington Director, Human Rights Watch/Asia,
Washington, DC

Freedom of the Press

Jeremy Paxman
Journalist, author and broadcaster; Presenter, *Newsnight*,
British Broadcasting Corporation, Television Centre,
London

Gender and Development

The Hon. Netumbo Nandi-Ndaitwah
Deputy Minister of Foreign Affairs,
Namibia

and

Eleni Stamiris
Director, Women's and Youth Affairs Division,
Commonwealth Secretariat,
London

Creating an Enabling Economic Environment for Development

Percy Mistry
Chairman, Oxford International,
Oxford

Facilitating the Proper Functioning of Parliament: The Role of the Commonwealth Parliamentary Association and Other Parliamentary Associations

Arthur Donahoe, QC
Secretary-General, Commonwealth Parliamentary
Association (CPA),
London

and

Sir Michael Marshall, MP
House of Commons, United Kingdom; former president,
Inter-Parliamentary Council

Discussion Groups

Indirect Democracy in Uganda

The Hon James Wapakabulo
Minister without Portfolio,
Kampala

and

The Hon. Dr Paul Ssemogerere
President-General, Democratic Party,
Kampala

148 *Democracy and Development*

The Singapore Model

Victor Perton, MP
Member of Parliament, Legislative Assembly, Victoria,
Australia

Aid and Good Governance

Bernard Berendsen
Director for Development Co-operation with Africa and the Middle East,
Ministry of Foreign Affairs,
Netherlands

Appendix 3 Discussion Group A: Indirect Democracy in Uganda

This discussion, ably chaired by Professor Peter Lyon, mirrored some of the key aspects of the constitutional debate in Uganda over the last four years as the country moves towards a new form of democracy which runs counter to the current global preference for multiparty, adversarial political systems. The group heard details of this new form of government from two eminent Ugandan political leaders: the Hon. James Wapakabulo, Minister without Portfolio in the National Resistance Movement government, who chaired the Constituent Assembly which drafted the country's new constitution, and Dr the Hon. Paul Ssemogerere, President-General of the Democratic Party, who left the government because of his opposition to aspects of the new constitution.

Uganda's political history since colonial times set precedents for some of the controversial aspects of the current government and of the new government which, under the 1995 constitution, must be in place by July 1996. Colonial councils contained both directly and indirectly elected members and served as a precedent for the continuation of indirect elections following independence in 1962. Indirect elections to the new National Assembly brought in representatives from the traditional Kingdom of Buganda to join the directly elected representatives from the competing political parties.

There was a difference of opinion in the group over whether parties were developing along religious lines and were therefore becoming divisive; but there was a consensus that Uganda then underwent close to two decades of authoritarian regimes under Milton Obote, Idi Amin and Milton Obote again. These regimes either abused or abolished democratic institutions and culminated in the brutal civil war which in 1986 brought into power the current government of the National Resistance Movement led by President Museveni.

This was followed by a consensual period in which it was agreed that partisan politics should be set aside so that peace and security could be restored, the economy could be revived, the infrastructure rebuilt and a democratic culture re-established.

During this period, the Museveni government sought to return Uganda to its tradition of indirect democracy by establishing a system in which only Village Committees were elected by direct voting using a queuing system, while all other government councils at the district, regional and national levels were indirectly elected from one council up to the next. Party politics were suspended for four years, later extended to nine years, as candidates for the Village Councils stood on their own merits, not on a party ticket.

To determine what form a more permanent government should take after this reconstruction period, a constitutional commission established in 1988 spent four years touring the country and hearing submissions. A Constituent Assembly elected in 1994 by a system of direct voting then debated and drafted the terms of the 1995 constitution based on the views received.

This new constitution retains an indirectly elected element, which is to represent such groups as women, the disabled and young people, although this is essentially small-scale token representation for groups other than women. The constitution generally provides for direct elections by universal adult suffrage and secret ballot for president and a parliament of members elected by the first-past-the-post system to represent single-member constituencies.

While it allows for the continuation of political parties, it further extends for another five years a ban on certain party activities. This was said to have been based on widespread public opposition to the reintroduction of adversarial politics which it is feared in some quarters would be divisive and lead to violence and instability. The National Resistance Movement led by President Museveni is not considered to be a political party.

Among the activities which parties are not allowed to conduct are: holding conferences to elect new leaders or formulate policies, holding public rallies, opening or operating party branches or sponsoring candidates in elections. New parties cannot be established for two years until the new parliament enacts enabling legislation. It was argued that these restrictions make parties lifeless and will therefore generate political frustration among those not in the National Resistance Movement. It was feared that this would lead to turmoil.

Bearing in mind the fact that some of the country's authoritarian leadership were uneducated – Idi Amin most notably – a further restriction was placed on the democratic system: candidates for the presidency and for seats in parliament will have to be high school graduates or hold an equivalent qualification. This latter condition has yet to be defined for a society which lacks universal mandatory secondary education.

It has not yet been decided when elections will be held, whether presidential and parliamentary votes will be held simultaneously and when public education programmes will begin or what form they will take.

However, an independent electoral commission is in place, the updating of the 1994 electoral register is being completed and international electoral assistance and observers will be welcomed. There is a question over the accuracy of the register.

The parliament to be elected in the coming months will be composed of individuals who will neither campaign on party tickets nor form into parties once they are elected. They will hold the usual parliamentary powers to legislate, scrutinize and approve government budgets and question the executive. Ministers do not have to be MPs, but all ministerial and other senior public appointments will be subject to parliamentary approval.

The effect of the absence of parties on parliament was debated. While it was argued that the absence of parties will undermine concerted and effective opposition to the government, it was also maintained that the absence of a disciplined government back bench will mean that ministers must win parliamentary support for each policy and Bill rather than being able to rely on party whipping.

Opposing perspectives also exist on the performance of the current government. Charges that Uganda is being governed by an intimidating personality cult are countered by contentions that ministers now fear a hostile Assembly where they have no guarantee that their programmes will be passed.

It was argued that the continued suspension of functional party politics was included in the constitution at the insistence of President Museveni, but it was also asserted that the vast majority of Ugandans support the political structure being put in place.

The constitution provides for an open debate in three years' time on whether adversarial party politics is to resume. This is to be followed by a referendum a year later. One view states that this gives Uganda's political leaders four years of parliamentary government to demonstrate to a cautious electorate that the excesses and divisions of the past will not be repeated. On the other hand, it is argued that 33 years of independence and an even longer history of advanced political culture make a further delay unnecessary and will simply further entrench the existing government.

While there were strongly held differences of opinion within the group, and apparently between opposing political leaders in Uganda, as well as a number of remaining grey areas, there was a consensus that the ability of

Ugandans to discuss their differences openly and in a parliamentary manner bodes well for the future of the country as a fully democratic member of the Commonwealth.

Report by Andrew Imlach, Editor, CPA Secretariat

Appendix 4 Discussion Group B: The Singapore Model

The session was chaired by the Hon. Johannah-Joy Phumaphi (Botswana) and introduced by Mr Victor Perton (Victoria).

The salient features of the Singapore school were outlined, as:

- The belief that human rights are not universal, but that they differ according to cultural factors and that Singaporean society is a mature expression of democracy with Asian values (i.e. the individual is important as part of a group, and not as the centrepiece of society; the emphasis is on the common good rather than on individual rights).
- That in order to develop, a country needs discipline rather than democracy, and that democracy is actually hostile to development.

The society produced by this model is apparently very ordered, clean and safe, and has a vibrant economy.

Elements of the model which cause unrest to Western observers include the fact that it has created a greater acceptance of a hierarchically structured society, and a situation wherein the dominant party can remain in power for upwards of 20 years. Opponents also draw attention to the practice of detention without trial, the coercion of government critics and opposition figures, various constraints on the freedom of the press, and censorship, which extends to reading lists in the National University.

Other criticisms centre on the perception that its economic success comes from its illiberal political structures and that its proclaimed consensus model is not true communitarianism as all obligations are imposed from above. Critics also complain that the emphasis on the citizens' 'Chineseness' is stressed to the detriment of other communities in Singapore (Malays and guest workers), whose rights are apparently often violated.

Group participants explored whether aspirations and values are the same the world over, or if there are beliefs and qualities that are peculiar to a particular nation or region. No clear consensus was reached on this, some delegates asserting that there were, others arguing that, while common values may exist, there are numerous manifestations of them.

Some delegates noted that the lack of democracy in Singapore so deplored by critics was the result of informed intelligent trade-offs made by individuals in order that they might progress economically. Singapore citizens have many rights, including the right to life, property rights and freedom of movement, but have willingly surrendered others for pragmatic reasons. It was noted that many Singaporean students study overseas but choose to return. Similarly, it was noted that if the regime was so intolerable the citizens were wealthy enough to leave, but do not do so, though other delegates disputed that it was as simple as that.

It was noted that democratic systems of government in some countries of the world were unable to furnish their citizens with the basic necessities of life, such as food, whereas in contrast the authoritarian Singapore regime provided a good standard of living for its citizens, with ample access to health care and education. It was argued that if democracy as a system of government results in the suppression of the aspirations of the majority (keeping them poor for ever) then it should be questioned.

It was noted that while the Singapore model was not intended to be transitory, change was inevitable. It was felt that many of the pettier restrictions (prohibitions against the chewing of gum, the playing of loud rock music and long hairstyles, etc.) would eventually right themselves as the wealthy children of once poor (and therefore more passive) parents will not tolerate such nonsense for ever.

Many delegates commented on the attractiveness of Singaporean society, noting that their own countries wished to emulate its economic success, along with several of its other features such as the cleanliness of the streets and the efficiency of its bureaucracy. Less authoritarian regimes have similar legislation to that on the statute books in Singapore (for example, laws relating to litter or graffiti), but fail to enforce it. Singaporean society is a disciplined society, which many delegates felt was an asset that their own societies lacked.

The discussion explored the definitions of various terms used – discipline and democracy, and also the nature of leadership – whether democracy is pliable and can be adapted in different cultures, and if self-professed democrats the world over had the right to interfere. The notion that authoritarian rule is necessary for economic growth was also explored, but no firm conclusions were reached.

The fact that some delegates were vehemently opposed to the Singapore model, while others acknowledged great admiration for the end-product produced by that model, meant that the discussion was lively and sustained and concluded with some delegates asserting that Singaporeans had the right to choose a system that delivered their avowed goals (even if that involved the surrender of certain rights) without endless criticism from outside, while others felt that it was not possible to know if the people are oppressed in a system where opposition parties are suppressed, or even if the system has been freely chosen by the Singaporeans, albeit for pragmatic reasons.

Report by Diana Reynolds, Assistant Editor, CPA Secretariat

Appendix 5 Discussion Group C: Aid and Good Governance

Mr Bernard Berendsen addressed the meeting by outlining the conditions that the World Bank and the International Monetary Fund (IMF) together with the donor countries would require for aid to be given.

Are the recipients of aid practising human civil rights programmes, electoral reforms and economic and social policies which would provide the three levels of conditions that would satisfy the World Bank and the International Monetary Fund?

- Firstly, that the country was a democratic capitalist country.
- Secondly, that the country had a political system that practised democracy, where there were free elections, social and economic reforms and an efficient civil service to administer the affairs of government.
- Thirdly, that aid had a political conditionality – it would only be given to countries with genuine systemic change to democracy.

There followed a full and frank discussion by members of the group, many of whom represented countries which receive aid.

A consensus of opinion was that conditional aid could be a hindrance to good government and that, in imposing conditions, the donor countries did not appreciate fully the social and economic requirements for aid of the recipient countries.

There was a feeling that, during the Cold War period, aid was given freely but that, with the demise of the Cold War, aid was now given conditionally upon good governance. This reflected Western values, without having sufficient regard to the longstanding culture of those countries.

The recipient countries did not totally disagree with conditionality, but felt that it had to be accepted by both parties, not imposed.

There was a view put forward that recipients of aid should have a greater say in the social and economic investment needs of their own countries; otherwise they perceive themselves as subservient to the donors with a consequent loss of sovereignty.

There was concern that donor nations do not practise what they preach when it comes to human rights. For instance, the USA has the death penalty while Namibia does not.

There was also concern that donor countries required the recipient countries to spend their aid with them, thereby reducing the recipient countries' ability to develop their own infrastructures to suit their social and economic needs.

Aid can be in conflict with good governance when that aid is suddenly withdrawn. Would it not be better to develop trade rather than aid, and allow developing countries to develop their infrastructures independently?

Good governance must be responsible for the budgetary choices that have to be made on behalf of its citizens. This can only be achieved in a parliamentary democracy whereby the transfer of power can be achieved in free and open elections when the people of a country by universal suffrage will determine who governs them.

Report by Deputy Jeremy Dorey, States of Jersey

SELECT BIBLIOGRAPHIES

1 Development and Human Rights

Abdullahi Ahmed An-Na'Im and Deng, Francis M., *Human Rights in Africa: Cross-Cultural Perspectives* (Washington, DC: Brookings Institution), 1990.

Afkami, Mahnaz (ed.), *Faith and Freedom: Women's Human Rights in the Muslim World* (London: I.B. Tauris), 1995.

Alhaji Sir Dawda Kairaba Jawara, 'The Commonwealth and Human Rights', *The Round Table*, no.321, January 1992, pp.37–42.

Amnesty International, *Human Rights are Women's Rights* (London: Amnesty International Publications), 1995.

Arat, Zehra F., *Democracy and Human Rights in Developing Countries* (Boulder, Col.: Lynne Rienner), 1991.

Arnolds, Eileen McCarthy (ed.), *Africa, Human Rights and the Global System: Political Economy of Human Rights in a Changing World* (Studies in Human Rights No.15) (London: Greenwood Press), 1994.

Baehr, P.R. (ed.), *Human Rights in Developing Countries: Year Book*, (Deventer, Netherlands: Kluwer Law and Taxation Publishers), 1994.

Barsh, R.L., 'Democratization and Development', *Human Rights Quarterly*, 14/1992, pp.120–34.

Baxi, Upendra, *Inhuman Wrongs and Human Rights: Unconventional Essays* (New Delhi: Har-Anand Publications), 1994.

Beetham, David (ed.), *Politics and Human Rights* (Oxford: Blackwell Publishers), 1995.

Blackburn, Robert and Taylor, John (eds), *Human Rights for the 1990s: Legal, Political and Ethical Issues* (London: Mansell), 1990.

Bobbio, Norberto, *The Age of Rights* (Cambridge: Polity Press), 1995.

Chan Heng Chee, 'Democracy, Human Rights and Social Justice as Key Factors in Balanced Development', *The Round Table,* no.329, January 1994, pp.27–36.

Cohen, Ronald, Hyden, Goran and Nagan, Winston P. (eds), *Human Rights and Governance in Africa* (Gainesville, Fla.: University Press of Florida), 1993.

Cook, Rebecca J. (ed.), *Human Rights of Women: National and International Perspectives* (Philadelphia: The University of Pennsylvania Press), 1993.

Craven, Mathew, *The International Covenant on Economic, Social and Cultural Rights: A Perspective on Its Development* (Oxford: Clarendon Press), 1995.

Diamond, Larry (ed.), *Democratic Revolution: Struggles for Freedom and Pluralism in the Developing World* (London: Freedom House), 1992.

Donnelly, Jack, *International Human Rights* (Boulder, Col.: Westview Press), 1993.
Elizabeth, Ann, *Islam and Human Rights: Tradition and Politics* (London: Pinter Publishers), 1995.
Fenwick, Helen, *Civil Liberties* (London: Cavendish Publishing Ltd), 1994.
Forsythe, David P., *Human Rights and Development: International Views* (Basingstoke: Macmillan), 1989.
Freedom House, *Freedom in the World: Political Rights and Civil Liberties 1993–94* (New York: Freedom House), 1994.
'Freedom and Prosperity', *The Economist*, vol.320, no.7713, 29 June 1991, pp.15–18.
Gaete, Rolando, *Human Rights and the Limits of Critical Reason* (Aldershot: Dartmouth), 1993.
Galtung, Johan, *Human Rights in Another Key* (Cambridge: Polity Press), 1994.
Human Rights Watch World Report 1995: Events of 1994 (New York: Human Rights Watch), 1994.
Inter-Parliamentary Union, *Parliamentary Human Rights Bodies, World Directory* (Geneva: Inter-Parliamentary Union), 1993.
Kymlicka, Will (ed.), *The Rights of Minority Cultures* (Oxford: Oxford University Press), 1995.
Mauzy, Diane K., 'Human Rights in Indonesia, Malaysia and Singapore: Contrasting Views from ASEAN, Canada and Australia', *The Round Table*, no.335, July 1995, pp.279–96.
McCarthy-Arnolds, Eileen, Penna, David R. and Sobrepena, Debra Joy Cruz (eds), *Africa, Human Rights and the Global System: The Political Economy of Human Rights in a Changing World* (Westport, Conn.: Greenwood), 1994.
Miller, William L. (ed.), *Alternatives to Freedom: Arguments and Opinions* (London: Longman Higher Education), 1995.
Monshipouri, Mahmood, *Democratization, Liberalization and Human Rights in the Third World* (Boulder, Col.: Lynne Rienner), 1995.
Nino, Carlos Santiago, *The Ethics of Human Rights* (Oxford: Clarendon Press), 1993.
Norman, Richard, *Studies in Equality* (Aldershot: Avebury), 1995.
Olson, M., 'Dictatorship, Democracy and Development', *American Political Science Review*, 87/1993, pp.567–76.
Owens, Edgar, *The Future of Freedom in the Developing World: Economic Development as Political Reform* (New York: Pergamon Press), 1987.
Paul, Ellen Frankel, Miller, Fred D. and Paul, Jeffrey, *Economic Rights* (Cambridge: Cambridge University Press), 1992.

Peters, Julie and Wolper, Andrea (eds), *Women's Rights, Human Rights: International Feminist Perspectives* (New York: Routledge), 1995.

Peterson, Spike V. and Runyan, Anne Sission, *Global Gender Issues* (Boulder, Col.: Westview Press), 1993.

Reoch, Richard (ed.), *Human Rights: The New Consensus* (London: Regency Press, in association with the United Nations High Commissioner for Refugees), 1994.

Savio, Roberto, Reoch, Richard and Dallas, Elaina (eds), *Human Rights: The New Consensus* (London: Regency Press), 1994.

Shute, Stephen and Hurley, Susan (eds), *On Human Rights* (New York: Basic Books), 1993.

Sorensen, G., *Democracy and Authoritarianism: Consequences for Economic Development* (Aarhus: Institute of Political Science), 1992.

Spindler, Z.A., 'Liberty and Development: A Further Empirical Perspective', *Public Choice*, 1991, pp.197–210.

Sunstein, Cass R., *Democracy and the Problem of Free Speech* (New York: Free Press), 1993.

Tang, James T.H. (ed.), *Human Rights and International Relations in the Asia Pacific Region* (London: Pinter Publishers), 1995.

Thamilmaran, V.T., *Human Rights in Third World Perspective* (New Delhi: Har-Anand Publications), 1992.

Tomasevski, Katarina, *Development Aid and Human Rights Revisited* (London: Pinter Publishers), 1993.

Tomasevski, Katarina, *Women and Human Rights* (London: Zed Books), 1993.

United Nations Centre for Human Rights, *Human Rights: A Compilation of International Instruments* (New York: United Nations Centre for Human Rights), 1994.

United Nations Centre for Human Rights, *United Nations Action in the Field of Human Rights* (New York: United Nations Centre for Human Rights), 1994.

United Nations Centre for Human Rights, *United Nations Reference Guide in the Field of Human Rights* (New York: United Nations Centre for Human Rights), 1993.

United Nations Centre for Social Development and Humanitarian Affairs, *Compendium of International Conventions Concerning the Status of Women* (New York: United Nations), 1988.

United Nations Centre for Social Development and Humanitarian Affairs, *The Impact of Economic and Political Reform on the Status of Women in Eastern Europe* (Proceedings of a United Nations Regional Seminar, Vienna, 8–12 April 1991) (New York: Centre for Social Development and Humanitarian Affairs), 1992.

Weede, E., 'The Impact of Democracy or Repressiveness on the Quality of Life, Income Distribution and Economic Growth Rates', *International Society*, 1993, pp.177–95.
Weiner, Myron, *The Global Migration Crisis: The Challenge to States and to Human Rights* (London: HarperCollins), 1995.
Working towards Gender Equality (Programme 1993–95) (London: The Commonwealth Secretariat).
Working towards Gender Equality: Programme Initiatives (London: The Commonwealth Secretariat).

2 Parliamentary Democracy and Development

Adam, Christopher, Cavendish, William and Mistry, Percy S., *Adjusting Privatization: Case Studies from Developing Countries* (London: James Currey), 1992.
Adedeji, Adebayo (ed.), *Africa within the World: Beyond Dispossession and Dependence* (London: Zed Books, in association with the African Centre for Development and Strategic Studies), 1993.
Adriaansen, Willem L.M. and Waardenburg, J. George (eds), *A Dual World Economy: Forty Years of Development Experience* (Bombay: Oxford University Press), 1992.
Agrawal, Pradeep et al., *Economic Restructuring in East Asia and India: Perspectives on Policy Reforms* (London: Macmillan), 1995.
Ahooja-Patel, Krishna, *Women and Sustainable Development: An International Dimension* (New Delhi: Ashish Publishing House), 1995.
Allen, Tim and Thomas, Alan, *Poverty and Development in the 1990s* (Oxford: Oxford University Press), 1992.
Apter, David E. and Rosberg, Carl G. (eds), *Political Development and the New Realism in Sub-Saharan Africa* (Charlottesville: University Press of Virginia), 1994.
Arat, Zehra F., *Democracy and Human Rights in Developing Countries* (Boulder, Col.: Lynne Rienner), 1991.
Archer, Robin, *Economic Democracy: the Politics of Feasible Socialism* (Oxford: Clarendon Press), 1995.
Archibugi, Damile and Held, David (eds), *Cosmopolitan Democracy: An Agenda for a New World Order* (Cambridge: Polity Press), 1995.
Arthur, J., *Democracy: Theory and Practice* (Andover, Hants: International Thomson Publishing Services Ltd), 1991.
Ashworth, Georgina, *When Will Democracy Include Women?* (London: Change), 1992.
Aslanbeigui, Nahid, Pressman, Steven and Summerfield, Gale, *Women in*

the Age of Economic Transformation: Gender Impact of Reforms in Post-Socialist and Developing Countries (London: Routledge), 1994.
Aslund, A. and Layard R. (eds), Changing the Economic System in Russia (New York: St Martin's Press), 1993.
Attfield, Robin and Wilkins, Barry (eds), International Justice and the Third World: Studies in the Philosophy of Development (London: Routledge), 1992.
Bagchi, Amiya Kumar (ed.), Democracy and Development (Proceedings of the IEA Conference held in Barcelona, Spain) (Basingstoke: Macmillan), 1995.
Bardhan, Pranab, Datta-Chaudhuri, Mrinal and Krishnan, T.N. (eds), Development and Change (Essays in honour of K.N. Raj) (Bombay: Oxford University Press), 1993.
Barsh, R.L., 'Democratization and Development', Human Rights Quarterly, 14/1992, pp.120–34.
Bayart, Jean-Francois, The State in Africa: the Politics of the Belly (London: Longman), 1993.
Beetham, David (ed.), Defining and Measuring Democracy (London: Sage Publications), 1994.
Berntzen, Einar, 'Democratic Consolidation in Central America: A Qualitative Comparative Approach', Third World Quarterly, vol.14, no.3, 1993, pp.589–604.
Beyene, Asmelash and Mutahaba, Galase (eds), The Quest for Constitutionalism in Africa: Selected Essays on Constitutionalism, the Nationality Problem, Military Rule and Party Politics (Frankfurt: Paul Lang), 1994.
Bhagwati, Jagdish, 'Democracy and Development: New Thinking on an Old Generation', Indian Economic Review, vol.30, no.1, January–June 1995, pp.1–8.
Bhagwati, J., India in Transition (Oxford: Clarendon Press), 1993.
Bhalla, A.S., Uneven Development in the Third World: A Study of China and India (2nd revised and enlarged edn) (Basingstoke: Macmillan), 1995.
Bienefeld, Manfred, 'The New World Order: Echoes of a New Imperialism', Third World Quarterly, vol.15, no.1, 1994, pp.31–48.
Bissio, Roberto Remo (ed.), The World: A Third World Guide 1995/96 (Montevideo: Institute del Tercer Mundo), 1996.
Borner, Silvio, Brunetti, Aymo and Weder, Beatrice, Political Credibility and Economic Development (Basingstoke: Macmillan), 1995.
Bremer, Stuart A. and Hughes, Barry B., Disarmament and Development: A Design for the Future (Englewood Cliffs, NJ: Prentice-Hall), 1990.
Bruno, M., Crisis, Stabilization and Economic Reform (Oxford: Clarendon Press), 1993.

Budge, Ian and McKay, David (eds), *Developing Democracy: Comparative Research in Honour of Jean Blondel* (London: Sage Publications), 1993.

Butcher, Tony, *Delivering Welfare: The Governance of the Social Services in the 1990s* (Buckingham: Open University Press), 1995.

Bystydzienski, Jill M. (ed.), *Women Transforming Politics: Worldwide Strategies for Empowerment* (Bloomington: Indiana University Press), 1992.

Campbell, Adrian, *The Challenge to the Centre* (London: Pitman Publishing), 1995.

Carew-Reid, Jeremy, Presscott-Allen, Robert, Bass, Stephen and Dalal-Clayton, Barry, *Strategies for National Sustainable Development* (London: Earthscan, in association with the World Conservation Union and the International Institute for Environment and Development), 1994.

Castells, M., *The Developmental City-State in an Open Economy: The Singapore Experience* (Berkeley Round Table on International Economy, Working Paper no.31) (Berkeley: University of California), 1988.

Chabal, Patrick, *Power in Africa: An Essay in Political Interpretation* (London: Macmillan), 1992.

Chalker, Lynda, 'Development and Democracy: What Should the Commonwealth be Doing?', *The Round Table*, no.329, January 1994, pp.23–6.

Change for the Better: Global Change and Economic Development (London: Commonwealth Secretariat), 1991.

Chan Heng Chee, 'Democracy, Human Rights and Social Justice as Key Factors in Balanced Development', *The Round Table*, no.329, January 1994, pp.27–36.

Chapman, David, *Reinventing Democracy* (London: Institute for Social Interventions), 1993.

Clapham, Christopher, 'The Collapse of Socialist Development in the Third World', *Third World Quarterly*, vol.13, no.1, 1992, pp.13–26.

Clapham, Christopher, 'Democratisation in Africa: Obstacles and Prospects', *Third World Quarterly*, vol.14, no.3, 1993, pp.423–38.

Cohen, Robin and Goulbourne, Harry (eds), *Democracy and Socialism in Africa* (Boulder, Col.: Westview Press), 1991.

Cohen, Ronald, Hyden, Goran and Nagan, Winston P. (eds), *Human Rights and Governance in Africa* (Gainesville, Fla.: University Press of Florida), 1993.

Colburn, Forrest D. and Rahmato, Dessalegn, 'Rethinking Socialism in the Third World', *Third World Quarterly*, vol.13, no.1, 1992, pp.159–74.

Copp, D., Hampton, J. and Roemer J. (eds), *The Idea of Democracy* (New York: Cambridge University Press), 1994.

Dahl, R., *Democracy and its Critics* (New Haven, Conn.: Yale University Press), 1989.

Danopoulos, Constantine P. (ed.), *Civilian Rule in the Developing World: Democracy on the March?* (Boulder, Col.: Westview Press), 1992.
Danopoulos, Constantine P., *From Military to Civilian Rule* (London: Routledge), 1991.
Davidian, Zaven N., *Economic Disparities among Nations: A Threat to Survival in a Globalized World* (Calcutta: Oxford University Press), 1994.
Decalo, Samuel, *Coups and Army Rule in Africa* (New Haven, Conn.: Yale University Press), 1990.
'Democracy and Growth', *The Economist*, vol.332, no.7878, 27 August 1994, pp.15–17.
'Democracy Works Best', *The Economist*, vol.332, no.7878, 27 August 1994, pp.9–10.
Devlin, John F. and Yap, Nomita T., 'Sustainable Development and the NICs: Cautionary Tales for the South in the New World (Dis)Order', *Third World Quarterly*, vol.15, no.1, 1994, pp.49–62.
Deyo, F.C. (ed.), *The Political Economy of the New Asian Industrialism* (Ithaca, NY: Cornell University Press), 1987.
Diamond, L., 'Economic Development and Democracy Reconsidered', *American Behavioural Scientist* 35 (4/5), 1992, pp.450–99.
Diamond, Larry (ed.), *Democracy in Developing Countries: Persistence, Failure and Renewal* (London: Adamantine Press Ltd), 1992.
Diamond, Larry (ed.), *Democratic Revolution: Struggles for Freedom and Pluralism in the Developing World* (London: Freedom House), 1992.
Diamond, Larry (ed.), *Political Culture and Democracy in Developing Countries* (Boulder, Col.: Lynne Rienner), 1993.
DiIulio, John J. Jr, *Deregulating the Public Policy: Can Government be Improved?* (Washington, DC: Brookings Institution), 1994.
Dixon, Chris and Drakakis-Smith, David (eds), *Economic and Social Development in Pacific Asia* (London: Routledge), 1993.
Doel, Hans Van and Velthoven, Ben Van, *Democracy and Welfare Economics* (Cambridge: Cambridge University Press), 1993.
Dominguez, Jorge I. (ed.), *Democracy in the Caribbean: Political, Economic and Social Perspectives* (Baltimore: Johns Hopkins University Press), 1993.
Dorraj, Manochagh (ed.), *The Changing Political Economy of the Third World* (Boulder, Col.: Lynne Rienner), 1995.
Dréze, J. and Sen A. (eds), *The Political Economy of Hunger* (vol.3) (Oxford: Clarendon Press), 1991.
Dunn, J. (ed.), *Democracy: The Unfinished Journey, 508 BC to AD 1993* (Oxford: Oxford University Press), 1992.
Edie, Carlena J. (ed.), *Democracy in the Caribbean: Myths and Realities* (Westport, Conn.: Praeger), 1994.

Eisenstadt, S.N. (ed.), *Democracy and Modernity* (Leiden: E.J. Brill), 1992.
Fenwick, J., *Managing Local Government* (London: International Thomson Business Press), 1995.
Field, Graham, *Economic Growth and Political Change in Asia* (Basingstoke: Macmillan), 1995.
Foreign and Commonwealth Office, *Good Government in Africa* (Wilton Park Paper 54) (London: HMSO), 1992.
Forsythe, David P., *Human Rights and Development: International Views* (Basingstoke: Macmillan), 1989.
Frank, André Gunder, *Capitalism and Underdevelopment in Latin America: Historical Studies of Chile and Brazil* (New York and London: Modern Reader Paperbacks), 1969.
Franke, Richard W. and Chasin, Barbara H. (eds), *Kerala: Development through Radical Reforms* (New Delhi: Promilla and Co., in collaboration with the Institute for Food and Development Policy), 1994.
'Freedom and Prosperity', *The Economist*, vol.320, no.7713, 29 June 1991, pp.15–18.
Friedman, Edward (ed.), *The Politics of Democratization: Generalizing East Asian Experiences* (Boulder, Col.: Westview Press), 1994.
Frimpong-Ansah, J.H. and Ingham, Barbara (eds), *Saving for Economic Recovery in Africa* (London: James Currey, for the African Centre for Economic Policy Research), 1992.
Fukuyama, Francis, 'Capitalism and Democracy: The Missing Link', *Journal of Democracy*, vol.3, no.3, July 1992.
Fukuyama, Francis, 'Democratization and International Security', *Adelphi Papers*, no.266, Winter 1991–2.
Fukuyama, Francis, *The End of History and the Last Man* (New York: Free Press), 1992.
Gibbon, Peter, *Social Change and Economic Reform in Africa* (Uppsala: Scandinavian Institute of African Studies), 1993.
Gills, Barry and Rocamora, Joel, 'Low Intensity Democracy', *Third World Quarterly*, vol.13, no.3, 1992, pp.501–23.
Gills, Barry and Rocamora, Joel, *Low Intensity Democracy: Political Power in the New World Order* (Oxford: Pluto Press), 1993.
Gills, Barry and Qadir, Shahid (eds), *Regimes in Crisis: the Post-Soviet Era and the Implications for Development* (London: Zed Books), 1995.
Goh, Keng-Swee, *Public Administration and Economic Development in LDCs* (London: TPRC), 1983.
Gould, Ron, Jackson, Christine and Wells, Loren, *Strengthening Democracy: A Parliamentary Perspective* (Aldershot: Dartmouth), 1995.
Graham, Norman A. (ed.), *Seeking Security and Development: the Impact of*

Military Spending and Arms Transfers (Boulder, Col.: Lynne Rienner), 1994.
Green, Philip (ed.), *Democracy* (New Jersey: Humanitio Press), 1993.
Greenberg, Douglas (ed.), *Constitutionalism and Democracy: Transitions in the Contemporary World* (American Council of Learned Societies, Comparative Constitutions Papers) (New York: Oxford University Press), 1993.
Griesgraber, Jo Marie and Gunter, Bernhard G. (eds), *Promoting Development: Effective Global Institutions for the Twenty-first Century* (London: Pluto Press, with Center of Concern, Washington, DC), 1995.
Griffin, Clifford E., 'Democracy in the Commonwealth Caribbean', *Journal of Democracy*, vol.4, no.2, April 1993, pp.84–94.
Grindle, Merilee S., *Challenging the State: Crisis and Innovation in Latin America and Africa* (Cambridge: Cambridge University Press), 1996.
Grugel, Jean, *Politics and Development in the Caribbean Basin: Central America and the Caribbean in the New World Order* (Basingstoke: Macmillan), 1995.
Guy, Arnold, *The End of the Third World* (Basingstoke: Macmillan), 1993.
Hadenius, Axel, *Democracy and Development* (Cambridge: Cambridge University Press), 1992.
Haggard, Stephen and Kaufman, Robert R., *The Political Economy of Democratic Transitions* (Princeton, NJ: Princeton University Press), 1995.
Haggard, Stephen and Kaufman, Robert R., *The Politics of Economic Adjustment* (Princeton, NJ: Princeton University Press), 1992.
Ha-Joon Chang and Rowthorn, Robert (eds), *The Role of the State in Economic Change* (Oxford: Clarendon Press), 1995.
Harrison, Ross, *Democracy* (London: Routledge), 1993.
Healey, John and Robinson, Mark, *Democracy, Governance and Economic Policy: Sub-Saharan Africa in Comparative Perspective* (London: Overseas Development Institute), 1994.
Held, David, *Democracy and the Global Order* (Oxford: Polity Press), 1995.
Held, David (ed.), *Prospects for Democracy: North, South, East, West* (Oxford: Polity Press), 1993.
Helliwell, J.F., *Empirical Linkages between Democracy and Economic Growth* (NBER Working Paper no.4066) (Cambridge, Mass.: National Bureau of Economic Research), 1992.
Himmelstrand, Ulf, Kinyanjui, Kabiru and Mburugu, Edward (eds), *African Perspectives on Development* (London: James Currey), 1994.
Hirst, Paul, *Associative Democracy: New Forms of Economic and Social Governance* (Cambridge: Polity Press), 1994.
Hodd, Michael, *The Economics of Africa: Geography, Population, History, Stability, Structure, Performance Forecasts* (Aldershot: Dartmouth), 1991.

Holden, Barry, *Understanding Liberal Democracy* (2nd edn) (New York: Harvester Wheatsheaf), 1993.

Holm, J. and Molutsi P. (eds), *Democracy in Botswana* (Athens, Ohio: Ohio University Press), 1989.

Hook, Steven W., *National Interest and Foreign Aid* (Boulder, Col.: Lynne Rienner), 1995.

Hopkinson, Nicholas, *Parliament and People* (Wilton Park Paper 100) (London: HMSO), 1995.

Hopkinson, Nicholas, *Strengthening Democracy throughout the World* (Wilton Park Paper 88) (London: HMSO), 1994.

Horowitz, David, 'Democracy in Divided Societies', *Journal of Democracy*, vol.4, no.4, October 1993, pp.18–38.

Huntington, Samuel P., *Third Wave: Democratization in the Late Twentieth Century* (Norman, Okla.: The University of Oklahoma Press), 1991.

Hyden, Goran and Bratton, Michael, *Governance and Politics in Africa* (Boulder, Col.: Lynne Rienner), 1992.

Inkeles, Alex (ed.), *On Measuring Democracy: Its Consequences and Concomitants* (Brunswick, NJ: Transaction Publishers), 1991.

Jain, R.B. and Asmero H.K. (eds), *Politics, Administration and Public Policy in Developing Countries: Examples from Africa, Asia and Latin America* (Netherlands: VUUP), 1993.

Jeffrey, Robin, *Politics, Women and Well-Being: How Kerala Became a 'Model'* (Basingstoke: Macmillan), 1992.

Johnson, John, 'Aid and Good Governance in Africa', *The Round Table*, no.320, October 1991, pp.395–400.

Jones, Alexandra D., *Global Good Governance: Legitimation through Popular Consent, International Credibility and Development Promotion* (London: University of London), 1994.

Joshi, Vijay, 'Democracy and Development in India', *The Round Table*, no.333, January 1995, pp.73–80.

Judge, David, *The Parliamentary State* (London: Sage Publications), 1993.

Karl, T.L., 'Dilemmas of Democratization in Latin America', *Comparative Politics*, 1990, pp.1–21.

Kasfir, Nelson, 'Popular Sovereignty and Popular Participation: Mixed Constitutional Democracy in the Third World', *Third World Quarterly*, vol.13, no.4, 1922, pp.587–606.

Keane, John, *Media and Democracy* (Oxford: Polity Press), 1991.

Keech, William R., *Economic Politics: The Costs of Democracy* (New York: Cambridge University Press), 1995.

Kennedy, Paul, *Preparing for the Twenty-First Century* (New York: Random House), 1993.

Khadiagala, Gilbert M., 'Thoughts on Africa and the New World Order', *The Round Table*, no.324, October 1992, pp.431–50.

Kiel, L. Douglas, *Managing Chaos and Complexity in Government: A New Paradigm for Managing Change, Innovation, and Organizational Renewal* (San Francisco: Jossey-Bass Publishers), 1994.

Kim, Bun Woong, Bell, David S. and Lee, Chang Bum, *Administrative Dynamics and Development* (Seoul: Kyobo Publishing), 1985.

Kinyanjui, Kabiru and Mburugu, Edward, *African Perspectives on Development: Controversies, Dilemmas and Openings* (London: Villiers Publications), 1994.

Kohli, Atul, 'Democracy amid Economic Orthodoxy: Trends in Developing Countries', *Third World Quarterly*, vol.14, no.4, November 1993, pp.671–90.

Kohli, Atul, *Democracy and Disorder: India's Growing Crisis of Governability* (Cambridge: Cambridge University Press), 1991.

Kornai, J., *The Socialist System: The Political Economy of Communism* (Oxford: Clarendon Press), 1992.

Kpundeh, Sahr J. and Riley, Stephen P., 'Political Choice and the New Democratic Politics in Africa', *The Round Table*, no.323, July 1992, pp.263–72.

Lee, M., *The Odyssey of Korean Democracy* (New York: Praeger), 1990.

Lee, Robin and Schlemmer, Lawrence (eds), *Transition to Democracy: Policy Perspectives* (Oxford: Oxford University Press), 1991.

Leftwich, Adrian, 'Governance, Democracy and Development in the Third World', *Third World Quarterly*, vol.14, no.3, 1993, pp.605–24.

Leftwich, Adrian, 'Bringing Politics Back In: Towards a Model of the Developmental State', *Journal of Developmental Studies*, 1995, pp.31, 400–27.

Leftwich, Adrian (ed.), *Democracy and Development: Theory and Practice* (Cambridge: Polity Press), 1996.

Lehmann, D., *Democracy and Development in Latin America* (Cambridge: Polity Press), 1990.

Levin, Bernard, *The Paradoxes of Democracy* (Kottayam: Malayala Manorama), 1993.

Lewellen, Ted C., *Dependence and Development: An Introduction to the Third World* (Westport, Conn.: Bergin and Garvey), 1995.

Lichtenberg, Judith (ed.), *Democracy and the Mass Media: A Collection of Essays* (Cambridge: Cambridge University Press), 1990.

Macintyre, Andrew (ed.), *Business and Government in Industrializing Asia* (Ithaca, NY: Cornell University Press), 1994.

Magang, David, 'A New Beginning: The Process of Democratization in Africa', *The Parliamentarian*, vol.LXXIII, no.4, October 1992, pp.235–9.

Mainwaring, Scott and Seully, Timothy R. (eds), *Building Democratic Institutions: Party System in Latin America* (Stanford, Calif.: Stanford University Press), 1995.
Mamdani, Mahmood and Wamba-dia-Wamba, Ernest (eds), *African Studies in Social Movements and Democracy* (Dakar, Senegal: CODESRIA), 1995.
Mandaza, Ibbo and Sachikonye, Lloyd (eds), *The One-Party State and Democracy: The Zimbabwe Debate* (Harare: SAPES Books), 1991.
Manley, Michael, *The Poverty of Nations: Imperialism and Underdevelopment in the Twentieth Century* (London: Pluto Press), 1991.
Manley, Michael, *The Poverty of Nations: Reflections on Underdevelopment and the World Economy* (London: Pluto Press), 1991.
Marks, Gary and Diamond, Larry (eds), *Re-examining Democracy: Essays in Honour of Seymour Martin Lipset* (Newbury Park: Sage Publications), 1992.
Mayall, James and Payne, Anthony (eds), *The Fallacies of Hope: The Post-Colonial Record of the Commonwealth Third World* (Manchester: Manchester University Press), 1990.
Mcarthy, Stephen, *Africa: The Challenge of Transformation* (London: I.B. Tauris), 1994.
McLellan, David and Sayers, Sean (eds), *Socialism and Democracy* (Basingstoke: Macmillan), 1991.
McMahon, Christopher, *Authority and Democracy: A General Theory of Government and Management* (Princeton, NJ: Princeton University Press), 1994.
Molombo, Mpho G. and Mokopakgosi, Brian T. (eds), *Multi-Party Democracy in Botswana* (Harare: SAPES Books), 1991.
Monshipouri, Mahmood, *Democratization, Liberalization and Human Rights in the Third World* (Boulder, Col.: Lynne Rienner), 1995.
Morley, J.W. (ed.), *Driven by Growth: Political Changes in the Asia-Pacific Region* (New York: M.E. Sharpe), 1993.
Morrissey, Oliver and Stewart, Frances (eds), *Economic and Political Reform in Developing Countries* (Basingstoke: Macmillan), 1995.
Mouffe, Chantal (ed.), *Dimensions of Radical Democracy: Pluralism, Citizenship, Community* (London: Verso), 1992.
Neher, Clark D. and Marlay, Ross, *Democracy and Development in Southeast Asia* (Boulder, Col.: Westview Press), 1995.
Norton, Philip, *Does Parliament Matter?* (Hemel Hempstead, Herts: Harvester Wheatsheaf), 1993.
Nwabueze, B.O., *Democratisation* (Lagos: Spectrum Books), 1994.
Nyong'o, Peter Anyang (ed.), *Thirty Years of Independence in Africa: The Lost Decades?* (Kenya: Academy Science Publishers), 1992.

O'Donnell, Guillermo, Schmitter, Phillippe C. and Whitehead, Lawrence (eds), *Transitions from Authoritarian Rule: Prospects for Democracy* (Baltimore: Johns Hopkins University Press), 1986.

Olson, David and Mezey, Michael, *Legislatures in the Policy Process: The Dilemmas of Economic Policy* (Cambridge: Cambridge University Press), 1991.

Olson, M., 'Dictatorship, Democracy and Development', *American Political Science Review*, 87/1993, pp.567–76.

Ottaway, M., *South Africa: The Struggle for a New Order* (Washington, DC: Brookings Institution), 1993.

Owens, Edgar, *The Future of Freedom in the Developing World: Economic Development as Political Reform* (New York: Pergamon Press), 1987.

Parry, Geraint and Moran, Michael (eds), *Democracy and Democratization* (London: Routledge), 1994.

Pastor, Robert A. (ed.), *Democracy in the Americas: Stopping the Pendulum* (New York: Holms and Meir), 1989.

Paul, Erik C., 'Prospects for Liberalization in Singapore', *Journal of Contemporary Asia*, vol.23, no.3, 1993, pp.291–305.

Payne, Anthony and Sulton, Paul, *Modern Caribbean Politics* (Baltimore: Johns Hopkins University Press), 1993.

Pereira, Luiz Carlos, Bresser, Maravall, Jose Maria and Przeworski, Adam, *Economic Reforms in New Democracies: A Social-Democratic Approach* (Cambridge: Cambridge University Press), 1993.

Peters, Donald C., *Democratic Systems in the Eastern Caribbean* (London: Greenwood Press), 1992.

Philip, George, 'The New Economic Liberalism and Democracy in Latin America: Friends or Enemies', *Third World Quarterly*, vol.14, no.3, 1993, pp.555–72.

Phillips, Anne, *Engendering Democracy* (Oxford: Polity Press), 1991.

Phillips, Anne, *Democracy and Difference* (Cambridge: Polity Press), 1993.

Pillai, Vijayan K., Shannon, Lyle W. and Mikim, Judith L. (eds), *Developing Areas: A Book of Readings and Research* (Oxford: Berg Publishers), 1995.

Pinkney, Robert, *Democracy in the Third World* (Buckingham: Open University Press), 1993.

Pourgerami, A., *Development and Democracy in the Third World* (Boulder, Col.: Westview Press), 1991.

Przeworski, A., *Democracy and the Market: Political and Economic Reforms in Eastern Europe and Latin America* (Cambridge: Cambridge University Press), 1991.

Przeworski, A. and Limongi, F., 'Political Regimes and Economic Growth', *Journal of Economic Perspectives*, vol.7, no.1, 1993, pp.51–69.

Quibria, M.G. (ed.), *Critical Issues in Asian Development: Theories, Experiences and Politics* (Hong Kong: Oxford University Press), 1995.

Raboy, Marc and Dagenais, Bernard (eds), *Media, Crisis and Democracy: Mass Communication and the Disruption of Social Order* (London: Sage Publications), 1992.

Ramphal, Shridath, *Our Country, the Planet: Forging a Partnership for Survival* (London: Lime Tree), 1992.

Ramphal, Shridath and Carlsson, Ingwar, *Our Global Neighbourhood: The Report of the Commission on Global Governance* (Oxford: Oxford University Press), 1995.

Randall, Vicky, 'The Media and Democratisation in the Third World', *Third World Quarterly*, vol.14, no.3, 1993, pp.625–46.

Randall, Vicky and Theobald, Robin (eds), *Political Change and Underdevelopment: A Critical Introduction to Third World Politics* (London: Sage Publications), 1988.

Ranger, Terence and Vaughan, Olufemi, *Legitimacy and the State in Twentieth Century Africa* (Basingstoke: Macmillan), 1993.

Rau, C.B., 'Managing Global Change: A Vision', *The Round Table*, no.33, April 1994, pp.149–67.

Remmer, K., 'Democracy and Economic Crisis: The Latin American Experience', *World Politics*, vol.42, no.3, pp.315–35.

Revel, Jean-François, *Democracy Against Itself: The Future of the Democratic Impulse* (translated by Roger Kaplan) (New York: Free Press), 1993.

Rich, Paul B. (ed.), *The Dynamics of Change in Southern Africa* (London: Macmillan), 1994.

Rijnierse, Elly, 'Democratisation in Sub-Saharan Africa? Literature Overview', *Third World Quarterly*, vol.14, no.3, 1993, pp.647–64.

Riley, S.P., *The Democratic Transition in Africa* (London: Research Institute for the Study of Conflict and Terrorism), 1991.

Riley, Stephen P., 'Political Adjustment or Domestic Pressure: Democratic Politics and Political Choice in Africa', *Third World Quarterly*, vol.13, no.3, 1992, pp.539–51.

Ronen, Dov (ed.), *Democracy and Pluralism in Africa* (Boulder, Col.: Lynne Rienner), 1986.

Rosow, Stephen J., Inayatullah, Naeem and Rupert, Mark (eds), *The Global Economy as Political Space* (Boulder, Col.: Lynne Rienner), 1994.

Ross, Robert R. (ed.), *East Asia in Transition: Towards a New Regional Order* (Armonk: M.E. Sharpe Inc.), 1995.

Rothchild, Donald and Chazan, Naomi (eds), *The Precarious Balance: State and Society in Africa* (Boulder, Col.: Westview Press), 1988.

Rothschild, E. and Steadman Jones, G. (eds), *History and Development* (Oxford: Oxford University Press), 1995.
Rotimi, Ajayi Ola, 'Democratic Impasse: Remilitarisation in Nigeria', *Third World Quarterly*, vol.15, no.4, December 1994, pp.669–90.
Rowat, Donald C. (ed.), *Public Administration in Developed Democracies: A Comparative Study* (New York: Marcel Dekker Inc.), 1988.
Rueschemeyer, D., Stephens, E.H. and Stephens, J.D., *Capitalist Development and Democracy* (Cambridge: Polity Press), 1992.
Ryrie, William, *First World, Third World* (Basingstoke: Macmillan), 1995.
Sahr, John Kpundeh (ed.), *Democratization in Africa: African Views, African Voices* (Plymouth: National Research Council), 1992.
Salmame, Ghasan (ed.), *Democracy without Democrats? The Renewal of Politics in the Muslim World* (London: I.B. Tauris), 1994.
Samuels, Warren J., *Essays on the Economic Role of Government (Volume 1): Fundamentals* (Basingstoke: Macmillan), 1992.
Samuels, Warren J., *Essays on the Economic Role of Government (Volume 2): Applications* (Basingstoke: Macmillan), 1992.
Sandbrook, Richard, *The Politics of Africa's Economic Recovery* (Cambridge: Cambridge University Press), 1993.
Sandhu, K.S. and Wheatey, Paul (eds), *Management of Success: The Moulding of Modern Singapore* (Singapore: Institute of South East-Asian Studies), 1989.
Scalapino, Robert, 'National Political Institutions and Leadership in Asia', *Washington Quarterly*, Autumn 1992.
Selden, M., *The Political Economy of Chinese Development* (New York: M.E. Sharpe), 1992.
Seligson, Mitchell A. and Passe-Smith, John T. (eds), *Development and Underdevelopment: The Political Economy of Inequality* (Boulder, Col.: Lynne Rienner), 1993.
Sen, Amartya, *Inequality Re-examined* (Oxford: Clarendon Press), 1992.
Shahid Qadir, Clapham, Christopher and Gills, Barry, 'Democratisation in the Third World: An Introduction', *Third World Quarterly*, vol.14, no.3, 1993, pp.415–22.
Shain, Yossi and Linz, Juan J., *Between States: Interim Governments and Democratic Transitions* (Cambridge: Cambridge University Press), 1995.
Shaw, Timothy M., 'Beyond any New World Order: The South in the 21st Century', *Third World Quarterly*, vol.15, no.1, 1994, pp.139–46.
Shin, D., Choy, M. and Cho M., *Korea in the Global Wave of Democratization* (Seoul: Seoul National Press), 1994.
Simone, Vera and Feraru, Anne Thompson, *The Asian Pacific: Political and Economic Development in a Global Context* (New York: Longman Publishers), 1995.

Sirowy, L. and Inkeles A., 'The Effects of Democracy on Economic Growth and Inequality', *Studies in Comparative International Development*, 1990, pp.126–57.

Sithole, Masipula, *Democracy and the One-Party State Debate: The Case of Zimbabwe* (Zimbabwe: Southern Africa Printing and Publishing House), 1993.

Skiair, Lesli (ed.), *Capitalism and Development* (London: Routledge), 1994.

Slater, Robert O., Schultz, Barry M. and Dorr, Steven R. (eds), *Global Transformation and the Third World* (Boulder, Col.: Lynne Rienner), 1993.

Slottje, D.J. et al., *Measuring the Quality of Life Across Countries: A Multi-dimensional Analysis*, (Boulder, Col.: Westview Press), 1991.

Sobhan, Rehman, *Rethinking the Role of the State in Development: Asian Perspectives* (Dhaka: University Press), 1993.

Soemardjan, Selo and Thompson, Kenneth W. (eds), *Culture, Development and Democracy: The Role of the Intellectual* (Tokyo: United Nations University Press), 1994.

Sorensen, G., *Democracy and Authoritarianism: Consequences for Economic Development* (Aarhus: Institute of Political Science), 1992.

Sorensen, Georg, *Democracy and Democratization: Processes and Prospects in a Changing World* (Boulder, Col.: Westview Press), 1993.

Spindler, Z.A., 'Liberty and Development: A Further Empirical Perspective', *Public Choice*, 1991, pp.197–210.

Spybey, Tony, *Social Change, Development and Dependency: Modernity, Colonialism and the Development of the West* (Cambridge: Polity Press), 1992.

Stallings, Barbara (ed.), *Global Change, Regional Response: The New International Context of Development* (Cambridge: Cambridge University Press), 1995.

Stedman, S.J. (ed.), *Botswana: the Political Economy of Democratic Development* (Boulder, Col.: Lynne Rienner), 1993.

Stubbs, Richard and Underhill, Geoffrey R.D. (eds), *Political Economy and the Changing Global Order* (Basingstoke: Macmillan), 1994.

Sunstein, Cass R., *Democracy and the Problem of Free Speech* (New York: Free Press), 1993.

Swedish International Development Authority (SIDA), *Making Government Work: Guidelines and Framework for SIDA Support to the Development of Public Administration* (Sweden: SIDA), 1991.

Tangri, Roger, *Politics in Sub-Saharan Africa* (London: Heinemann/Currey), 1985.

'The Democratic Challenge', *The Parliamentarian*, vol.LXXIII, no.4, October 1992, pp.249–54.

Thompson, Mark R., 'The Limits of Democratization in ASEAN', *Third World Quarterly*, vol.14, no.3, 1993, pp.469–84.
Todaro, Michael P., *Economics for a Developing World: An Introduction to Principal Problems and Policies for Development* (3rd edn) (London: Longman), 1992.
Tordoff, William, *Government and Politics in Africa* (2nd edn) (London: Macmillan), 1993.
Turok, Ben (ed.), *Debt and Democracy* (London: Institute for African Alternatives), 1991.
Usher, Dan, *The Economic Prerequisite to Democracy* (New York: Columbia University Press), 1991.
Vanhanen, Tatu, *Strategies of Democratization* (London: Taylor & Francis), 1994.
Wade, R., *Governing the Market: Economic Theory and the Role of Government in East Asian Industrialization* (Princeton, NJ: Princeton University Press), 1990.
Warner, David, 'CPA: Commonwealth Parliamentary Aid, Responding to World Changes', *The Parliamentarian*, vol.LXXIV, no.4, October 1993, pp.193–5.
Watson, Hilbourne A. (ed.), *The Caribbean in the Global Political Economy* (Boulder, Col.: Lynne Rienner), 1994.
Waylen, Georgina, 'Women's Movements and Democratisation in Latin America', *Third World Quarterly*, vol.14, no.3, 1993, pp.573–84.
Weede, E., 'The Impact of Democracy or Repressiveness on the Quality of Life, Income Distribution and Economic Growth Rates', *International Society*, 1993, pp.177–95.
Wekkin, Gary D., *Building Democracy in a One-Party System: Theoretical Problems and Cross-Nation Experiences* (New York: Praeger), 1993.
Werunga, Murumba, 'Parliamentary Democracy in Africa: The 25th Conference of the Africa Region of the Commonwealth Parliamentary Association', *The Parliamentarian*, vol.LXXV, no.4, October 1994, pp.247–51.
White, G. (ed.), *The Chinese State in the Era of Economic Reforms* (London: Macmillan), 1994.
White, Gordon (ed.), *Developmental States in East Asia* (London: Macmillan), 1988.
Wilson, Henry S., *African Decolonization* (London: Edward Arnold), 1994.
Winner, Langdon (ed.), *Democracy in a Technological Society* (Dordrecht: Kluwer Academic Publishers), 1992.
Wiseman, John A., 'Democracy and the New Political Pluralism in Africa: Causes, Consequences and Significance', *Third World Quarterly*, vol.14, no.3, 1993, pp.439–50.
Women and the Democratization Process in Africa: Report of UNESCO

Regional Meeting of Experts, Windhoek, Namibia, 18 to 22 October 1994 (Windhoek and Dakar Offices: UNESCO).

Wood, B. Dan and Waterman, Richard W., *Bureaucratic Dynamics: the Role of Bureaucracy in a Democracy* (Boulder, Col.: Westview Press), 1994.

World Bank, *Governance and Development* (Washington, DC: World Bank), 1992.

World Bank, *Social Indicators of Development, 1990* (Baltimore: Johns Hopkins University Press), 1991.

Wright, Richard Kozul, *Walking on Two Legs: Strengthening Democracy and Productive Entrepreneurship in the Transition Economies* (Geneva: UNCTAD), 1995.

3 Facilitating the Proper Functioning of Parliament: the Role of the Commonwealth Parliamentary Association and other Parliamentary Associations

Commonwealth Parliamentary Association: Aims, Organization, Activities (London: CPA Headquarters Secretariat), 1996.

Gould, Ron, Jackson, Christine and Wells, Loren, *Strengthening Democracy: A Parliamentary Perspective* (Aldershot: Dartmouth), 1995.

Grey, Ian, *The Parliamentarians: The History of the Commonwealth Parliamentary Association, 1911–1985* (Aldershot: Gower Publishing), 1986.

Hopkinson, Nicholas, *Parliament and People* (Wilton Park Paper 100) (London: HMSO), 1995.

Hopkinson, Nicholas, *Strengthening Democracy throughout the World* (Wilton Park Paper 88) (London: HMSO), 1994.

Inter-Parliamentary Union, *Distribution of Seats between Men and Women in National Parliaments: Statistical Data from 1945 to 30 June 1991* (Geneva: Inter-Parliamentary Union), 1991.

Inter-Parliamentary Union, *Inter-Parliamentary Union, 1993* (Geneva: Inter-Parliamentary Union), 1993.

Inter-Parliamentary Union, *Parliamentary Human Rights Bodies, World Directory* (Geneva: Inter-Parliamentary Union), 1993.

Inter-Parliamentary Union, *Distribution of Seats between Men and Women in the 178 National Parliaments existing as at 30 June 1994* (Geneva: Inter-Parliamentary Union), 1994.

Inter-Parliamentary Union, *Plan of Action to Correct Present Imbalance in the Participation of Men and Women in Political Life* (Geneva: Inter-Parliamentary Union), 1994.

Inter-Parliamentary Union, *Women in Parliaments 1950–1995: A World Statistical Survey* (Geneva: Inter-Parliamentary Union), 1995.

Sawicki, Joan, 'CPA and the Parliamentary Profession', *Canadian Parliamentary Review*, vol.15, no.3, Autumn 1992, pp.12–13.
Warner, David, 'CPA: Commonwealth Parliamentary Aid, Responding to World Changes', *The Parliamentarian*, vol.LXXIV, no.4, October 1993, pp.193–5.
Zarjevski, Yefime, *The People Have the Floor: A History of the Inter-Parliamentary Union* (Translated from the French by Nicholas Albredcht) (Aldershot: Dartmouth), 1989.

4 Freedom of the Press

Altschull, J. Herbert, *Agents of Power: the Media and Public Policy* (New York: Longman), 1995.
Barbrook, Richard, *Media Freedom: The Contradictions of Communication in the Age of Modernity* (London: Pluto Press), 1995.
Davidson, Diane, 'Parliamentary Privilege and Freedom of the Press', *Canadian Parliamentary Review*, vol.16, no.2, Summer 1993, pp.10–12.
Graber, Daris A., *Media Power in Politics* (2nd edn) (New Delhi: Macmillan), 1990.
Hiebert, Ray Eldon (ed.), *Impact of Mass Media: Current Issues* (3rd edn) (New York: Longman), 1995.
Keane, John, *Media and Democracy* (Oxford: Polity Press), 1991.
Lichtenberg, Judith (ed.), *Democracy and the Mass Media: A Collection of Essays* (Cambridge: Cambridge University Press), 1990.
Raboy, Marc and Dagenais, Bernard (eds), *Media, Crisis and Democracy: Mass Communication and the Disruption of Social Order* (London: Sage Publications), 1992.
Randall, Vicky, 'The Media and Democratisation in the Third World', *Third World Quarterly*, vol.14, no.3, 1993, pp.625–46.
Sorlin, Pierre, *Mass Media* (London: Routledge), 1994.
'The Media: The Worst of Friends, the Best of Enemies', *The Parliamentarian*, vol.LXXIII, no.4, October 1992, p.254.
Werunga, Murumba, 'Legislators and the Mass Media', *The Parliamentarian*, vol.LXXI, no.2, April 1990, pp.119–20.

5 The Relationship between Government and the Military

Beyene, Asmelash and Mutahaba, Galase (eds), *The Quest for Constitutionalism in Africa: Selected Essays on Constitutionalism, the Nationality Problem, Military Rule and Party Politics* (Frankfurt: Paul Lang), 1994.

Chabal, Patrick, *Power in Africa: An Essay in Political Interpretation* (London: Macmillan), 1992.
Danopoulos, Constantine P. (ed.), *Civilian Rule in the Developing World: Democracy on the March?* (Boulder, Col.: Westview Press), 1992.
Danopoulos, Constantine P., *From Military to Civilian Rule* (London: Routledge), 1991.
Decalo, Samuel, *Coups and Army Rule in Africa* (New Haven, Conn.: Yale University Press), 1990.
Graham, Norman A. (ed.), *Seeking Security and Development: the Impact of Military Spending and Arms Transfers* (Boulder, Col.: Lynne Rienner), 1994.
Rotimi, Ajayi Ola, 'Democratic Impasse: Remilitarisation in Nigeria', *Third World Quarterly*, vol.15, no.4, December 1994, pp.669–90.

6 The Singapore Model

Agrawal, Pradeep et al., *Economic Restructuring in East Asia and India: Perspectives on Policy Reforms* (London: Macmillan), 1995.
Asian Development Outlook 1994 (Oxford: Oxford University Press), 1994.
Asian Development Bank, *Asian Development Outlook 1995 and 1996* (Oxford: Oxford University Press), 1995.
Asian Development Bank, *Human Resource Policy and Economic Development: Selected Country Studies* (Manila: Asian Development Bank), 1991.
'Asian Values', *The Economist*, vol.331, no.7867, May 28, 1994, pp.9–10.
Banuri, Tariq (ed.), *Economic Liberalization No Panacea: the Experience of Latin America and Asia* (Oxford: Clarendon Press), 1991.
Bello, W.F. and Rosenfeld S., *Dragons in Distress: Asia's Miracle Economies in Crisis* (San Francisco: Institute for Food and Development Policy), 1990.
Beng-Huat Chua, 'Arrested Development: Democratisation in Singapore', *Third World Quarterly*, vol.15, no.4, 1994, pp.655–68.
Beng-Huat Chua, *Communitarian Ideology and Democracy in Singapore* (London: Routledge), 1995.
Berger, P.L. and Hsiao, H.M. (eds), *In Search of an East Asian Development Model* (New Brunswick: Transaction Books), 1988.
Castells, M., *The Developmental City-State in an Open Economy: The Singapore Experience* (Berkeley Round Table on International Economy, Working Paper no.31) (Berkeley: University of California), 1988.
Chew, Ernest C.T. and Lee, Edwin, *A History of Singapore* (Singapore: Oxford University Press), 1991.

Chew, Rosalind, *Employment Driven Industrial Relations Regimes: The Singapore Experience* (Aldershot: Avebury), 1995.
Chong-Yah Lim et al., *Policy Options for the Singapore Economy* (Singapore: McGraw-Hill), 1988.
Chowdhury, A. and Islam, I., *The Newly Industrialising Economies of East Asia* (London: Routledge), 1993.
Deyo, F.C. (ed.), *The Political Economy of the New Asian Industrialism* (Ithaca, NY: Cornell University Press), 1987.
Economic and Social Commission for Asia and the Pacific, *Econometric Modelling and Forecasting in Asia* (Proceedings of a Regional Seminar organized in collaboration with the Research and Information System for the Non-aligned and Other Developing Countries, New Delhi, 27 February–1 March 1989), Bangkok, 1991.
Economic and Social Commission for Asia and the Pacific, *Economic and Social Survey of Asia and the Pacific 1995* (New York: Economic and Social Commission for Asia and the Pacific), 1995.
Economic and Social Commission for Asia and the Pacific, *Strengthening of Regional Co-operation in Human Resources Development in Asia and the Pacific* (with Special Reference to the Social Implications of Sustainable Economic Growth) (United Nations, Economic and Social Commission for Asia and the Pacific), 1995.
Field, Graham, *Economic Growth and Political Change in Asia* (Basingstoke: Macmillan), 1995.
Friedman, Edward (ed.), *The Politics of Democratization: Generalizing East Asian Experiences* (Boulder, Col.: Westview Press), 1994.
Gereffi, G. and Wyman D. (eds), *Manufacturing Miracles: Paths of Industrialization in Latin America and East Asia* (Princeton, NJ: Princeton University Press), 1990.
Heron, Richard Le and Park, Sam Ock (eds), *The Asian Pacific Rim and Globalization: Enterprises, Governance and Territoriality* (Aldershot: Avebury), 1995.
Hill, Michael and Lian Kwen Fee, *The Politics of Nation Building and Citizenship in Singapore* (London: Routledge), 1995.
Hussin Mutalib, 'Singapore's December 1992 By-elections: Interpreting the Results and the Signals', *The Round Table*, no.326, April 1993, pp.159–68.
Iwasaki, Teruyuki, Mori, Takeshi and Yamaguchi, Hiroichi (eds), *Development Strategies for the 21st Century* (Papers and Proceedings of the Institute of Developing Economies, 30th Anniversary Symposium on Development Strategies for the 21st Century, held 10–12 December 1990) (Tokyo: Institute of Developing Economies), 1992.
James, William E., Naya, Seiji and Meier, Gerald M., *Asian Development:*

Economic Success and Policy Lessons (Wisconsin: The University of Wisconsin Press), 1989.

LePoer, Barbara Leitch (ed.), *Singapore: A Country Study* (Washington, DC: United States Government Printer), 1991.

Lim, L. and Pang, E.F., *Foreign Direct Investment and Industrialization in Malaysia, Singapore, Taiwan and Thailand* (Paris: OECD Development Centre), 1991.

Mary, Turnbull C., *History of Singapore, 1819–1988* (Oxford: Oxford University Press), 1990.

Mauzy, Diane K., 'Human Rights in Indonesia, Malaysia and Singapore: Contrasting Views from ASEAN, Canada and Australia', *The Round Table*, no.335, July 1995, pp.279–96.

Milne, R.S., 'Singapore's Growth Triangle', *The Round Table*, no.327, July 1993, pp.291–304.

Milne, R.S. and Mauzy, Diane K., *Singapore: The Legacy of Lee Kuan Yew* (Plymouth, Mass.: Westview Press), 1990.

Morley, J.W. (ed.), *Driven by Growth: Political Changes in the Asia-Pacific Region* (New York: M.E. Sharpe), 1993.

Nagel, Stuart S. (ed.), *Asian Development and Public Policy* (Basingstoke: Macmillan), 1994.

Naisbitt, John, *Megatrends in Asia: The Eight Asian Megatrends that are Changing the World* (London: Nicholas Brealey Publishing), 1995.

Neher, Clark D., *Southeast Asia in the New International Era* (Boulder, Col.: Westview Press), 1991.

Neher, Clark D. and Marlay, Ross, *Democracy and Development in Southeast Asia* (Boulder, Col.: Westview Press), 1995.

Nguyen Duc-Tho and Roy, Kartik C. (eds), *Economic Reform, Liberalisation and Trade in the Asia-Pacific Region* (New Delhi: Wiley Eastern), 1994.

Paul, Erik C., 'Prospects for Liberalization in Singapore', *Journal of Contemporary Asia*, vol.23, no.3, 1993, pp.291–305.

Quibria, M.G. (ed.), *Critical Issues in Asian Development: Theories, Experiences and Politics* (Hong Kong: Oxford University Press), 1995.

Rodan, G., *The Political Economy of Singapore's Industrialization: National, State and International Capital* (New York: St Martin's Press), 1989.

Rodan, Garry (ed.), *Singapore Changes Guard: Social, Political and Economic Directions in the 1990s* (London: Longman), 1994.

Ross, Robert R. (ed.), *East Asia in Transition: Towards a New Regional Order* (Armonk: M.E. Sharpe Inc.), 1995.

Sandhu, K.S. and Wheatey, Paul (eds), *Management of Success: The Moulding of Modern Singapore* (Singapore: Institute of South-East Asian Studies), 1989.

Scalapino, Robert, 'National Political Institutions and Leadership in Asia', *Washington Quarterly*, Autumn 1992.
Simone, Vera and Feraru, Anne Thompson, *The Asian Pacific: Political and Economic Development in a Global Context* (New York: Longman Publishers), 1995.
'Singapore after Lee', *The Economist*, vol.317, no.7678, 27 October 1990, pp.19–20, 23.
Sobhan Rehman, *Rethinking the Role of the State in Development: Asian Perspectives* (Dhaka: University Press), 1993.
Somjee, A.H. and Somjee, Geeta, *Development Success in Asia Pacific: An Exercise in Normative-Pragmatic Balance* (London: Macmillan), 1995.
Stallings, Barbara (ed.), *Global Change, Regional Response: The New International Context of Development* (Cambridge: Cambridge University Press), 1995.
Tambunlertchai, Somsak and Gupta, S.P. (eds), *Development Planning in Asia* (Kuala Lumpur: Asian and Pacific Development Centre), 1993.
Tan, Gerald, 'The Next NICs of Asia', *Third World Quarterly*, vol.14, no.1, 1993, pp.57–74.
Tang, James T.H. (ed.), *Human Rights and International Relations in the Asia Pacific Region* (London: Pinter Publishers), 1995.
Thompson, Mark R., 'The Limits of Democratization in ASEAN', *Third World Quarterly*, vol.14, no.3, 1993, pp.469–84.
Tremwam, Christopher, *The Political Economy of Social Control in Singapore* (London: Macmillan), 1994.
Wade, R., *Governing the Market: Economic Theory and the Role of Government in East Asian Industrialization* (Princeton, NJ: Princeton University Press), 1990.
Watanabe, Toshio, *Asia: Its Growth and Agony* (Honolulu: East-West Center), 1992.
White, Gordon (ed.), *Developmental States in East Asia* (London: Macmillan), 1988.
World Bank, *The East Asian Miracle: Economic Growth and Public Policy* (New York: Oxford University Press), 1993.

7 Development and Democracy in the Island States of the Caribbean

Bryan, Anthony T., Green, J. Edward and Shaw, Timothy M., *Peace, Development and Security in the Caribbean: Perspectives to the Year 2000* (Basingstoke: Macmillan), 1990.
Clarke, Colin G., *Society and Politics in the Caribbean* (London: Macmillan), 1991.

Dominguez, Jorge I. (ed.), *Democracy in the Caribbean: Political, Economic and Social Perspectives* (Baltimore: Johns Hopkins University Press), 1993.
Dookeran, Winston, 'Caribbean Integration: An Agenda for Open Regionalism', *The Round Table*, no.330, April 1994, pp.205–11.
Dookeran, Winston, 'NAFTA, the EC and the Uruguay Round: Does the Caribbean Have a Place in the New Economic Order?', *The Round Table*, no.326, April 1993, pp.153–8.
Economic Commission for Latin America and the Caribbean, *Economic Survey of Latin America and the Caribbean 1992* (Santiago: Economic Commission for Latin America and the Caribbean), 1994.
Economic Commission for Latin America and the Caribbean, *Major Changes and Crises: the Impact of Women in Latin America and the Caribbean* (Santiago: Economic Commission for Latin America and the Caribbean), 1992.
Edie, Carlena J. (ed.), *Democracy in the Caribbean: Myths and Realities* (Westport, Conn.: Praeger), 1994.
Erisman, H. Michael, *Pursuing Post-Dependency Politics: South–South Relations in the Caribbean* (Boulder, Col.: Lynne Rienner), 1992.
Griffin, Clifford E., 'Democracy in the Commonwealth Caribbean', *Journal of Democracy*, vol.4, no.2, April 1993, pp.84–94.
Grugel, Jean, *Politics and Development in the Caribbean Basin: Central America and the Caribbean in the New World Order* (Basingstoke: Macmillan), 1995.
McAfee, Kathy, *Storm Signals: Structural Adjustment and Development Alternatives in the Caribbean* (London: Zed Books), 1991.
Payne, Anthony and Sulton, Paul, *Modern Caribbean Politics* (Baltimore: Johns Hopkins University Press), 1993.
Peters, Donald C., *Democratic Systems in the Eastern Caribbean* (London: Greenwood Press), 1992.
Stewart, Frances, *Protecting the Poor during Adjustment in Latin America and the Caribbean in the 1980s: How Adequate was the World Bank Response?* (Development Studies Working Papers) (Oxford: International Development Centre), 1992.
Watson, Hilbourne A. (ed.), *The Caribbean in the Global Political Economy* (Boulder, Col.: Lynne Rienner), 1994.

8 Indirect Democracy in Uganda

Beyene, Asmelash and Mutahaba, Galase (eds), *The Quest for Constitutionalism in Africa: Selected Essays on Constitutionalism, the Nationality Problem, Military Rule and Party Politics* (Frankfurt: Paul Lang), 1994.

Cohen, Ronald, Hyden, Goran and Nagan, Winston P. (eds), *Human Rights and Governance in Africa* (Gainesville, Fla.: University Press of Florida), 1993.
Cornia, Giovanni Andrea, Van der Hoeven, Rolph and Mkandawire, Thandika (eds), *Africa's Recovery in the 1990s: from Stagnation and Adjustment to Human Development* (London: Macmillan), 1992.
Decalo, Samuel, *Coups and Army Rule in Africa* (New Haven, Conn.: Yale University Press), 1990.
Hansen, Holger Bernt and Twaddle, Michael, *Changing Uganda: The Dilemmas of Structural Adjustment and Revolutionary Change* (London: James Currey), 1991.
Hansen, Holger Bernt and Twaddle, Michael (eds), *From Chaos to Order: the Politics of Constitution-making in Uganda* (Kampala: Fountain Publishers), 1994.
Himmelstrand, Ulf, Kinyanjui, Kabiru and Mburugu, Edward (eds), *African Perspectives on Development* (London: James Currey), 1994.
Hodd, Michael, *The Economics of Africa: Geography, Population, History, Stability, Structure, Performance Forecasts* (Aldershot: Dartmouth), 1991.
Hyden, Goran and Bratton, Michael, *Governance and Politics in Africa* (Boulder, Col.: Lynne Rienner), 1992.
Instruments for Economic Policy in Africa (London: James Currey, for the African Centre for Monetary Studies and Association of African Central Banks), 1992.
Mutibwa, Phares, *Uganda Since Independence: A Story of Unfulfilled Hopes* (London: Hurst), 1992.
Ranger, Terence and Vaughan, Olufemi, *Legitimacy and the State in Twentieth-Century Africa* (Basingstoke: Macmillan), 1993.
Riley, S.P., *The Democratic Transition in Africa* (London: Research Institute for the Study of Conflict and Terrorism), 1991.
Riley, Stephen P., 'Political Adjustment or Domestic Pressure: Democratic Politics and Political Choice in Africa', *Third World Quarterly*, vol.13, no.3, 1992, pp.539–51.
Ronen, Dov (ed.), *Democracy and Pluralism in Africa* (Boulder, Col.: Lynne Rienner), 1986.
Rothchild, Donald and Chazan, Naomi (eds), *The Precarious Balance: State and Society in Africa* (Boulder, Colorado: Westview Press), 1988.
Sahr, John Kpundeh (ed.), *Democratization in Africa: African Views, African Voices* (Plymouth: National Research Council), 1992.
Tordoff, William, *Government and Politics in Africa* (2nd edn) (London: Macmillan), 1993.

9 Gender and Development

Afkami, Mahnaz (ed.), *Faith and Freedom: Women's Human Rights in the Muslim World* (London: I.B. Tauris), 1995.

Ahooja-Patel, Krishna, *Women and Sustainable Development: An International Dimension* (New Delhi: Ashish Publishing House), 1995.

Amnesty International, *Human Rights are Women's Rights* (London: Amnesty International Publications), 1995.

Ashworth, Georgina, *When Will Democracy Include Women?* (London: Change), 1992.

Aslanbeigui, Nahid, Pressman, Steven and Summerfield, Gale, *Women in the Age of Economic Transformation: Gender Impact of Reforms in Post-Socialist and Developing Countries* (London: Routledge), 1994.

Astwood, Norma Cox, 'Women in Politics: A Challenge to Tradition', *The Parliamentarian*, vol.LXXI, no.3, July 1990, pp.153–6.

Beckman, Peter R. and D'amico, Francine (eds), *Women, Gender and World Politics: Perspectives, Policies and Prospects* (London: Bergin and Garvey), 1995.

Boserup, Ester, *Women's Role in Economic Development* (London: Earthscan), 1989.

Brill, Alida (ed.), *Rising Public Voice: Women in Politics Worldwide* (Lancaster: Gazelle Book Services), 1995.

Brown, Jan, 'Changing the Gender Agenda of Politics', *Canadian Parliamentary Review*, vol.17, no.2, Summer 1994, pp.8–10.

Bryson, Valerie, *Feminist Political Theory: An Introduction* (Basingstoke: Macmillan), 1992.

Bystydzienski, Jill M. (ed.), *Women Transforming Politics: Worldwide Strategies for Empowerment* (Bloomington: Indiana University Press), 1992.

Calman, Leslie J., *Toward Empowerment: Women and Movement Politics in India* (Boulder, Col.: Westview Press), 1992.

Chalker, Lynda, 'Women in Politics: That's no Lady, That's my MP', *The Parliamentarian*, vol.LXXI, no.3, July 1990, pp.157–9.

Clarke, Alice W. (ed.), *Gender and Political Economy: Exploration of South Asian Systems* (Delhi: Oxford University Press), 1993.

Cook, Rebecca J. (ed.), *Human Rights of Women: National and International Perspectives* (Philadelphia: The University of Pennsylvania Press), 1993.

Coole, Diana H., *Women in Political Theory: From Ancient Misogyny to Contemporary Feminism* (2nd rev. edn) (Basingstoke: Macmillan), 1993.

Cottam, Christine M. and Rao, Sudha V. (eds), *Women, Aid and Development* (Essays in Honour of Professor T. Scarlett Epstein) (Delhi: Hindustan Publishing), 1993.

Dagenais, Huguette and Piche, Denise, *Women, Feminism and Development* (London: McGill–Queen's University Press), 1994.
Darcy, R. et al., *Women, Elections and Representation* (2nd rev. edn) (Lincoln: University of Nebraska Press), 1994.
Duke, Lois Lovelace (ed.), *Women in Politics: Outsiders or Insiders?* (NJ: Prentice-Hall), 1993.
Dysart, Shirley, 'Barriers to Women's Participation in Parliament', *Canadian Parliamentary Review*, vol.17, no.3, Autumn 1994, pp.12–14.
Economic Commission for Latin America and the Caribbean, *Major Changes and Crises: the Impact of Women in Latin America and the Caribbean* (Santiago: Economic Commission for Latin America and the Caribbean), 1992.
Franke, Richard W. and Chasin, Barbara H. (eds), *Kerala: Development through Radical Reforms* (New Delhi: Promilla and Co., in collaboration with the Institute for Food and Development Policy), 1994.
Githens, Marianne et al., *Different Roles, Different Voices: Women and Politics in the United States and Europe* (London: HarperCollins), 1994.
Goetz, Anne Marie, *Politics of Integrating Gender to State Development Processes: Trends, Opportunities and Constraints in Bangladesh, Chile, Jamaica, Mali, Morocco and Uganda* (Geneva: United Nations Research Institute for Social Development), 1995.
Harcourt, Wendy (ed.), *Feminist Perspectives on Sustainable Development* (London: Zed Books, in association with the Society for International Development, Rome), 1994.
Hawley, John Stralton (ed.), *Fundamentalism and Gender* (New York: Oxford University Press), 1994.
Heptulla, Najma (ed.), *Reforms for Women: Future Options* (New Delhi: Oxford and IBH Publishing Company), 1992.
Heptulla, Najma, 'The Unrepresented Electorate: Women in Indian Politics', *The Parliamentarian*, vol.LXXII, no.3, July 1991, pp.193–6.
Inter-Parliamentary Union, *Distribution of Seats between Men and Women in National Parliaments: Statistical Data from 1945 to 30 June 1991* (Geneva: Inter-Parliamentary Union), 1991.
Inter-Parliamentary Union, *Distribution of Seats between Men and Women in the 178 National Parliaments existing as at 30 June 1994* (Geneva: Inter-Parliamentary Union), 1994.
Inter-Parliamentary Union, *Plan of Action to Correct Present Imbalance in the Participation of Men and Women in Political Life* (Geneva: Inter-Parliamentary Union), 1994.
Inter-Parliamentary Union, *Women in Parliaments 1950–1995: A World Statistical Survey* (Geneva: Inter-Parliamentary Union), 1995.

Jacobson, Jodi L., *Gender Bias: Roadblock to Sustainable Development* (Worldwatch Paper 110) (USA: Worldwatch Institute), 1992.

Jahan, Rounaq, *The Elusive Agenda: Mainstreaming Women in Development* (London: Zed Books), 1995.

Jeffrey, Robin, *Politics, Women and Well-Being: How Kerala Became a 'Model'* (Basingstoke: Macmillan), 1992.

Kabeer, Naila, *Reversed Realities: Gender Hierarchies in Development Thought* (London: Verso), 1994.

Kalbagh, Chetana (ed.), *Women and Development* (7 vols) (New Delhi: Discovery Publishing House), 1991.

Kaushik, Susheela (ed.), *Women's Participation in Politics* (New Delhi: Vikas Publishing House), 1993.

Laslett, Barbara, Brenner, Johanna and Arat, Yesim (eds), *Rethinking the Political: Gender, Resistance and the State* (Chicago: Chicago University Press), 1995.

Lockwood, Matthew, *Engendering Adjustment or Adjusting Gender? Some New Approaches to Women and Development in Africa* (Brighton: Institute of Development Studies, University of Sussex), 1992.

Lorber, Judith, *Paradoxes of Gender* (New Haven, Conn.: Yale University Press), 1994.

Lovenduski, Joni and Norris, Pippa (eds), *Gender and Political Parties* (London: Sage), 1993.

Lynn, Naomi (ed.), *Women, Politics and the Constitution* (London: Harrington Park Press), 1991.

Macdonald, Mandy, *Gender Planning in Development Agencies: Meeting the Challenge* (Oxford: Oxfam), 1994.

Massiah, Joycelin (ed.), *Women in Developing Economies: Making Visible the Invisible* (Providence, Rhode Island: Berg Publishers, Inc., in cooperation with UNESCO), 1993.

Moghadam, Valentine M., 'Development and Women's Emancipation: Is There a Connection?', *Development and Change*, vol.23, no.3, 1992.

Moghadam, Valentine M. (ed.), *Gender and National Identity: Women and Politics in Muslim Societies* (London: Zed Books), 1994.

Moghadam, Valentine M. (ed.), *Identity Politics and Women: Cultural Reassertions and Feminism in International Perspective* (Boulder, Col.: Westview Press), 1994.

Moser, Caroline O.N., *Gender, Planning and Development: Theory, Practice and Training* (London: Routledge), 1993.

Mosse, Julia Cleves, *Half the World, Half a Chance: An Introduction to Gender and Development* (Oxford: Oxfam), 1994.

Mujuru, J.T.R., 'Women in Zimbabwe's Political Life', *The Parliamentarian*, vol.LXXI, no.3, July 1990, pp.187–8.

Nelson, Barbara J. and Chowdhury, Najma (eds), *Women and Politics Worldwide* (New Haven, Conn.: Yale University Press), 1994.
Nuna, Sheel C., *Women and Development* (New Delhi: National Institute of Educational Planning and Administration), 1990.
Palmer, Ingrid, *Gender and Population in the Adjustment of African Economies: Planning for Change* (Geneva: ILO), 1991.
Peters, Julie and Wolper, Andrea (eds), *Women's Rights, Human Rights: International Feminist Perspectives* (New York: Routledge), 1995.
Peterson, Spike V. and Runyan, Anne Sission, *Global Gender Issues* (Boulder, Col.: Westview Press), 1993.
Pickles, Carolyn, 'Barriers to Electing More Women to Parliament and Some Solutions', *The Parliamentarian*, vol.LXXVI, no.4, October 1995, pp.290–3.
Pietila, Hilkka and Vickers, Jeanne, *Making Women Matter: Role of the United Nations* (London: Zed Books), 1990.
Ranjana Kumari (ed.), *Women in Decision-Making* (New Delhi: Vikas Publishing House), 1992.
Ranjana Kumari and Dubey, Anju, *Women Parliamentarians: A Study in the Indian Context* (New Delhi: Har-Anand Publications), 1994.
Rinehart, Sue Tolleson, *Gender Consciousness and Politics* (New York: Routledge), 1992.
Rounaq Jahan, *The Elusive Agenda: Mainstreaming Women in Development* (Dhaka: University Press), 1995.
Snyder, Margaret C. and Tadesse, Mary, *African Women and Development – A History: the Story of the African Training and Research Centre* (London: Zed Books), 1995.
Stiftung, Friedrich Ebert, *Women in Politics: Forms and Processes* (New Delhi: Har-Anand Publications), 1993.
Sutherland, Sally J.M. (ed.), *Bridging Worlds: Studies on Women in South Asia* (Delhi: Oxford University Press), 1992.
Symonds, Ann, 'It's Still a Man's World: Women and Parliament', *The Parliamentarian*, vol.LXXII, no.4, October 1991, pp.278–81.
The 1995 Commonwealth Plan of Action on Gender and Development: A Commonwealth Vision (London: Commonwealth Secretariat).
The Polity Reader in Gender Studies (Cambridge: Polity Press), 1994.
Thomas, Sue, *How Women Legislate?* (New York: Oxford University Press), 1994.
Tomasevski, Katarina, *Women and Human Rights* (London: Zed Books), 1993.
Uchendu, Patrick Kenechukwu, *Role of Nigerian Women in Politics: Past and Present* (Nigeria: Fourth Dimension Publishing Co.), 1994.

United Nations, *The World's Women 1995: Trends and Statistics* (New York: United Nations), 1995.

United Nations Centre for Social Development and Humanitarian Affairs, *Compendium of International Conventions Concerning the Status of Women* (New York: United Nations), 1988.

United Nations Centre for Social Development and Humanitarian Affairs, *The Impact of Economic and Political Reform on the Status of Women in Eastern Europe* (Proceedings of a United Nations Regional Seminar, Vienna, 8–12 April 1991) (New York: Centre for Social Development and Humanitarian Affairs), 1992.

United Nations Centre for Social Development and Humanitarians Affairs, *The World's Women, 1970–1990: Trends and Statistics* (New York: United Nations), 1991.

United Nations Department for Policy Co-ordination and Sustainable Development, *Women in a Changing Global Economy: 1994, World Survey on the Role of Women in Development* (New York: Department for Policy Co-ordination and Sustainable Development, United Nations), 1995.

Vickers, Jeanne, *Women and the World Economic Crisis* (London: Zed Books), 1994.

Wallace, Tina and March, Candida, *Changing Perceptions: Writings on Gender and Development* (Oxford: Oxfam), 1991.

Waylen, Georgina, 'Women's Movements and Democratisation in Latin America', *Third World Quarterly*, vol.14, no.3, 193, pp.573–84.

Weeks-Vagliani, Winifred, *Participatory Development and Gender: Articulating Concepts and Cases* (Paris: OECD), 1994.

Women and Men in Namibia (Windhoek: Central Statistics Office, National Planning Commission), 1995.

Women and the Democratization Process in Africa: Report of UNESCO Regional Meeting of Experts, Windhoek, Namibia, 18 to 22 October 1994 (Windhoek and Dakar Offices: UNESCO).

Working towards Gender Equality (Programme 1993–95) (London: The Commonwealth Secretariat).

Working towards Gender Equality: Programme Initiatives (London: The Commonwealth Secretariat).

Wormald, Eileen and Thomas, Laura, *Women and Political Structures: Constraints on Access and the Role of the 300 Group* (Worcester: Worcester College of Higher Education), 1992.

10 Creating an Enabling Economic Environment for Development

Adam, Christopher, Cavendish, William and Mistry, Percy S., *Adjusting Privatization: Case Studies from Developing Countries* (London: James Currey), 1992.
Adams, Patricia, *Odious Debts: Loose Lending, Corruption and the Third World's Environmental Legacy* (London: Earthscan), 1991.
Adedeji, Adebayo (ed.), *Africa within the World: Beyond Dispossession and Dependence* (London: Zed Books, in association with the African Centre for Development and Strategic Studies), 1993.
Adriaansen, Willem L.M. and Waardenburg, J. George (eds), *A Dual World Economy: Forty Years of Development Experience* (Bombay: Oxford University Press), 1992.
Agrawal, Pradeep et al., *Economic Restructuring in East Asia and India: Perspectives on Policy Reforms* (London: Macmillan), 1995.
Ahooja-Patel, Krishna, *Women and Sustainable Development: An International Dimension* (New Delhi: Ashish Publishing House), 1995.
Allen, Tim and Thomas, Alan, *Poverty and Development in the 1990s* (Oxford: Oxford University Press), 1992.
Amsden, A.H., *Asia's Next Giant: South Korea and Late Industrialization* (New York: Oxford University Press), 1989.
Archer, Robin, *Economic Democracy: the Politics of Feasible Socialism* (Oxford: Clarendon Press), 1995.
Archibugi, Damile and Held, David (eds), *Cosmopolitan Democracy: An Agenda for a New World Order* (Cambridge: Polity Press), 1995.
Asian Development Outlook 1994 (Oxford: Oxford University Press), 1994.
Asian Development Bank, *Asian Development Outlook 1995 and 1996* (Oxford: Oxford University Press), 1995.
Asian Development Bank, *Human Resource Policy and Economic Development: Selected Country Studies* (Manila: Asian Development Bank), 1991.
'Asian Values', *The Economist*, vol.331, no.7867, 28 May 1994, pp.9–10.
Aslanbeigui, Nahid, Pressman, Steven and Summerfield, Gale, *Women in the Age of Economic Transformation: Gender Impact of Reforms in Post-Socialist and Developing Countries* (London: Routledge), 1994.
Aslund, A. and Layard R. (eds), *Changing the Economic System in Russia* (New York: St Martin's Press), 1993.
Attfield, Robin and Wilkins, Barry (eds), *International Justice and the Third World: Studies in the Philosophy of Development* (London: Routledge), 1992.
Auty, Richard M., *Economic Development and Industrial Policy: Korea, Brazil, Mexico, India and China* (London: Mansell), 1994.

Auty, Richard M., *Patterns of Development: Resources, Policy and Economic Growth* (London: Edward Arnold), 1995.

Bagchi, Amiya Kumar (ed.), *Democracy and Development* (Proceedings of the IEA Conference held in Barcelona, Spain) (Basingstoke: Macmillan), 1995.

Balgoun, M. Jide and Mutahaba, Gelase (eds), *Economic Restructuring and African Public Administration: Issues, Actions and Future Choices* (Conn.: Kumarian Press), 1991.

Banuri, Tariq (ed.), *Economic Liberalization No Panacea: the Experience of Latin America and Asia* (Oxford: Clarendon Press), 1991.

Bardhan, Pranab, Datta-Chaudhuri, Mrinal and Krishnan, T.N. (eds), *Development and Change* (Essays in honour of K.N. Raj) (Bombay: Oxford University Press), 1993.

Barsh, R.L., 'Democratization and Development', *Human Rights Quarterly*, 14/1992, pp.120–34.

Bayart, Jean-Francois, *The State in Africa: the Politics of the Belly* (London: Longman), 1993.

Bayoumi, Tamim and Hewitt, Daniel, *Economic Consequences of Lower Military Spending: Some Simulation Results* (Washington: IMF), 1993.

Bayoumi, Tamim and Hewitt, Daniel, *Impact of Worldwide Military Spending Cuts on Developing Countries* (Washington: IMF), 1993.

Bello, W.F. and Rosenfeld S., *Dragons in Distress: Asia's Miracle Economies in Crisis* (San Francisco: Institute for Food and Development Policy), 1990.

Beng-Huat Chua, 'Arrested Development: Democratization in Singapore', *Third World Quarterly*, vol.15, no.4, 1994, pp.655–68.

Beng-Huat Chua, *Communitarian Ideology and Democracy in Singapore* (London: Routledge), 1995.

Berberoglu, Berch, *The Political Economy of Development: Development Theory and the Prospects for Change in the Third World* (Albany: State University of New York Press), 1992.

Berger, Mark T., 'The End of the Third World', *Third World Quarterly*, vol.15, no.2, 1994, pp.257–76.

Berger, P.L. and Hsiao, H.M. (eds), *In Search of an East Asian Development Model* (New Brunswick: Transaction Books), 1988.

Bhagwati, Jagdish, 'Democracy and Development: New Thinking on an Old Generation', *Indian Economic Review*, vol.30, no.1, January–June 1995, pp.1–8.

Bhagwati, J., *India in Transition* (Oxford: Clarendon Press), 1993.

Bhalla, A.S., *Uneven Development in the Third World: A Study of China and India* (2nd revised and enlarged edn) (Basingstoke: Macmillan), 1995.

Bienefeld, Manfred, 'The New World Order: Echoes of a New Imperialism', *Third World Quarterly*, vol.15, no.1, 1994, pp.31–48.
Bird, Graham, *IMF Lending to Developing Countries: Issues and Evidence* (London: Routledge), 1995.
Bissio, Roberto Remo (ed.), *The World: A Third World Guide 1995/96* (Montevideo: Institute del Tercer Mundo), 1996.
Blake, David H. and Walters, Robert S., *The Politics of Global Economic Relations* (3rd edn) (Englewood Cliffs, NJ: Prentice-Hall), 1987.
Borner, Silvio, Brunetti, Aymo and Weder, Beatrice, *Political Credibility and Economic Development* (Basingstoke: Macmillan), 1995.
Boserup, Ester, *Women's Role in Economic Development* (London: Earthscan), 1989.
Boyko, Maxim, Sehleifer, Andrei and Vishny, Robert, *Privatizing Russia* (London: MIT Press), 1995.
Bradbury, Mark, *Aid Under Fire: Redefining Relief and Development Assistance in Unstable Situations* (Wilton Park Paper 104) (London: HMSO), 1995.
Bremer, Stuart A. and Hughes, Barry B., *Disarmament and Development: A Design for the Future* (Englewood Cliffs, NJ: Prentice-Hall), 1990.
Brown, Michael Barratt, *Africa's Choices: After Thirty Years of the World Bank* (London: Penguin Books), 1995.
Brown, Michael Barratt and Tiffen, Pauline, *Shortchanged: Africa and World Trade* (London: Pluto Press), 1992.
Bruno, M., *Crisis, Stabilization and Economic Reform* (Oxford: Clarendon Press), 1993.
Bryan, Anthony T., Green, J. Edward and Shaw, Timothy M., *Peace, Development and Security in the Caribbean: Perspectives to the Year 2000* (Basingstoke: Macmillan), 1990.
Budge, Ian and McKay, David (eds), *Developing Democracy: Comparative Research in Honour of Jean Blondel* (London: Sage Publications), 1993.
Butcher, Tony, *Delivering Welfare: The Governance of the Social Services in the 1990s* (Buckingham: Open University Press), 1995.
Callaghy, Thomas M. and Ravenhill, John (eds), *Hemmed In: Responses to Africa's Economic Decline* (New York: Columbia University Press), 1994.
Cameron, John, Ramharak, Hans and Cole, Ken (eds), *Poverty and Power: the Role of Institutions and the Market in Development* (Delhi: Oxford University Press), 1995.
Campbell, Adrian, *The Challenge to the Centre* (London: Pitman Publishing), 1995.
Carew-Reid, Jeremy, Presscott-Allen, Robert, Bass, Stephen and Dalal-Clayton, Barry, *Strategies for National Sustainable Development* (London:

Earthscan, in association with the World Conservation Union and the International Institute for Environment and Development), 1994.

Castells, M., *The Developmental City-State in an Open Economy: The Singapore Experience* (Berkeley Round Table on International Economy, Working Paper no.31) (Berkeley: University of California), 1988.

Cassen, Robert, *Does Aid Work? Report to an Intergovernmental Task Force* (2nd edn) (Oxford: Clarendon Press), 1994.

Chalker, Lynda, 'Development and Democracy: What Should the Commonwealth be Doing?', *The Round Table*, no.329, January 1994, pp.23–6.

Chan, Steven (ed.), *Foreign Direct Investment in a Changing Global Political Economy* (Basingstoke: Macmillan), 1995.

Chandra, Rajesh, *Industrialization and Development in the Third World* (London: Routledge), 1992.

Change for the Better: Global Change and Economic Development (London: Commonwealth Secretariat), 1991.

Chan Heng Chee, 'Democracy, Human Rights and Social Justice as Key Factors in Balanced Development', *The Round Table*, no.329, January 1994, pp.27–36.

Chew, Rosalind, *Employment-Driven Industrial Relations Regimes: The Singapore Experience* (Aldershot: Avebury), 1995.

Chong-Yah Lim et al., *Policy Options for the Singapore Economy* (Singapore: McGraw-Hill), 1988.

Chowdhury, A. and Islam, I., *The Newly Industrialising Economies of East Asia* (London: Routledge), 1993.

Clague, Christopher and Rausser, Gordon C. (eds), *The Emergence of Market Economies in Eastern Europe* (Cambridge: Blackwell), 1992.

Clapham, Christopher, 'The Collapse of Socialist Development in the Third World', *Third World Quarterly*, vol.13, no.1, 1992, pp.13–26.

Clarke, Alice W. (ed.), *Gender and Political Economy: Exploration of South Asian Systems* (Delhi: Oxford University Press), 1993.

Cline, William R., *International Debt Re-examined* (Washington, DC: Institute for International Economics), 1995.

Cohen, Robin and Goulbourne, Harry (eds), *Democracy and Socialism in Africa* (Boulder, Col.: Westview Press), 1991.

Colburn, Forrest D. and Rahmato, Dessalegn, 'Rethinking Socialism in the Third World', *Third World Quarterly*, vol.13, no.1, 1992, pp.159–74.

Cornia, Giovanni Andrea, Van der Hoeven, Rolph and Mkandawire, Thandika (eds), *Africa's Recovery in the 1990s: from Stagnation and Adjustment to Human Development* (London: Macmillan), 1992.

Cottam, Christine M. and Rao, Sudha V. (eds), *Women, Aid and Development* (Essays in Honour of Professor T. Scarlett Epstein) (Delhi: Hindustan Publishing), 1993.

da Cunha, Derek (ed.), *Debating Singapore: Reflective Essays* (Singapore: Institute of South East Asian Studies), 1994.
Daffern, Peter et al., *Financial Management in the Public Sector* (London: Pitman Publishing), 1995.
Dagenais, Huguette and Piche, Denise, *Women, Feminism and Development* (London: McGill–Queen's University Press), 1994.
Dahl, R., *Democracy and its Critics* (New Haven, Conn.: Yale University Press), 1989.
Dasgupta, Abhijit and Lechner, Georg (eds), *Development Aid Today* (New Delhi: Mosaic Books), 1995.
Dasgupta, P., *An Inquiry into Well-being and Destitution* (Oxford: Clarendon Press), 1993.
Davidian, Zaven N., *Economic Disparities among Nations: A Threat to Survival in a Globalized World* (Calcutta: Oxford University Press), 1994.
Debt-Conversion Schemes in Africa: Lessons from the Experience of Developing Countries (London: James Currey, for the African Centre for Monetary Studies and Association of African Central Banks), 1992.
'Democracy and Growth', *The Economist*, vol.332, no.7878, 27 August 1994, pp.15–17.
'Democracy Works Best', *The Economist*, vol.332, no.7878, 27 August 1994, pp.9–10.
Devlin, John F. and Yap, Nomita T., 'Sustainable Development and the NICs: Cautionary Tales for the South in the New World (Dis)Order', *Third World Quarterly*, vol.15, no.1, 1994, pp.49–62.
Deyo, F.C. (ed.), *The Political Economy of the New Asian Industrialism* (Ithaca, NY: Cornell University Press), 1987.
Diamond, L., 'Economic Development and Democracy Reconsidered', *American Behavioural Scientist* 35 (4/5), 1992, pp.450–99.
Diamond, Larry (ed.), *Democracy in Developing Countries: Persistence, Failure and Renewal* (London: Adamantine Press), 1992.
DiIulio, John J. Jr, *Deregulating the Public Policy: Can Government be Improved?* (Washington, DC: Brookings Institution), 1994.
Dixon, Chris and Drakakis-Smith, David (eds), *Economic and Social Development in Pacific Asia* (London: Routledge), 1993.
Doel, Hans Van and Velthoven, Ben Van, *Democracy and Welfare Economics* (Cambridge: Cambridge University Press), 1993.
Dominguez, Jorge I. (ed.), *Democracy in the Caribbean: Political, Economic and Social Perspectives* (Baltimore: Johns Hopkins University Press), 1993.
Drokeran, Winston, 'NAFTA, the EC and the Uruguay Round: Does the Caribbean Have a Place in the New Economic Order?', *The Round Table*, no.326, April 1993, pp.153–8.

Dorraj, Manochagh (ed.), *The Changing Political Economy of the Third World* (Boulder, Col.: Lynne Rienner), 1995.

Dréze, J. and Sen A. (eds), *The Political Economy of Hunger* (vol.3) (Oxford: Clarendon Press), 1991.

Economic and Social Commission for Asia and the Pacific, *Econometric Modelling and Forecasting in Asia* (Proceedings of a Regional Seminar organized in collaboration with the Research and Information System for the Non-aligned and Other Developing Countries, New Delhi, 27 February–1 March 1989) (Bangkok), 1991.

'Economic Growth: Explaining the Mystery', *The Economist*, vol.322, no.7740, 4 January 1992, pp.17–20.

Eisenstadt, S.N. (ed.), *Democracy and Modernity* (Leiden: E.J. Brill), 1992.

Erisman, H. Michael, *Pursuing Post-Dependency Politics: South–South Relations in the Caribbean* (Boulder, Col.: Lynne Rienner), 1992.

Fenwick, J., *Managing Local Government* (London: International Thomson Business Press), 1995.

Field, Graham, *Economic Growth and Political Change in Asia* (Basingstoke: Macmillan), 1995.

Foreign and Commonwealth Office, *Good Government in Africa* (Wilton Park Paper 54) (London: HMSO), 1992.

Forsythe, David P., *Human Rights and Development: International Views* (Basingstoke: Macmillan), 1989.

Frank, André Gunder, *Capitalism and Underdevelopment in Latin America: Historical Studies of Chile and Brazil* (New York and London: Modern Reader Paperbacks), 1969.

Franke, Richard W. and Chasin, Barbara H. (eds), *Kerala: Development through Radical Reforms* (New Delhi: Promilla and Co., in collaboration with the Institute for Food and Development Policy), 1994.

'Freedom and Prosperity', *The Economist*, vol.320, no.7713, 29 June 1991, pp.15–18.

'Freeing India's Economy', *The Economist*, vol.323, no.7760, 23 May 1992, pp.21–3.

Friedman, Edward (ed.), *The Politics of Democratization: Generalizing East Asian Experiences* (Boulder, Col.: Westview Press), 1994.

Frimpong-Ansah, J.H. and Ingham, Barbara (eds), *Saving for Economic Recovery in Africa* (London: James Currey, for the African Centre for Economic Policy Research), 1992.

Froot, Kenneth A. (ed.), *Foreign Direct Investment* (Chicago: University of Chicago Press), 1993.

Fukuyama, Francis, 'Capitalism and Democracy: The Missing Link', *Journal of Democracy*, vol.3, no.3, July 1992.

Fukuyama, Francis, *The End of History and the Last Man* (New York: Free Press), 1992.
General Agreement on Tariffs and Trade (GATT), *International Trade: Trends and Statistics* (GATT), 1994.
George, Robert Lloyd, *The East–West Pendulum* (New York: Woodhead-Faulkner), 1992.
George, Susan and Sabelli, Fabrizio, *Faith and Credit: The World Bank's Secular Empire* (London: Penguin Books), 1994.
Gereffi, G. and Wyman D. (eds), *Manufacturing Miracles: Paths of Industrialization in Latin America and East Asia* (Princeton, NJ: Princeton University Press), 1990.
German, Tony and Randel, Judith (eds), *The Reality of Aid 1995: An Independent Review of International Aid* (London: Earthscan), 1995.
Gibbon, Peter, *Social Change and Economic Reform in Africa* (Uppsala: Scandinavian Institute of African Studies), 1993.
Gills, Barry and Rocamora, Joel, *Low Intensity Democracy: Political Power in the New World Order* (Oxford: Pluto Press), 1993.
Gills, Barry and Qadir, Shahid (eds), *Regimes in Crisis: the Post-Soviet Era and the Implications for Development* (London: Zed Books), 1995.
Goetz, Anne Marie, *Politics of Integrating Gender to State Development Processes: Trends, Opportunities and Constraints in Bangladesh, Chile, Jamaica, Mali, Morocco and Uganda* (Geneva: United Nations Research Institute for Social Development), 1995.
Goh, Keng-Swee, *Public Administration and Economic Development in LDCs* (London: TPRC), 1983.
Graham, Norman A. (ed.), *Seeking Security and Development: the Impact of Military Spending and Arms Transfers* (Boulder, Col.: Lynne Rienner), 1994.
Griesgraber, Jo Marie and Gunter, Bernhard G. (eds), *Promoting Development: Effective Global Institutions for the Twenty-first Century* (London: Pluto Press, with Center of Concern, Washington, DC), 1995.
Grindle, Merilee S., *Challenging the State: Crisis and Innovation in Latin America and Africa* (Cambridge: Cambridge University Press), 1996.
Grugel, Jean, *Politics and Development in the Caribbean Basin: Central America and the Caribbean in the New World Order* (Basingstoke: Macmillan), 1995.
Guy, Arnold, *The End of the Third World* (Basingstoke: Macmillan), 1993.
Hadenius, Axel, *Democracy and Development* (Cambridge: Cambridge University Press), 1992.
Haggard, Stephen and Kaufman, Robert R., *The Political Economy of Democratic Transitions* (Princeton, NJ: Princeton University Press), 1995.

Haggard, Stephen and Kaufman, Robert R., *The Politics of Economic Adjustment* (Princeton, NJ: Princeton University Press), 1992.
Ha-Joon Chang and Rowthorn, Robert (eds), *The Role of the State in Economic Change* (Oxford: Clarendon Press), 1995.
Hansen, Holger Bernt and Twaddle, Michael, *Changing Uganda: The Dilemmas of Structural Adjustment and Revolutionary Change* (London: James Currey), 1991.
Harcourt, Wendy (ed.), *Feminist Perspectives on Sustainable Development* (London: Zed Books, in association with the Society for International Development, Rome), 1994.
Hartley, Keith, *Economic Aspects of Disarmament: Disarmament as an Investment Process* (New York: United Nations), 1993.
Harvey, C. and Lewis, S.R., *Policy Choice and Development Performance in Botswana* (London: Macmillan), 1990.
Healey, John and Robinson, Mark, *Democracy, Governance and Economic Policy: Sub-Saharan Africa in Comparative Perspective* (London: Overseas Development Institute), 1994.
Held, David, *Democracy and the Global Order* (Oxford: Polity Press), 1995.
Helleiner, G.K. (ed.), *The International Monetary and Financial System: Developing Country Perspectives* (Basingstoke: Macmillan), 1996.
Helliwell, J.F., *Empirical Linkages between Democracy and Economic Growth* (NBER Working Paper no.4066) (Cambridge, Mass.: National Bureau of Economic Research), 1992.
Henry, Paul-Marc (ed.), *Poverty, Progress and Development* (Paris: Kegan Paul International), 1991.
Herera, Remy, *Statistics on Military Expenditure in Developing Countries: Concepts, Methodological Problems and Sources* (Paris: OECD), 1994.
Heron, Richard Le and Park, Sam Ock (eds), *The Asian Pacific Rim and Globalization: Enterprises, Governance and Territoriality* (Aldershot: Avebury), 1995.
Hill, Michael and Lian Kwen Fee, *The Politics of Nation Building and Citizenship in Singapore* (London: Routledge), 1995.
Himmelstrand, Ulf, Kinyanjui, Kabiru and Mburugu, Edward (eds), *African Perspectives on Development* (London: James Currey), 1994.
Hintjens, Helen M. and Newitt, Malyn D.D. (eds), *The Political Economy of Small Tropical Islands: The Importance of Being Small* (Exeter: University of Exeter Press), 1992.
Hirst, Paul, *Associative Democracy: New Forms of Economic and Social Governance* (Cambridge: Polity Press), 1994.
Hodd, Michael, *The Economics of Africa: Geography, Population, History, Stability, Structure, Performance Forecasts* (Aldershot: Dartmouth), 1991.

Hook, Steven W., *National Interest and Foreign Aid* (Boulder, Col.: Lynne Rienner), 1995.
Hout, Wil, *Capitalism and the Third World: Development, Dependence and the World System* (Aldershot: Edward Elgar), 1993.
Howell, J., *China Opens its Doors: The Politics of Economic Transition* (Boulder, Col.: Lynne Rienner), 1993.
Huntington, Samuel P., *Third Wave: Democratization in the Late Twentieth Century* (Norman, Okla.: University of Oklahoma Press), 1991.
Hyden, Goran and Bratton, Michael, *Governance and Politics in Africa* (Boulder, Col.: Lynne Rienner), 1992.
Ihonvbere, Julius O. and Turner, Terisa E., 'Africa in the Post-Containment Era: Constraints, Pressures and Prospects for the 21st Century', *The Round Table*, no.328, October 1993, pp.443–59.
Inkeles, Alex (ed.), *On Measuring Democracy: Its Consequences and Concomitants* (Brunswick, NJ: Transaction Publishers), 1991.
Instruments for Economic Policy in Africa (London: James Currey, for the African Centre for Monetary Studies and Association of African Central Banks), 1992.
International Monetary Fund, *Issues and Developments in International Trade Policy* (Washington: International Monetary Fund), 1992.
Iwasaki, Teruyuki, Mori, Takeshi and Yamaguchi, Hiroichi (eds), *Development Strategies for the 21st Century* (Papers and Proceedings of the Institute of Developing Economies, 30th Anniversary Symposium on Development Strategies for the 21st Century, held on 10–12 December 1990 (Tokyo: Institute of Developing Economies), 1992.
Jacobson, Jodi L., *Gender Bias: Roadblock to Sustainable Development* (Worldwatch Paper 110) (USA: Worldwatch Institute), 1992.
Jahan, Rounaq, *The Elusive Agenda: Mainstreaming Women in Development* (London: Zed Books), 1995.
Jain, R.B. and Asmero H.K. (eds), *Politics, Administration and Public Policy in Developing Countries: Examples from Africa, Asia and Latin America* (Netherlands: VUUP), 1993.
James, William E., Naya, Seiji and Meier, Gerald M., *Asian Development: Economic Success and Policy Lessons* (Wisconsin: University of Wisconsin Press), 1989.
Jeffrey, Robin, *Politics, Women and Well-Being: How Kerala Became a 'Model'* (Basingstoke: Macmillan), 1992.
Johnson, John, 'Aid and Good Governance in Africa', *The Round Table*, no.320, October 1991, pp.395–400.
Jones, Alexandra D., *Global Good Governance: Legitimation through Popular Consent, International Credibility and Development Promotion* (London: University of London), 1994.

Joshi, Vijay, 'Democracy and Development in India', *The Round Table*, no.333, January 1995, pp.73–80.
Kabeer, Naila, *Reversed Realities: Gender Hierarchies in Development Thought* (London: Verso), 1994.
Kalbagh, Chetana (ed.), *Women and Development* (7 vols) (New Delhi: Discovery Publishing House), 1991.
Karl, T.L., 'Dilemmas of Democratization in Latin America', *Comparative Politics*, 1990, pp.1–21.
Kay, Cristobal, *Latin American Theories of Development and Underdevelopment* (London: Routledge), 1989.
Keech, William R., *Economic Politics: The Costs of Democracy* (New York: Cambridge University Press), 1995.
Kennedy, Paul, *Preparing for the Twenty-First Century* (New York: Random House), 1993.
Khadiagala, Gilbert M., 'Thoughts on Africa and the New World Order', *The Round Table*, no.324, October 1992, pp.431–50.
Khan, Mohsin S., Montiel, Peter J. and Haque, Nadeem U. (eds), *Macroeconomic Models for Adjustment in Countries* (Washington, DC: International Monetary Fund), 1991.
Kiel, L. Douglas, *Managing Chaos and Complexity in Government: A New Paradigm for Managing Change, Innovation, and Organizational Renewal* (San Francisco: Jossey-Bass Publishers), 1994.
Kim, Bun Woong, Bell, David S. and Lee, Chang Bum, *Administrative Dynamics and Development* (Seoul: Kyobo Publishing), 1985.
Kinyanjui, Kabiru and Mburugu, Edward, *African Perspectives on Development: Controversies, Dilemmas and Openings* (London: Villiers Publications), 1994.
Klein, Lawrence R., Fu-Chen Lo and Mckibbin, Warwick J. (eds), *Arms Reduction: Economic Implications in the Post-Cold War Era* (Tokyo: United Nations University Press), 1995.
Knight, Malcolm, Loayza, Norman et al., *Peace Dividend: Military Spending Cuts and Economic Growth* (Washington, DC: International Monetary Fund), 1995.
Kohli, Atul, 'Democracy amid Economic Orthodoxy: Trends in Developing Countries', *Third World Quarterly*, vol.14, no.4, November 1993, pp.671–90.
Kohli, Atul, *Democracy and Disorder: India's Growing Crisis of Governability* (Cambridge: Cambridge University Press), 1991.
Kornai, J., *The Socialist System: The Political Economy of Communism* (Oxford: Clarendon Press), 1992.
Kothari, S.S., *New Fiscal and Economic Strategies for Growth in Developing Countries* (Delhi: Oxford University Press), 1992.

Lall, K.B., *International Economic Relations: Struggle for Change* (rev. edn) (New Delhi: Allied Publishers), 1992.
Lasserre, Philippe and Schutte, Hellmutt, *Strategies for Asia Pacific* (Basingstoke: Macmillan), 1995.
Leftwich, Adrian, 'Governance, Democracy and Development in the Third World', *Third World Quarterly*, vol.14, no.3, 1993, pp.605–24.
Leftwich, Adrian, 'Bringing Politics Back In: Towards a Model of the Developmental State', *Journal of Developmental Studies*, 1995, pp.31, 400–27.
Leftwich, Adrian (ed.), *Democracy and Development: Theory and Practice* (Cambridge: Polity Press), 1996.
Lehmann, D., *Democracy and Development in Latin America* (Cambridge: Polity Press), 1990.
Lewellen, Ted C., *Dependence and Development: An Introduction to the Third World* (Westport, Conn.: Bergin and Garvey), 1995.
Lim, C.Y., *Development and Underdevelopment* (Singapore: Longman), 1991.
Lim, David, *Explaining Economic Growth: A New Analytical Framework* (Cheltenham: Edward Elgar), 1996.
Lim, L. and Pang, E.F., *Foreign Direct Investment and Industrialization in Malaysia, Singapore, Taiwan and Thailand* (Paris: OECD Development Centre), 1991.
Lindenberg, M. and Ramirez N. (eds), *Managing Adjustment in Developing Countries* (San Francisco: ICS Press), 1989.
Lipton, Michael, 'The State–Market Dilemma, Civil Society, and Structural Adjustment: Any Cross-Commonwealth Lessons?', *The Round Table*, no.317, January 1991, pp.21–31.
Lockwood, Matthew, *Engendering Adjustment or Adjusting Gender? Some New Approaches to Women and Development in Africa* (Brighton: Institute of Development Studies, University of Sussex), 1992.
Macintyre, Andrew (ed.), *Business and Government in Industrialising Asia* (Ithaca, NY: Cornell University Press), 1994.
Manley, Michael, *The Poverty of Nations: Imperialism and Underdevelopment in the Twentieth Century* (London: Pluto Press), 1991.
Manley, Michael, *The Poverty of Nations: Reflections on Underdevelopment and the World Economy* (London: Pluto Press), 1991.
Martin Khor Kok Peng, *The Uruguay Round and Third World Sovereignty* (Penang: Third World Network), 1990.
Massiah, Joycelin (ed.), *Women in Developing Economies: Making Visible the Invisible* (Providence, RI: Berg Publishers, in co-operation with UNESCO), 1993.
Mayall, James and Payne, Anthony (eds), *The Fallacies of Hope: The Post-*

Colonial Record of the Commonwealth Third World (Manchester: Manchester University Press), 1990.

McAfee, Kathy, *Storm Signals: Structural Adjustment and Development Alternatives in the Caribbean* (London: Zed Books), 1991.

McCarthy-Arnolds, Eileen, Penna, David R. and Sobrepena, Debra Joy Cruz (eds), *Africa, Human Rights and the Global System: The Political Economy of Human Rights in a Changing World* (Westport, Conn.: Greenwood), 1994.

McCarthy, Mary and McCarthy, Tom, *Third World Debt: Towards an Equitable Solution* (Dublin: Macmillan), 1994.

McLellan, David and Sayers, Sean (eds), *Socialism and Democracy* (Basingstoke: Macmillan), 1991.

McMahon, Christopher, *Authority and Democracy: A General Theory of Government and Management* (Princeton, NJ: Princeton University Press), 1994.

Mengisteab, Kidane and Logan, Ikubolajeh (eds), *Beyond Economic Liberalization in Africa: Structural Adjustment and the Alternatives* (London: Zed Books), 1995.

Milne, R.S., 'Singapore's Growth Triangle', *The Round Table,* no.327, July 1993, pp.291–304.

Milne, R.S. and Mauzy, Diane K., *Singapore: The Legacy of Lee Kuan Yew* (Plymouth: Westview Press), 1990.

Mittelman, James H., 'The Globalization Challenge', *Third World Quarterly*, vol.15, no.3, September 1994, pp.427–44.

Moghadam, Valentine M., 'Development and Women's Emancipation: Is There a Connection?', *Development and Change*, vol.23, no.3, 1992.

Momsen, Janet H. and Kinnaird, Vivian (eds), *Different Places, Different Voices: Gender and Development in Africa, Asia and Latin America* (London: Routledge), 1993.

Monshipouri, Mahmood, *Democratization, Liberalization and Human Rights in the Third World* (Boulder, Col.: Lynne Rienner), 1995.

Morishima, M., *Why has Japan 'Succeeded?'* (Cambridge: Cambridge University Press), 1982.

Morley, J.W. (ed.), *Driven by Growth: Political Changes in the Asia-Pacific Region* (New York: M.E. Sharpe), 1993.

Morrissey, Oliver and Stewart, Frances (eds), *Economic and Political Reform in Developing Countries* (Basingstoke: Macmillan), 1995.

Moser, Caroline O.N., *Gender, Planning and Development: Theory, Practice and Training* (London: Routledge), 1993.

Mosley, Paul (ed.), *Development Finance and Policy Reform: Essays in the Theory and Practice of Conditionality in Less Developed Countries* (New York: St Martin's Press), 1992.

Mosley, Paul, Harrigan, Jana and Toye, John, *Aid and Power: The World Bank and Policy-Based Lending* (London: Routledge), 1991.
Mosse, Julia Cleves, *Half the World, Half a Chance: An Introduction to Gender and Development* (Oxford: Oxfam), 1994.
Munck, Ronaldo, 'South Africa: the Great Economic Debate', *Third World Quarterly*, vol.15, no.2, June 1994, pp.205–18.
Munslow, Barry and Fitzgerald, Patrick, 'South Africa: the Sustainable Development Challenge', *Third World Quarterly*, vol.15, no.2, June 1994, pp.227–42.
Murinde, Victor, *Macroeconomic Policy Modelling for Developing Countries* (Aldershot: Avebury), 1995.
Mutahaba, Gelase, *Reforming Public Administration for Development: Experiences from Eastern Africa* (Conn.: Kumarian Press), 1989.
Mutahaba, Gelase, Baguma, Rweikiza and Halfani, Mohamed, *Vitalizing African Public Administration for Recovery and Development* (Conn.: Kumarian Press), 1993.
Mwase, Ngila, 'Economic Integration for Development in Eastern and Southern Africa', *The Round Table*, no.336, October 1995, pp.477–94.
Myrdal, Gunnar, *Asian Drama* (New York: Pantheon), 1968.
Nagel, Stuart S. (ed.), *Asian Development and Public Policy* (Basingstoke: Macmillan), 1994.
Naisbitt, John, Megatrends in Asia: *The Eight Asian Megatrends that are Changing the World* (London: Nicholas Brealey Publishing), 1995.
Nanda, Ved P., Shepherd, George W. and Arnolds-McCarthy, Eileen (eds), *World Debt and the Human Condition: Structural Adjustment and the Right to Development* (Westport, Conn.: Greenwood Press), 1993.
Neher, Clark D., *Southeast Asia in the New International Era* (Boulder, Col.: Westview Press), 1991.
Neher, Clark D. and Marlay, Ross, *Democracy and Development in Southeast Asia* (Boulder, Col.: Westview Press), 1995.
Nelson, J. (ed.), *Economic Crisis and Policy Choice: The Politics of Adjustment in the Third World* (Princeton, NJ: Princeton University Press), 1990.
Nguyen Duc-Tho and Roy, Kartik C. (eds), *Economic Reform, Liberalization and Trade in the Asia-Pacific Region* (New Delhi: Wiley Eastern), 1994.
Nissanke, Machiko and Hewitt, Adrian (eds), *Economic Crisis in Developing Countries: New Perspectives on Commodities, Trade and Finance* (Essays in Honour of Alfred Maizels), (London: Pinter Publishers), 1993.
Nuna, Sheel C., *Women and Development* (New Delhi: National Institute of Educational Planning and Administration), 1990.
Olson, David and Mezey, Michael, *Legislatures in the Policy Process: The*

Dilemmas of Economic Policy (Cambridge: Cambridge University Press), 1991.
Olson, M., 'Dictatorship, Democracy and Development', *American Political Science Review*, 87/1993, pp.567–76.
Organisation for Economic Co-operation and Development (OECD), *Geographical Distribution of Financial Flows to Aid Recipients – 1989/1993* (Paris: OECD), 1995.
Ottaway, M., *South Africa: The Struggle for a New Order* (Washington, DC: Brookings Institution), 1993.
Ould-Mey, Mohameden, 'Global Adjustment: Implications for Peripheral States', *Third World Quarterly*, vol.15, no.2, June 1994, pp.319–36.
Overseas Development Administration, *ODA Guide to Social Analysis/Projects in Developing Countries* (London: HMSO), 1995.
Owens, Edgar, *The Future of Freedom in the Developing World: Economic Development as Political Reform* (New York: Pergamon Press), 1987.
Page, Sheila, *Trade, Finance and Developing Countries: Strategies and Constraints in the 1990s* (London: Harvester Wheatsheaf), 1990.
Palmer, Ingrid, *Gender and Population in the Adjustment of African Economies: Planning for Change* (Geneva: ILO), 1991.
Paul, Ellen Frankel, Miller, Fred D. and Paul, Jeffrey, *Economic Rights* (Cambridge: Cambridge University Press), 1992.
Paul, Erik C., 'Prospects for Liberalization in Singapore', *Journal of Contemporary Asia*, vol.23, no.3, 1993, pp.291–305.
Pereira, Luiz Carlos, Bresser, Maravall, Jose Maria and Przeworski, Adam, *Economic Reforms in New Democracies: A Social-Democratic Approach* (Cambridge: Cambridge University Press), 1993.
Persaud, Vishnu, 'Developing Countries can Compete in International Capital Markets', *The Round Table*, no.323, July 1992, pp.359–68.
Philip, George, 'The New Economic Liberalism and Democracy in Latin America: Friends or Enemies', *Third World Quarterly*, vol.14, no.3, 1993, pp.555–72.
Picard, Louis A. and Garrity, Michele (eds), *Policy Reform for Sustainable Development in Africa: The Institutional Imperative* (Boulder, Col.: Lynne Rienner), 1994.
Pourgerami, A., *Development and Democracy in the Third World* (Boulder, Col.: Westview Press), 1991.
Przeworski, A., *Democracy and the Market: Political and Economic Reforms in Eastern Europe and Latin America* (Cambridge: Cambridge University Press), 1991.
Przeworski, A. and Limongi, F., 'Political Regimes and Economic Growth', *Journal of Economic Perspectives*, vol.7, no.1, 1993, pp.51–69.

Quibria, M.G. (ed.), *Critical Issues in Asian Development: Theories, Experiences and Politics* (Hong Kong: Oxford University Press), 1995.

Ramphal, Shridath, *Our Country, the Planet: Forging a Partnership for Survival* (London: Lime Tree), 1992.

Ramphal, Shridath and Carlsson, Ingwar, *Our Global Neighbourhood: The Report of the Commission on Global Governance* (Oxford: Oxford University Press), 1995.

Randall, Vicky and Theobald, Robin (eds), *Political Change and Underdevelopment: A Critical Introduction to Third World Politics* (London: Sage Publications), 1988.

Remmer, K., 'Democracy and Economic Crisis: The Latin American Experience', *World Politics*, vol.42, no.3, pp.315–35.

Riddell, Roger, *Foreign Aid Reconsidered* (3rd edn) (London: Overseas Development Institute), 1995.

Riley, Stephen P. (ed.), *The Politics of Global Debt* (Basingstoke: Macmillan), 1993.

Rodan, G., *The Political Economy of Singapore's Industrialization: National, State and International Capital* (New York: St Martin's Press), 1989.

Rodan, Garry (ed.), *Singapore Changes Guard: Social, Political and Economic Directions in the 1990s* (London: Longman), 1994.

Rosow, Stephen J., Inayatullah, Naeem and Rupert, Mark (eds), *The Global Economy as Political Space* (Boulder, Col.: Lynne Rienner), 1994.

Ross, Robert R. (ed.), *East Asia in Transition: Towards a New Regional Order* (Armonk: M.E. Sharpe Inc.), 1995.

Rothschild, E. and Steadman Jones, G. (eds), *History and Development* (Oxford: Oxford University Press), 1995.

Rounaq Jahan, *The Elusive Agenda: Mainstreaming Women in Development* (Dhaka: University Press), 1995.

Rudner, Martin, *Malaysian Development: A Retrospect* (Ottawa: Carleton University Press), 1994.

Rueschemeyer, D., Stephens, E.H. and Stephens, J.D., *Capitalist Development and Democracy* (Cambridge: Polity Press), 1992.

Ryrie, William, *First World, Third World* (Basingstoke: Macmillan), 1995.

Saeed, Khalid, *Development Planning and Policy Design: A System Dynamics Approach* (Aldershot: Avebury), 1994.

Sahn, David E. (ed.), *Adjusting to Policy Failure in African Economies* (Ithaca, NY: Cornell University Press), 1994.

Sakong, I., *Korea in the World Economy* (Washington, DC: Institute for International Economics), 1993.

Samuels, Warren J., *Essays on the Economic Role of Government (Volume 1): Fundamentals* (Basingstoke: Macmillan), 1992.

Samuels, Warren J., *Essays on the Economic Role of Government (Volume 2): Applications* (Basingstoke: Macmillan), 1992.

Sandbrook, Richard, *The Politics of Africa's Economic Recovery* (Cambridge: Cambridge University Press), 1993.

Sandhu, K.S. and Wheatey, Paul (eds), *Management of Success: The Moulding of Modern Singapore* (Singapore: Institute of South East-Asian Studies), 1989.

Schneider, Bertrand, *The Scandal and the Shame: Poverty and Underdevelopment* (New Delhi: Vikas Publishing House), 1995.

Seabrook, Jeremy, *Victim of Development: Resistance and Alternatives* (London: Verso), 1993.

Selden, M., *The Political Economy of Chinese Development* (New York: M.E. Sharpe), 1992.

Seligson, Mitchell A. and Passe-Smith, John T. (eds), *Development and Underdevelopment: The Political Economy of Inequality* (Boulder, Col.: Lynne Rienner), 1993.

Sen, Amartya, *Inequality Re-examined* (Oxford: Clarendon Press), 1992.

Shaw, Timothy M., 'Beyond any New World Order: The South in the 21st Century', *Third World Quarterly*, vol.15, no.1, 1994, pp.139–46.

Short-term Economic Indicators, Transition Economies: Sources and Definitions (Paris: Centre for Co-operation with the Economies in Transition/Organisation for Economic Co-operation and Development), 1995.

Simon, David, et al. (eds), *Structurally Adjusted Africa: Poverty, Debt and Basic Needs* (London: Pluto Press), 1995.

Simone, Vera and Feraru, Anne Thompson, *The Asian Pacific: Political and Economic Development in a Global Context* (New York: Longman Publishers), 1995.

Sirowy, L. and Inkeles A., 'The Effects of Democracy on Economic Growth and Inequality', *Studies in Comparative International Development*, 1990, pp.126–57.

Sivard, Ruth Leger, *World Military and Social Expenditures, 1991* (Washington: World Priorities), 1991.

Skiair, Lesli (ed.), *Capitalism and Development* (London: Routledge), 1994.

Slater, Robert O., Schultz, Barry M. and Dorr, Steven R. (eds), *Global Transformation and the Third World* (Boulder, Col.: Lynne Rienner), 1993.

Slottje, D.J. et al., *Measuring the Quality of Life Across Countries: A Multidimensional Analysis*, (Boulder, Col.: Westview Press), 1991.

Sobhan Rehman, 'Changing Patterns of Interdependence: The Need for Symmetry in North–South Adjustment Processes', *The Round Table*, no.324, October 1992, pp.417–29.

Sobhan, Rehman, *Rethinking the Role of the State in Development: Asian Perspectives* (Dhaka: University Press), 1993.
Sobhan Rehman (ed.), *Structural Adjustment Policies in the Third World: Design and Experience* (Dhaka: University Press), 1991.
Soemardjan, Selo and Thompson, Kenneth W. (eds), *Culture, Development and Democracy: The Role of the Intellectual* (Tokyo: United Nations University Press), 1994.
Somjee, A.H. and Somjee, Geeta, *Development Success in Asia Pacific: An Exercise in Normative-Pragmatic Balance* (London: Macmillan), 1995.
Song, B.N., *The Rise of the Korean Economy* (Hong Kong: Oxford University Press), 1990.
Sorensen, G., *Democracy and Authoritarianism: Consequences for Economic Development* (Aarhus: Institute of Political Science), 1992.
Spindler, Z.A., 'Liberty and Development: A Further Empirical Perspective', *Public Choice*, 1991, pp.197–210.
Spybey, Tony, *Social Change, Development and Dependency: Modernity, Colonialism and the Development of the West* (Cambridge: Polity Press), 1992.
Stallings, Barbara (ed.), *Global Change, Regional Response: The New International Context of Development* (Cambridge: Cambridge University Press), 1995.
Starke, Lynda (ed.), *State of the World 1992* (A Worldwatch Institute Report on Progress towards a Sustainable Society), (Washington, DC: Worldwatch Institute), 1992.
Stedman, S.J. (ed.), *Botswana: the Political Economy of Democratic Development* (Boulder, Col.: Lynne Rienner), 1993.
Stewart, Frances, *Protecting the Poor during Adjustment in Latin America and the Caribbean in the 1980s: How Adequate was the World Bank Response?* (Development Studies Working Papers) (Oxford: International Development Centre), 1992.
Stewart, John, *Understanding the Management of Local Government* (2nd edn) (London: Pitman Publishing), 1995.
Streeten, Paul Patrick, *Thinking About Development* (Cambridge: Cambridge University Press), 1995.
Stubbs, Richard and Underhill, Geoffrey R.D. (eds), *Political Economy and the Changing Global Order* (Basingstoke: Macmillan), 1994.
Tambunlertchai, Somsak and Gupta, S.P. (eds), *Development Planning in Asia* (Kuala Lumpur: Asian and Pacific Development Centre), 1993.
Tan, Gerald, 'The Next NICs of Asia', *Third World Quarterly*, vol.14, no.1, 1993, pp.57–74.
Thirlwall, A.P., *Growth and Development* (London: Macmillan), 1994.

The 1995 Commonwealth Plan of Action on Gender and Development: A Commonwealth Vision (London: Commonwealth Secretariat), 1995.
The Reality of Aid 1995 (London: Earthscan), 1995.
Thompson, Mark R., 'The Limits of Democratization in ASEAN', *Third World Quarterly*, vol.14, no.3, 1993, pp.469–84.
Tisch, Sarah J. and Wallace, Michael B., *Dilemmas of Development Assistance: The What, Why and Who of Foreign Aid* (Boulder, Col.: Westview Press), 1994.
Todaro, Michael P., *Economics for a Developing World: An Introduction to Principal Problems and Policies for Development* (3rd edn) (London: Longman), 1992.
Tomasevski, Katarina, *Development Aid and Human Rights Revisited* (London: Pinter Publishers), 1993.
Tremwam, Christopher, *The Political Economy of Social Control in Singapore* (London: Macmillan), 1994.
Turok, Ben (ed.), *Debt and Democracy* (London: Institute for African Alternatives), 1991.
United Nations Centre for Social Development and Humanitarian Affairs, *The Impact of Economic and Political Reform on the Status of Women in Eastern Europe* (Proceedings of a United Nations Regional Seminar, Vienna, 8–12 April 1991) (New York: Centre for Social Development and Humanitarian Affairs), 1992.
United Nations Centre for Social Development and Humanitarians Affairs, *The World's Women, 1970–1990: Trends and Statistics* (New York: United Nations), 1991.
United Nations Conference on Trade and Development (UNCTAD), *Accelerating the Development Process: Challenges for National and International Policies in the 1990s* (New York: United Nations), 1991.
United Nations Conference on Trade and Development (UNCTAD), *Trade and Development Report, 1994: Overview* (by the Secretary-General of UNCTAD) (New York and Geneva: United Nations), 1994.
United Nations Conference on Trade and Development (UNCTAD), *Trade and Development Report, 1995* (New York: United Nations), 1995.
United Nations Department of Humanitarian Affairs, *Aid Under Fire: Relief and Development in an Unstable World* (Geneva: United Nations Department of Humanitarian Affairs), 1995.
United Nations Department for Policy Co-ordination and Sustainable Development, *Women in a Changing Global Economy: 1994, World Survey on the Role of Women in Development* (New York: Department for Policy Co-ordination and Sustainable Development, United Nations), 1995.
United Nations Department of Economic and Social Information and Policy Analysis, *World Economic Survey 1993: Current Trends and Policies in*

the World Economy (New York: Department of Economic and Social Information and Policy Analysis), 1993.
United Nations Department of Economic and Social Information and Policy Analysis, *World Economic and Social Survey 1994: Current Trends and Policies in the World Economy* (New York: United Nations), 1994.
United Nations Development Programme (UNDP), *Human Development Report 1990* (New York: Oxford University Press), 1990.
United Nations Development Programme (UNDP), *Human Development Report 1991* (New York: Oxford University Press), 1991.
United Nations Development Programme (UNDP), *Human Development Report 1992* (New York: Oxford University Press), 1992.
United Nations Development Programme (UNDP), *Human Development Report 1993* (New York: Oxford University Press), 1993.
United Nations Development Programme (UNDP), *Human Development Report 1994* (New York: Oxford University Press), 1994.
United Nations Development Programme (UNDP), *Human Development Report 1995* (New York: Oxford University Press), 1995.
Usher, Dan, *The Economic Prerequisite to Democracy* (New York: Columbia University Press), 1991.
Vickers, Jeanne, *Women and the World Economic Crisis* (London: Zed Books), 1994.
Wade, R., *Governing the Market: Economic Theory and the Role of Government in East Asian Industrialization* (Princeton, NJ: Princeton University Press), 1990.
Wallace, Tina and March, Candida, *Changing Perceptions: Writings on Gender and Development* (Oxford: Oxfam), 1991.
Watanabe, Toshio, *Asia: Its Growth and Agony* (Honolulu: East–West Center), 1992.
Watkins, Kevin, *The Oxfam Poverty Report* (Oxford: Oxfam), 1995.
Watson, Hilbourne A. (ed.), *The Caribbean in the Global Political Economy* (Boulder, Col.: Lynne Rienner), 1994.
Weede, E., 'The Impact of Democracy or Repressiveness on the Quality of Life, Income Distribution and Economic Growth Rates', *International Society*, 1993, pp.177–95.
Weeks-Vagliani, Winifred, *Participatory Development and Gender: Articulating Concepts and Cases* (Paris: OECD), 1994.
White, G., *Riding the Tiger: The Politics of Economic Reforms in China* (London: Macmillan), 1993.
White, Gordon (ed.), *Developmental States in East Asia* (London: Macmillan), 1988.
White, G. (ed.), *The Chinese State in the Era of Economic Reforms* (London: Macmillan), 1994.

Williams, Marc, *International Economic Organisations and the Third World* (New York: Harvester), 1994.
Winner, Langdon (ed.), *Democracy in a Technological Society* (Dordrecht: Kluwer Academic Publishers), 1992.
Wood, A., *China's Economic System* (London: London School of Economics), 1991.
World Bank, *Social Indicators of Development, 1990* (Baltimore: Johns Hopkins University Press), 1991.
World Bank, *Governance and Development* (Washington, DC: World Bank), 1992.
World Bank, *The East Asian Miracle: Economic Growth and Public Policy* (New York: Oxford University Press), 1993.
World Bank, *Strengthening the Effectiveness of Aid: Lessons for Donors* (Washington: World Bank), 1995.
World Bank, *World Development Report 1991* (New York: Oxford University Press), 1991.
World Bank, *World Development Report 1992* (New York: Oxford University Press), 1992.
World Bank, *World Development Report 1993* (Oxford: Oxford University Press), 1993.
World Bank, *World Development Report 1994* (Oxford: Oxford University Press), 1994.
World Bank, *World Development Report 1995* (Oxford: Oxford University Press), 1995.
Wright, Richard Kozul, *Walking on Two Legs: Strengthening Democracy and Productive Entrepreneurship in the Transition Economies* (Geneva: UNCTAD), 1995.

11 Aid and Good Governance

Bird, Graham, *IMF Lending to Developing Countries: Issues and Evidence* (London: Routledge), 1995.
Bissio, Roberto Remo (ed.), *The World: A Third World Guide 1995/96* (Montevideo: Institute del Tercer Mundo), 1996.
Blake, David H. and Walters, Robert S., *The Politics of Global Economic Relations* (3rd edn) (Englewood Cliffs, NJ: Prentice-Hall), 1987.
Brown, Michael Barratt, *Africa's Choices: After Thirty Years of the World Bank* (London: Penguin Books), 1995.
Brown, Michael Barratt and Tiffen, Pauline, *Shortchanged: Africa and World Trade* (London: Pluto Press), 1992.

Butcher, Tony, *Delivering Welfare: The Governance of the Social Services in the 1990s* (Buckingham: Open University Press), 1995.
Cassen, Robert, *Does Aid Work? Report to an Intergovernmental Task Force* (2nd edn) (Oxford: Clarendon Press), 1994.
Chan, Steven (ed.), *Foreign Direct Investment in a Changing Global Political Economy* (Basingstoke: Macmillan), 1995.
Cline, William R., *International Debt Re-examined* (Washington, DC: Institute for International Economics), 1995.
Cohen, Ronald, Hyden, Goran and Nagan, Winston P. (eds), *Human Rights and Governance in Africa* (Gainesville, Fla.: University Press of Florida), 1993.
Cottam, Christine M. and Rao, Sudha V. (eds), *Women, Aid and Development* (Essays in Honour of Professor T. Scarlett Epstein) (Delhi: Hindustan Publishing), 1993.
Dasgupta, Abhijit and Lechner, Georg (eds), *Development Aid Today* (New Delhi: Mosaic Books), 1995.
Dasgupta, P., *An Inquiry into Well-being and Destitution* (Oxford: Clarendon Press), 1993.
Davidson, Diane, 'Parliamentary Privilege and Freedom of the Press', *Canadian Parliamentary Review*, vol.16, no.2, Summer 1993, pp.10–12.
Debt-Conversion Schemes in Africa: Lessons from the Experience of Developing Countries (London: James Currey, for the African Centre for Monetary Studies and Association of African Central Banks), 1992.
Foreign and Commonwealth Office, *Good Government in Africa* (Wilton Park Paper 54) (London: HMSO), 1992.
Froot, Kenneth A. (ed.), *Foreign Direct Investment* (Chicago: University of Chicago Press), 1993.
George, Susan and Sabelli, Fabrizio, *Faith and Credit: The World Bank's Secular Empire* (London: Penguin Books), 1994.
German, Tony and Randel, Judith (eds), *The Reality of Aid 1995: An Independent Review of International Aid* (London: Earthscan), 1995.
Heron, Richard Le and Park, Sam Ock (eds), *The Asian Pacific Rim and Globalization: Enterprises, Governance and Territoriality* (Aldershot: Avebury), 1995.
Hirst, Paul, *Associative Democracy: New Forms of Economic and Social Governance* (Cambridge: Polity Press), 1994.
Hook, Steven W., *National Interest and Foreign Aid* (Boulder, Col.: Lynne Rienner), 1995.
Hyden, Goran and Bratton, Michael, *Governance and Politics in Africa* (Boulder, Col.: Lynne Rienner), 1992.
Johnson, John, 'Aid and Good Governance in Africa', *The Round Table*, no.320, October 1991, pp.395–400.

Jones, Alexandra D., *Global Good Governance: Legitimation through Popular Consent, International Credibility and Development Promotion* (London: University of London), 1994.
Leftwich, Adrian, 'Governance, Democracy and Development in the Third World', *Third World Quarterly*, vol.14, no.3, 1993, pp.605–24.
Lewellen, Ted C., *Dependence and Development: An Introduction to the Third World* (Westport, Conn.: Bergin and Garvey), 1995.
Lim, L. and Pang, E.F., *Foreign Direct Investment and Industrialization in Malaysia, Singapore, Taiwan and Thailand* (Paris: OECD Development Centre), 1991.
Lindenberg, M. and Ramirez N. (eds), *Managing Adjustment in Developing Countries* (San Francisco: ICS Press), 1989.
McCarthy, Mary and McCarthy, Tom, *Third World Debt: Towards an Equitable Solution* (Dublin: Macmillan), 1994.
Mengisteab, Kidane and Logan, Ikubolajeh (eds), *Beyond Economic Liberalization in Africa: Structural Adjustment and the Alternatives* (London: Zed Books), 1995.
Mosley, Paul (ed.), *Development Finance and Policy Reform: Essays in the Theory and Practice of Conditionality in Less Developed Countries* (New York: St Martin's Press), 1992.
Mosley, Paul, Harrigan, Jana and Toye, John, *Aid and Power: The World Bank and Policy-Based Lending* (London: Routledge), 1991.
Nanda, Ved P., Shepherd, George W. and Arnolds-McCarthy, Eileen (eds), *World Debt and the Human Condition: Structural Adjustment and the Right to Development* (Westport, Conn.: Greenwood Press), 1993.
Nissanke, Machiko and Hewitt, Adrian (eds), *Economic Crisis in Developing Countries: New Perspectives on Commodities, Trade and Finance* (Essays in Honour of Alfred Maizels), (London: Pinter Publishers), 1993.
Organisation for Economic Co-operation and Development (OECD), *Geographical Distribution of Financial Flows to Aid Recipients – 1989/1993* (Paris: OECD), 1995.
Ould-Mey, Mohameden, 'Global Adjustment: Implications for Peripheral States', *Third World Quarterly*, vol.15, no.2, June 1994, pp.319–36.
Overseas Development Administration, *ODA Guide to Social Analysis/ Projects in Developing Countries* (London: HMSO), 1995.
Page, Sheila, *Trade, Finance and Developing Countries: Strategies and Constraints in the 1990s* (London: Harvester Wheatsheaf), 1990.
Ramphal, Shridath, *Our Country, the Planet: Forging a Partnership for Survival* (London: Lime Tree), 1992.
Ramphal, Shridath and Carlsson, Ingwar, *Our Global Neighbourhood: The Report of the Commission on Global Governance* (Oxford: Oxford University Press), 1995.

Riddell, Roger, *Foreign Aid Reconsidered* (3rd edn) (London: Overseas Development Institute), 1995.
Riley, Stephen P. (ed.), *The Politics of Global Debt* (Basingstoke: Macmillan), 1993.
Rosow, Stephen J., Inayatullah, Naeem and Rupert, Mark (eds), *The Global Economy as Political Space* (Boulder, Col.: Lynne Rienner), 1994.
Ryrie, William, *First World, Third World* (Basingstoke: Macmillan), 1995.
Simon, David, et al. (eds), *Structurally Adjusted Africa: Poverty, Debt and Basic Needs* (London: Pluto Press), 1995.
Sobhan Rehman, 'Changing Patterns of Interdependence: The Need for Symmetry in the North–South Adjustment Process', *The Round Table*, no.324, October 1992, pp.417–29.
Spybey, Tony, *Social Change, Development and Dependency: Modernity, Colonialism and the Development of the West* (Cambridge: Polity Press), 1992.
The Reality of Aid 1995 (London: Earthscan), 1995.
Tisch, Sarah J. and Wallace, Michael B., *Dilemmas of Development Assistance: The What, Why and Who of Foreign Aid* (Boulder, Col.: Westview Press), 1994.
Tomasevski, Katarina, *Development Aid and Human Rights Revisited* (London: Pinter Publishers), 1993.
Turok, Ben (ed.), *Debt and Democracy* (London: Institute for African Alternatives), 1991.
United Nations Department of Humanitarian Affairs, *Aid Under Fire: Relief and Development in an Unstable World* (Geneva: United Nations Department of Humanitarian Affairs), 1995.
Williams, Marc, *International Economic Organisations and the Third World* (New York: Harvester), 1994.
World Bank, *Governance and Development* (Washington, DC: World Bank), 1992.
World Bank, *Strengthening the Effectiveness of Aid: Lessons for Donors* (Washington, DC: World Bank), 1995.

12 Promoting an Efficient and Independent Public Administration

Baker, Randall, *Public Administration in Small and Island States* (Conn.: Kumarian Press), 1992.
Balgoun, M. Jide and Mutahaba, Gelase (eds), *Economic Restructuring and African Public Administration: Issues, Actions and Future Choices* (Conn.: Kumarian Press), 1991.

Butcher, Tony, *Delivering Welfare: The Governance of the Social Services in the 1990s* (Buckingham: Open University Press), 1995.

Cameron, John, Ramharak, Hans and Cole, Ken (eds), *Poverty and Power: the Role of Institutions and the Market in Development* (Delhi: Oxford University Press), 1995.

Campbell, Adrian, *The Challenge to the Centre* (London: Pitman Publishing), 1995.

Daffern, Peter et al., *Financial Management in the Public Sector* (London: Pitman Publishing), 1995.

DiIulio, John J. Jr, *Deregulating the Public Policy: Can Government be Improved?* (Washington, DC: Brookings Institution), 1994.

Fenwick, J., *Managing Local Government* (London: International Thomson Business Press), 1995.

Goh, Keng-Swee, *Public Administration and Economic Development in LDCs* (London: TPRC), 1983.

Jain, R.B. and Asmero H.K. (eds), *Politics, Administration and Public Policy in Developing Countries: Examples from Africa, Asia and Latin America* (Netherlands: VUUP), 1993.

Kiel, L. Douglas, *Managing Chaos and Complexity in Government: A New Paradigm for Managing Change, Innovation, and Organizational Renewal* (San Francisco: Jossey-Bass Publishers), 1994.

McMahon, Christopher, *Authority and Democracy: A General Theory of Government and Management* (Princeton, NJ: Princeton University Press), 1994.

Mutahaba, Gelase, *Reforming Public Administration for Development: Experiences from Eastern Africa* (Conn.: Kumarian Press), 1989.

Mutahaba, Gelase, Baguma, Rweikiza and Halfani, Mohamed, *Vitalizing African Public Administration for Recovery and Development* (Conn.: Kumarian Press), 1993.

Peters, B. Guy, *The Politics of Bureaucracy* (3rd edn) (New York: Longman), 1989.

Pierre, Jon (ed.), *Bureaucracy in the Modern State: An Introduction to Comparative Public Administration* (Aldershot: Edward Elgar), 1995.

Rowat, Donald C. (ed.), *Public Administration in Developed Democracies: A Comparative Study* (New York: Marcel Dekker, Inc.), 1988.

Salleh, Sirajuddin H. and Othman, Norlella (eds), *Emerging Trends of Public Administration in SAARC Countries: Proceedings of the Second South Conference on Public Administration, Islamabad, Pakistan, 18–20 September 1989* (Kuala Lumpur: Asian and Pacific Development Centre), 1992.

Stewart, John, *Understanding the Management of Local Government* (2nd edn) (London: Pitman Publishing), 1995.

Swedish International Development Authority (SIDA), *Making Government Work: Guidelines and Framework for SIDA Support to the Development of Public Administration* (Sweden: SIDA), 1991.

Wood, B. Dan and Waterman, Richard W., *Bureaucratic Dynamics: the Role of Bureaucracy in a Democracy* (Boulder, Col.: Westview Press), 1994.

Index

accountability 7, 74, 75
Africa
  electoralism 4–5
  military interventions 77–9, 84, 86
  public spending 7
  state intervention 4
  see also Uganda
aid
  denial of 39, 41
  and good governance 37–8, 39–40, 157–8
  political conditionalities 40–3
Alhaji Sir Dawda Kairaba Jawara:
  on Africa 9
  on human rights 42
Amin, Idi 108, 109
Anyaoku, Emeka: on CPA 127
Argentina
  background 80–1
  military rule 81
  military under civilian control 81–2
  miltary and UN 82
  reform measures 82
  regional co-operation 83–4
ASEAN (Association of South-East Asian Nations) 36–7, 73
Asia 72–3
  see also East Asia; Singapore model; South Asia; South-East Asia
'Asian values' 36–7, 91–2
Association of South-East Asian Nations (ASEAN) 36–7, 73
Astwood, Norma Cox: on gender politics 52
authoritarianism 4, 6, 32
  Singapore model 95
  see also Argentina; Uganda
Ayittey, George: on military control in Africa 78

Beijing Parliamentary Declaration 55, 56
Beng-Huat Chua: on communitarianism 92, 94
birth rate see human development indicators
Bretton Woods system 37
Brown, Jan: on gender politics 52–3
Buganda 107, 108, 111, 114
bureaucracy see public administration, bureaucracy in democracy

capitalism 2–3, 17
capitalist class 2, 5
Caribbean Common Market and Community (CARICOM) 103, 104
Caribbean island states
  Commonwealth 99, 100, 104–5
  economic development 101–3
  regional co-operation and integration 103–5
  see also Jamaica
CARICOM (Caribbean Common Market and Community) 103, 104
Chalker, Lynda: on gender politics 52
charismatic leaders 65, 102
Christie, Kenneth: on 'human rights' dichotomy 41, 42
civil services 24, 73–5

civil vs economic rights 33, 34, 35, 41
civil-government relationships 26–7
civil-military relationships *see* military-civil relationships
Clarke, Colin: on Caribbean societies 99
Commonwealth Caribbean *see* Caribbean island states
Commonwealth community
  human rights 42
  women's status 50–1, 54–5
Commonwealth Parliamentary Association (CPA) 120–1
  conferences 121–3, 126, 127
    regional 124
    for small countries 123
  election monitoring 125
  future role 126–7
  organization 121
  publications 124–5
  seminars 124
  staff training 125–6
  women 123, 125
Commonwealth Women Parliamentarians Group (CWPG) 123
communitarianism 92, 94–5
competitiveness 11
  and democracy 3–4
  global 28–9
  policies 28–30
conflicts of interest 24, 26–7
corruption 11, 24, 29, 74, 78–9
  prevention in civil service 75
CPA *see* Commonwealth Parliamentary Association (CPA)
CWPG (Commonwealth Women Parliamentarians Group) 123

decolonization 71, 100, 120
democracy
  accountability 7
  and capitalism 2–3, 17
  and competitiveness 3–4
  definition 2
  economic growth and political stability 3
  electoralism and economic reforms 4–5
  and media 65–7
  relationship with development 7–10, 17
  role of bureaucracy 69–71, 73–5
democratization
  and economic growth 6–7
  and media 60
development
  administration 71
  definitions 2, 21, 22
  enabling environment for 21–30
  and human rights 32–5
  lessons from experience 22–3
  see also economic development; economic reforms; human development
Development Decades 31–2
dictatorships *see* authoritarianism
diplomacy 131–2
distribution of gains 23
Donahue, Arthur: on CPA 123, 127
Dookeran, Winston: on Caribbean economies 104, 105
Dunn, John: on good governance 38

East Asia ('miracle economies') 3–4, 21
  characteristics 12–13
  corruption 24
  economic vs civil rights 34, 35
economic co-operation 72–3, 103–5
economic development 22
  and democratization 6–7
  and distribution of gains 23
  and political stability 3
  sustained 23–30
economic reforms 8
  and electoralism 4–5
  and governmental accountability 7
  India 5–6
economic vs civil rights 33, 34, 35, 41
education
  girls' 46, 49, 53
  media responsibility for 60–1

elected representatives
  and media 61–2
  women 50–1, 52, 54
election monitoring 125
electoralism and economic reforms 4–5
employment
  Asia 73
  women 46, 48, 49–50, 53
export-oriented industries 34–5, 101, 105

Finer, Samuel: civil-military relationships 79
foreign investors 27
foreign policies 25, 27–8
freedom of the press 59–67

GAD (Gender and Development) 46
gender *see* women
Gender and Development (GAD) 46
global competitiveness 28–9
Global Competitiveness Report 11
globalization 28, 31, 65
  and liberalization 74–5, 85
good governance 8, 24–6
  and aid 37–8, 39–40, 157–8
  definitions 38–40
government-civil relationships 26–7
government-military relationships 77–87
Grugel, Jean: on Caribbean island states 100, 101, 102, 105

Haggard, S. & Kaufman, R.: on democracy and economic reforms 8
Harker, Trevor: on Caribbean integration 104
Healey, John: on capitalist class 2, 5
human development 10–11
human development indicators 13, 14–17, 101
Human Development Report 10–11, 14, 46, 51
  Singapore 89
  strategy for women's development 55

human resources development 73
human rights
  and aid 37–8, 39–40, 40–3
  and 'Asian values' 91
  in Commonwealth community 42
  and development 32–5
  and good governance 38–40
  political conditionalities 37, 40–3
  right to development 31, 33–4, 35, 42
  South Asia 35–7
human rights violations
  military 78, 80, 82
  punishnment for 80, 82
  Singapore 91, 93
Hunter, Wendy: on Argentina 83–4
Huntington, Samuel: on military takeover 77

IMF (International Monetary Fund) 36, 37
India 2–3, 72
  Kerala 13–17
  political system and culture 5–6
indicators of development *see* human development indicators
infant mortality rate *see* human development indicators
information dissemination
  media 59, 60–1, 63
  parliamentary groups 124–5, 131
information technology 31, 65, 126–7
infrastructure 26, 70
Inter-Parliamentary Union (IPU) 119–20
  aims and objectives 128
  conferences 128, 129–30, 132
    regional 130
  diplomacy 132
  information dissemination 131
  seminars 131
  staff training 131
  technical programme 130–1
  and UN 131–2
  women parliamentarians 47, 53, 56, 130

interest groups 26–7, 28, 63
International Monetary Fund (IMF) 36, 37
international relations *see* foreign policies
IPU *see* Inter-Parliamentary Union (IPU)

Jamaica 2–3, 4, 7

Kaufman, R. & Haggard, S.: on democracy and economic reforms 8
Kerala 13–17

Latin America 4, 6, 54
see also Argentina
Lawyers Committee for Human Rights 42
LEDCs (less economically developed countries) 2–3, 11
Lee Kwan Yew: on democracy and development 96
Leftwich, Adrian: on democracy and development variables 9–10
less economically developed countries (LEDCs) 2–3, 11
Lippmann, Walter: on media 66, 67
literacy *see* education, girls'; human development indicators

market systems 22, 23
Mauzy, Diane: on 'human rights' dichotomy 41
media
  and democracy 65–7
  and democratization 60
  educational responsibility 60–1
  and government 63
  political reporting 61–2
  politicians as information sources 63–4
  and politics 59–60
  privileges 64–5
  television 62, 65
military interventions
  Africa 77–9, 84, 86
  disengagement 80
  modes of 79–80
military rule 39, 41, 81, 109
  prevention of 84–6
military-civil relationships 77, 79–80
  see also Argentina
'miracle economies' *see* East Asia ('miracle economies')
Murdock, Graham: on 'newsworthiness' 66
Museveni, President 109, 110, 111, 112, 113, 114, 115, 116

National Resistance Movement (NRM) 109, 111, 112, 114, 116
Nelson, Joan: on good governance 8
newly industrialized countries (NICs) 3, 21, 34
NGOs (non-governmental organizations) 26, 36, 42–3
NICs (newly industrialized countries) 3, 21, 34
non-governmental organizations (NGOs) 26, 36, 42–3
North-South relations 40–2
NRM (National Resistance Movement) 109, 111, 112, 114, 116

Obote, Milton 108, 109
Oyewole, Bode: on education and media 60–1

PAP (People's Action Party) 90–1, 92–3, 96
Parliamentarian, The 124
Parliamentary Associations 119–34
Paul, Eric: 96
  on democracy and development 7–8
  on state intervention 93
People's Action Party (PAP) 90–1, 92–3, 96
Pickles, Caroline: on gender politics 52
political conditionalities 37, 40–3
political reporting 61–2
political stability 3, 72–3
politicians and media 63–5

poverty 1, 46
Preston, Lewis: on East Asia 12, 13
private investment 26, 27
private sector 25, 36
privileges, parliament and media 64–5
property rights 24, 26
public administration
  bureaucracy in democracy 69–71, 73–5
  development of 71–2
  human resources development 73
  socio-political stability 72–3
public spending 7

refugees 1–2
right to development 31, 33–4, 35, 42

SAARC (South Asian Association for Regional Co-operation) 132–3
Sawicki, Joan: on CPA 127
Schudson, Michael: on media in America 61
Shepherd, Sir Colin:
  on CPA 121
  on media and politicans 64–5
Singapore model 3, 12–13, 33, 72
  Asian values 91–2
  communitarianism 92, 94–5
  discussion group 153–5
  early years 90–1
  future of PAP 96
  human rights violations 91, 93
  political component 91
  shared values 92–3
  statistics 89–90
'Singapore school' supporters 91, 94–5
single-party regimes *see* authoritarianism
socio-political stability 3, 72–3
SOEs (state-owned enterprises) 25, 29, 36
Sorensen, Georg: on democracy and development 8–9
South Asia 4
  human rights 35–7
  women leaders 50–1

see also India; Sri Lanka
South Asian Association for Regional Co-operation (SAARC) 132–3
South-East Asia 34, 35, 73
see also ASEAN (Association of South-East Asian Nations); Singapore model
sovereignty 40–3
special interest groups 26–7, 28, 63
Sri Lanka 3, 4, 7, 13, 72
Ssemogerere, Dr Paul 114, 115, 116
Stamiris, Eleni: barriers to women's political participation 47–8
state intervention 4, 22, 23, 25–6
see also public administration
state-owned enterprises (SOEs) 25, 29, 36
sustained economic development 23–30
Symonds, Ann: on women in parliament 54

tax policies 23
television 62, 65
Tiruchelvam, Neelan:
  on aid and good governance 37
  on human rights 43
trade unions 26, 34–5, 36, 50
transparency 24
Transparency International 11
tribalism 107, 111, 113–14

Uganda
  Amin 108, 109
  background 107
  Constitutional Commission 113–15
  independence movement 108
  indirect democracy 110–11, 116
  discussion group 149–52
  Museveni 109, 110, 111, 112, 113, 114, 115, 116
  Obote 108, 109
  political developments 116
  post-independence politics 108
  Resistance Councils 112
Ugandan Peoples Congress (UPC) 108, 109

United Nations (UN)
  Declaration on the Right to Develop 33–4
  gender issues 45, 47, 51
  human rights 31–2
  and IPU 131–2
  peace-keeping activities 82
UPC (Ugandan Peoples Congress) 108, 109

Warner, David: on communication networks 126–7
Waylen, Georgina: on women's movements 54
Weber, Max: on bureaucracy 74
Werunga, Murumba: on media and politicans 64
'Western values' 40–1
Westminster model 29
  in Caribbean 100, 102–3, 104, 105

WID (Women in Development) 45–6
women
  barriers to political participation 47–51
  CPA study 125
  empowerment strategies 51–6
  in Commonwealth community 50–1, 54–5
  in decision-making 47, 48
    corporate 50
  employment 46, 48, 49–50, 53
  parliamentarians 47, 53, 56, 123, 125, 130
  statistics 46
Women in Development (WID) 45–6
work *see* employment
World Bank 12, 36, 37, 38–9
World Human Rights Conference 39
World Women's Conferences 45, 55, 56